EILEAN GIBLIN

EILEAN GIBLIN

A feminist between the wars

Patricia Clarke

"No woman's life is a single story"
Sarah Pritchard *Revealing Women's Life Stories*

© Copyright 2013 Patricia Clarke
All rights reserved. Apart from any uses permitted by Australia's Copyright Act 1968, no part of this book may be reproduced by any process without prior written permission from the copyright owners. Inquiries should be directed to the publisher.

Monash University Publishing
Building 4, Monash University
Clayton, Victoria 3800, Australia
www.publishing.monash.edu

Monash University Publishing brings to the world publications which advance the best traditions of humane and enlightened thought.

Monash University Publishing titles pass through a rigorous process of independent peer review.

www.publishing.monash.edu/books/eg-9781921867842.html

Series: Australian History

Design: Les Thomas

Front cover images: Eilean Giblin, from a photograph of the 1902 Wycombe Abbey hockey team, reproduced courtesy of Wycombe Abbey School; and a detail of the Georgina Sweet Wing of the University Women's College, reproduced courtesy of the University College Archives.

Back cover image: The Australian delegation to the International Woman Suffrage Alliance Conference, 1923. Reproduced courtesy of the National Library of Australia (BibID: 3279316).

National Library of Australia Cataloguing-in-Publication entry:
Author: Clarke, Patricia, author.
Title: Eilean Giblin : a feminist between the wars /
                Patricia Clarke.
ISBN: 9781921867842 (paperback)
Notes: Includes bibliographical references and index.
Subjects: Giblin, Eilean Mary.
                Women social reformers--Australia--Biography.
                Feminists--Australia--Biography.
                Suffragists--Australia--Biography.
                Women's rights--Australia--History.
                Human rights workers--Australia--Biography.
Dewey Number: 324.6230994

Printed in Australia by Griffin Press an Accredited ISO AS/NZS 14001:2004 Environmental Management System printer.

The paper this book is printed on is certified against the Forest Stewardship Council ® Standards. Griffin Press holds FSC chain of custody certification SGS-COC-005088. FSC promotes environmentally responsible, socially beneficial and economically viable management of the world's forests

Contents

Acknowledgments..vii
List of acronyms...ix
Foreword – Dale Spender..xi
Introduction...xv

1   Radical waves in a sea of conformity........................1
    London 1884–1912

2   Searching for the unknown..................................19
    Australia 1913–1916

3   Love in wartime..36
    England 1917–1919

4   'A woman's place is in the world'..........................55
    Hobart 1920s

5   *A Room of One's Own*..79
    Melbourne 1930s

6   War and the *Dunera* 'enemy aliens'.......................103
    Canberra, Hay, Hobart 1940

7   A studio pottery in a time of war..........................126
    Canberra 1940s

8   The country under threat...................................145
    Australia 1942

9   War and peace...166
    Canberra, Hobart 1943–1951

10 'My roots are in England'...................................185
    Australia, England 1951–1955

Bibliography..193
Index 201
About the author..215

Acknowledgments

My initial research on the life of Eilean Giblin began with her diaries held in the Giblin Papers in the Manuscripts Room at the National Library of Australia. I am grateful to the late Violet Giblin, Sandy Bay, Tasmania for permission to use these diaries, for family information and for her encouragement of my project.

I would not have been able to progress further had I not eventually contacted Eilean Giblin's niece, Gillian Pole-Carew in Devon, England, who was extraordinarily generous in making available to me information on the Burton family including a copy of a typescript family history written by her father Clive Mence Burton. She also provided me with Burton family photographs and put me in touch with her brother, Peter Burton, Addo, Cape Province, South Africa and Biddy Compton Boyd, Great Eversden, Cambridge, a granddaughter of Eilean's brother, Brigadier Colin Burton. All were generous in providing information and photographs. I am particularly grateful to Peter Burton for copies of a few letters, invaluable because of their rarity.

Similarly I am very grateful to Margot Giblin, Battery Point, Hobart for copies of a few letters Eilean Giblin wrote to Margot's father Cyril ('Copper') Giblin during the last part of her life. I also thank other Giblin relatives particularly Diana Giblin, Sandy Bay, Hobart, L.F. Giblin's niece, Elaine Ross, Hawthorn East, Vic. who provided information and photographs, and also other nieces Deidre Mackinnon and Audrey Salter. Alison Heath, Archivist, Wycombe Abbey was very helpful with information and photographs on Eilean's schooling. I am also grateful to Dr Terry Rogers, Archivist, Marlborough College for information on the school; Beverley Cook, Museum of London for suffragettes' records; Professor Michael Roe, Sandy Bay, Tasmania, for Tasmanian background and St Michael's School, St Kilda for information on an elusive person.

I thank Ian Forster, Archivist, University College, for his most generous help from the time I began researching Eilean Giblin's role in the building of University Women's College at the University of Melbourne and for supplying photographs; I am most grateful for his continuing interest. In Canberra I acknowledge with thanks help from Peter Bailey for his recollections, and also Dawn Waterhouse; Angela Mawbey for Burton family research in English records; Gary Kent for shipping records; Victor Isaacs for information on train timetables in 1940 and for showing me a prototype of the rail motor Eilean Giblin would have travelled on from Narrandera to Hay in 1940, and in Queensland Katie Dean and Jim and Terry Lindsay for information on 'Shirley' station. The late Shirley Storey, Deakin ACT was a great help in explaining pottery processes to me and lending me books on pottery and Sandy Gillam, Archivist, RMIT University, supplied information on early pottery courses. The National Gallery of Australia arranged for me to view, with Shirley Storey, Eilean Giblin's pottery in the Collection Study Area and lent an illustration of some of her pieces.

As with all my research I most happily acknowledge the great help and interest of staff of the National Library of Australia in the Petherick, Manuscripts and Newspaper reading rooms. The friendly and helpful atmosphere of the Petherick Room, where I did most of the research for this book, is legendary among researchers. It has made possible my output of books and articles since I first became a Petherick reader in 1982, more than three decades ago.

Patricia Clarke

List of acronyms

ACT	Australian Capital Territory
AGPS	Australian Government Publishing Service
AIF	Australian Imperial Force
ALP	Australian Labor Party
ANU	Australian National University
ANZAAS	Australian and New Zealand Association for the Advancement of Science
ARP	Air Raids Precautions
AWL	Absent Without Leave
BBC	British Broadcasting Corporation
CMG	Companion of the Order of St Michael and St George
CP	Country Party
CSIR	Council for Scientific and Industrial Research (to 1949)
DORA	Defence of the Realm Act (UK)
DSO	Distinguished Service Order
EMG	(Gramophone) E.M. Ginn
ICOMOS	International Council on Monuments and Sites
IWSA	International Woman Suffrage Alliance
HMAS	His Majesty's Australian Ship
HMAT	His Majesty's Australian Transport
JP	Justice of the Peace
KC	King's Counsel
MC	Military Cross
MP	Member of Parliament
MS	Manuscript
MUP	Melbourne University Press

NAA	National Archives of Australia
NCW	National Council of Women
NGA	National Gallery of Australia
NLA	National Library of Australia
NSW	New South Wales
RAAF	Royal Australian Air Force
RAF	Royal Air Force (UK)
RASC	Royal Army Service Corps (UK)
RMIT	Royal Melbourne Institute of Technology University (formerly Melbourne Technical College)
RMS	Royal Mail Steamer
UAP	United Australia Party
UC	University College, University of Melbourne (from 1975)
USA	United States of America
UWC	University Women's College, University of Melbourne (to 1975)
VIREC	Victorian International Refugee Emergency Council
VWCM	Victorian Women's Citizenship Movement
WA	Western Australia
WNPPL	Women's Non-Party Political League (Tasmania)
WSPU	Women's Social and Political Union
WWI	World War I
YWCA	Young Women's Christian Association

Foreword

Today, when the majority of university graduates are women, it is difficult to imagine the time – when not so long ago – women had to win many arguments and quite a few votes before they were entitled to education – and careers. The status of women in the early years of the 20th century – in Britain and Australia was predominantly that of wives and mothers who had little public influence.

It is worth reminding ourselves that the gains women enjoy in the 21st century did not always come easily; that we now take for granted the achievements of women in the public sphere – at the highest levels – is an indication of the extraordinary success of the campaigns that were undertaken for equal opportunities and equal citizenship.

Many unsung women devoted their lives to women's rights and independence yet few have found an honoured place in our history. This account of Eilean Giblin's life helps to remedy the omissions.

Born in London in 1884, into a comfortably wealthy family, Eilean Burton's values were formed by her 'cosmopolitan' family (with highly conservative father) and her attendance at Wycombe Abbey school which had 'advanced' views on female education. It was one of the few schools that prepared girls for university.

(Some family members and friends objected to the school on the grounds that it did not teach girls to be 'ladies'. Such assessments were probably quite accurate if Eilean is a representative example: a cultured, well-informed and unconventional woman – she had little interest in polite conversation, much preferring political debate.)

Other family members helped to provide more activist role models. Her unmarried aunts led the way – taking up interesting if not dangerous careers (one served as a nursing sister in the Boer War) others choosing a life of comparably interesting and dangerous political activities.

Two aunts, Georgina and Helen MacRae, were staunch supporters of Votes For Women and joined the Women's Social and Political Union (WSPU), became suffragettes, and engaged in persistent civil disobedience – which consisted primarily of a great deal of window breaking and consequent arrest.

Georgina was arrested on Black Friday (an event reasonably well recorded in British history when police used undue force in arresting unarmed, protesting women) at the age of 50 when she threw stones at the homes of influential (male, of course) politicians, who refused to vote for Votes for Women. In Georgina's case it was the home of Winston Churchill that had its windows broken. She refused to pay the fine and was sent to prison; and it was no picnic.

Aunt Helen was also arrested after another famous broken windows incident when most of the shop windows in London's Oxford Street were shattered in a coordinated exercise, and women hid a variety of implements in their muffs, including 'toffee hammers'. Along with 125 other women, Aunt Helen was tried and sent to prison. Expecting such an outcome, most of the women had arrived well prepared with all their luggage, and this caused a further furore with critics claiming that the courthouse looked more like a railway station.

In prison, many of the women went on hunger strike – and were forcibly fed. This was an horrendous practice (which could lead to death) where the women were held down, their jaw was clamped open with a barbarous steel instrument, and a feeding tube forced down either their throat or their nose. You had to be very committed to the cause of women's rights to endure such torture.

Ada Burton, Eilean's mother didn't engage in window breaking (maybe she was constrained by the presence of six children) but she did instruct cook to make a cake that held a secret cylinder containing a message, and which was delivered to Helen. (Unfortunately the cake was cut open by the prison guards and Ada herself was lucky to escape arrest!) Ada did however work in the WSPU office distributing pamphlets etc; there was no doubting her commitment even though she avoided a criminal record.

Eilean didn't join in these family patterns of window breaking but they certainly left an imprint. Apart from politics and public service (working with the underprivileged) she had numerous other interests – particularly in the areas of the arts, music, and literature. She was quite at home with some members of the Bloomsbury set.

But she was also very interested in how women could live their lives in the 20th century; while they were still without the vote in England – there was one country where women did vote, and Eilean was curious as to how women had gained the vote and as a result, what they were doing with it.

In a period when women of her class were still being chaperoned, she set sail for Australia and arrived in Melbourne in 1913. She set off for Hobart which at the time was regarded as a very civilised city, and she was not disappointed. She did meet her future husband in Tasmania – Lyndhurst Giblin; he clearly shared her interest in politics and horticulture (he had an orchard) and was probably considered as unorthodox as she was eccentric. (Older than Eilean, he was a brilliant scholar and outspoken rational thinker who – when war broke out – suggested to the loyal locals that they would be better served by using their monies to defend their own shores rather than send it to the British to buy warships.)

Giblin went off to war and Eilean went off to find out about Australia. By 1915 she was in North Queensland and clearly 'roughing it'. She took copious notes and wrote numerous letters with a view to publishing them when she returned to England. While off fighting a war he didn't condone, and being wounded (more than once) Giblin made suggestions as to possible publishers for her book on Australia – a book which he clearly approved of. Although a few attempts were made to find a publisher – the book did not appear in print.

Surviving the war, Giblin returned to England and he and Eilean were married in July 1918. It was quite obvious that he did not expect that his wife would be submissive or dutiful!

They both returned to Australia after the war had finished, but on separate ships. Eilean travelled with other 'war brides' but was undoubtedly distinguished from most of them. As Patricia Clarke remarks in this meticulously researched and fascinating account, 'Eilean was almost certainly unique among war brides in being offered a week at a Labor Party conference as her introduction to Australia'.

Throughout the following years, Eilean and Lyndhurst had a most modern marriage – with their interests determining that they often led separate lives. And Eilean served as a marvellous role model for many women in Australian society. At a time when women rarely drove, she set out in her little Morris on her own and travelled to all parts of the country.

When they lived in Melbourne, she became very interested in women's education – and the absence of a non-denominational women's college at Melbourne University (when such colleges existed in Sydney and Brisbane).

She was soon chair of the committee determined to build such a college, and after years of postponement was able to see the college come to fruition – at the last moment out-manoeuvring a ploy by some of the men to have the allotted ground re-allocated for use as a cricket pitch.

When Giblin's work took him to Canberra she was curious about the newly created capital and decided to join him; it was typical of her that when he thought they might not be able to find a suitable house, she proposed that they set up camp!

Her musings about Canberra – where she found an almost unbridgeable gender divide – make interesting reading and provide an unusual account of the days when its nomination as the seat of government was more name than reality. And where she felt the enormous absence of cultural activities; no theatre or music.

Eilean's sense of isolation was heightened during the Second World War; many of the reported battles 'overseas' were at places that were familiar to her. She subscribed to the *New Statesman and Nation*, the *Manchester Guardian*, the *London Times*, the *Sydney Morning Herald* and the *Canberra Times* (a feeble little paper) and read the (censored) accounts of the devastation of the country of her birth. She could envisage the waste and the awful destruction of Europe.

With a few exceptions, Canberra wives were more preoccupied with apparently petty conventions and rarely shared her political concerns: she directed her considerable energy into creating her 'pottery studio'. (The trouble she took to find the best clay for her kiln, speaks not only of her perseverance – but of her concern for artistry and merit. She may have been eccentric but she is immensely likeable.)

Eilean Giblin led the life of an independent woman well before the modern women's movement. She was a pioneer who opened a door of possibility for women. She transformed an issue of equality into a reality – and the more we know about women like her and the role they played – the more we can appreciate the contribution they made to the rights we take for granted today.

Patricia Clarke is to be congratulated for reclaiming this exemplary woman whose great achievement was to live as a feminist between the wars.

Dale Spender

Introduction

Eilean Giblin travelled from England to Australia in 1919 on the *Katoomba* with a shipload of war brides, almost certainly the only woman not wearing a wedding ring. She had refused to accept a ring for the marriage ceremony – she believed both husband and wife should have rings or neither. She was older than the majority of war brides on the *Katoomba* and unlike many of them she had no baby or young child. She travelled alone while many of the others had their Australian soldier husbands with them. Eilean's husband, Major Lyndhurst Falkiner Giblin DSO MC, had returned to Australia from the First World War on another ship. He believed it was his duty to stay with his men, the surviving soldiers of the Tasmanian 40th AIF battalion, whom he had led in terrible battles on the Western Front. Eilean Giblin was an unusual war bride, an unconventional feminist whose life had been shaped by the radical social and political movements of late nineteenth and early twentieth century England. In Australia she pursued feminist objectives in the superficially becalmed period between the headlines of the suffrage campaigns during the first wave of feminist activism and the transformative influences of the second wave beginning in the 1960s.

I first became interested in her through diaries she kept in Canberra during the Second World War, a world she observed as an outsider, a person out of tune with many of the conformist ideas of the 1940s. I wanted to know who this diarist was, what life experiences made her who she was and how she related to the era in which she lived. Initially the only clues came through these diaries filed in the National Library of Australia's Manuscript Collection among the Giblin papers of her noted economist husband.[1] Although a largely hidden resource they were no secret to people interested in the social history of Canberra. Several writers had dipped into their

---

[1] NLA MS366/6/1-2, Eilean Giblin diaries, Papers L. F. Giblin.

contents, usually for a specific aspect of her observations: Jim Gibbney for the wartime chapter in his history of Canberra,[2] Nicholas Brown for Dick Downing's early years as a young economist.[3] I had used them myself in a paper for an ICOMOS conference at Old Parliament House.[4] They provide a unique glimpse of Canberra society at a time of heightened awareness of the National Capital as the seat of government in the crisis of war. The diarist's agonised reaction to the immense human suffering and futility of war recurs constantly as she counterpoises her unobtrusive recording of the calm life of the city against the disasters of lost battles in Europe and the Middle East, the lightning Japanese advance through Asia, the threat of invasion and the dislocations caused by war regulations and restrictions.

They give few clues to the diarist's background or to her personal life, however. Apart from the war, the most recurrent references are to the natural world. She recorded the changing seasons – the flowering of spring, the colours of autumn, the dead leaves of winter and the heat of summer – the sounds of birds, the fruit trees in backyard gardens and the neat front hedges and grass verges trimmed, to her amazement, by government employees in the midst of a world war. It is possible only in an incidental way to deduce some sense of her marriage. In her diaries, it appears a union between two compatible people, considerate and adaptive towards each other, but with no indications of intimacy or endearment. It is obvious that both had highly developed social consciences and respect for individual freedom and that they shared similar views on world events. Their views were informed by their reading of the English press, particularly periodicals such as the radical *New Statesman and Nation*; they both read widely and were up to date with the latest books, both literary and political.

I followed the few personal leads in her diaries including one which appeared, almost incongruously, in the midst of appalling war news. This was the day-to-day record of her attempts to establish a studio pottery in Canberra. Further research on this apparently out of character private pursuit revealed that she was not only a pioneer in this field but that some of her pottery was in the National Gallery of Australia's collection.[5] The most important public story to emerge from her diaries was the record of

---

[2] Jim Gibbney, *Canberra 1913–1953*, AGPS, Canberra, 1988, Ch. 10.
[3] Nicholas Brown, *Richard Downing:Economics, advocacy and social reform in Australia*, MUP, Carlton Vic., 2001.
[4] NLA MS8363, Acc06.025, Papers P. Clarke, 'Canberra in diaries and fiction', Folder 21.
[5] NGA 90.563.1-5.

her concerted efforts to help the 'enemy aliens', deported from England in 1940 on the *Dunera*, to be interned in Australia. She was one of a small minority who supported the internees, many of them Jewish refugees from Nazi regimes, at a time when Australian public opinion had little time for such sympathy. Her support was not passive and extended to making a lone 500 kilometre journey to investigate their remote internment camp. Researching this subject eventually led me to some understanding of her English connections.

Many aspects of Eilean Giblin's life remained a mystery. A diarist, a woman with a highly developed social conscience, a potter and the wife of a well-known man (the last a description she would not have welcomed): in all other ways she was unknown. As I read her diaries I came across references that were not immediately explicable. I knew nothing about the family members in England she mentioned occasionally and little of the significance of her visits to University Women's College in Melbourne or the people and places she mentioned when she visited Hobart. It was one brief incidental mention of the school she went to in England that enabled me to begin researching her early life. Conversely it was easy to find out a great deal about her husband, Professor Lyndhurst Falkiner Giblin. He has been the subject of many articles and a comparatively recent book[6] documenting his role as adviser to governments between the two world wars and during the Second World War, and identifying him as an original economic thinker – including the claim that his multiplier theory predated the economic theories of British economist Maynard Keynes. His wife is rarely mentioned in these publications. When she is, information about her is usually confined to the fact of her marriage in London towards the end of the First World War. The scarcity of even photographic records of her points starkly to her invisibility, in contrast with her husband who was painted by the famous Australian painter William Dobell. (The portrait is in the Ian Potter Museum and a print hangs in the Giblin/Eunson Library, University of Melbourne.)

Her invisibility made her an intriguing enigma. After her husband's death she deposited more than 400 of his letters to her in the National Library but there are none of the ones she wrote in reply. The diaries she kept in Canberra are the only substantial written evidence of her life. On almost every page these diaries raise questions about her identity. In the

---

[6] William Coleman, Selwyn Cornish, Alf Hagger, *Giblin's Platoon: The Trials and Triumphs of the Economist in Australian Public Life*, ANU E Press, Canberra ACT, 2006.

now vague memories of people who knew her she appears rather plain and unfashionable, uninterested in dress or appearance. She was often coupled with her husband in this – his eccentricities of dress were often recorded, his coats without lapels, his dubbined boots, his floppy ex-digger's hat, and always his homemade red tie, interpreted as a marker of his socialist sympathies. In the few photographic records of her, Eilean is plainly dressed, her dark hair parted in the middle and drawn severely back and she seems unlikely to have ever worn make-up. She believed the manufacture of cosmetics should have been abandoned as unnecessary during the Second World War.[7] To her husband's relatives she was a quiet person who didn't like people who talked a lot – she referred to them as 'empty rattles'. They remembered her as undomesticated, a woman who did little cooking but who always knitted singlets as presents for babies of nieces and nephews. Like her husband she was an inveterate smoker; they each had their plugs of tobacco which they chopped up, she to roll into cigarettes, he to pack into his pipe. At public events she presented as a woman with 'an arresting personality' who spoke 'with a quiet forceful manner'.[8]

It is obvious from her diaries that the Giblins led a simple life, they grew vegetables and kept hens and preserved fruit and made jam. Eilean sewed most of her own clothes and some of her husband's; her dresses were often not much more than pieces of straight striped material sewn together at the sides and over them in cold weather she wore a long coat and a hat. Their homes were marked by spartan good taste. Her first action in one rented house was to remove the paintings she found on the walls.[9] Their furniture was severely utilitarian, some of it made by Eilean herself. Lyndhurst Giblin always slept on a verandah or in a sleep-out in a makeshift bed, even in the severest of Canberra winters – he was reputed to have slept in a tree when staying with his friend the Commonwealth Statistician, Roland Wilson, but this was an exaggerated rumour.[10] Their only heating was a wood fire. Some of these ways of living were familiar to Canberra residents of the 1940s especially after wartime austerity took hold but there was an extra edge to the spartan quality of the Giblins' household. Their sparse lifestyle was so much part of their way of living that Giblin joked about it after a robbery at

---

[7] MS366/6/2, 17 January 1943.
[8] *Daily News* (Perth WA), 12 January 1932, p. 7.
[9] MS366/6/1, 31 August 1940.
[10] (Sir) Roland Wilson, 'L.F. Giblin: A Man for All Seasons', The Giblin Memorial Lecture, *47th ANZAAS Congress Papers*, Section 24, Hobart, 12 May 1976, p. 19.

their house in the Melbourne suburb of South Yarra, where they lived before moving to Canberra. 'It makes rather a good story,' he wrote to Eilean. 'Ransacked the house of a Director of the Commonwealth Bank & could find nothing worth taking away.' He was relieved that one of their very few treasured possessions, the gramophone Eilean had brought back from one of her trips to England, was untouched.[11]

It was a surprisingly 'modern' marriage for the very conformist world of the first half of the twentieth century when many women remained tied to domestic roles. Within the confines of moves that were dictated by her husband's career, Eilean Giblin maintained the freedom and independence that allowed her to follow her own interests wherever she found herself. She was financially independent and in peacetime travelled overseas regularly, sometimes for long periods. In Australia she drove her own car at a time when only a small minority of Australian women owned cars and she made her own decisions about where she would travel, undertaking long and demanding drives in her small Morris car.

As I researched her background I discovered that she arrived with a commitment to women's rights and social justice developed through work with victims of poverty and deprivation in the slums of south London and through the intellectual appeal of left-wing political ideas and the emancipation of women. She came as the wife of a war hero whose radical political and social views belied his establishment background in Tasmanian society. Her first home, Hobart, was an uneasy milieu in which to find a feminist role. Moreover the period between the two world wars was a steady rather than a spectacular period for women's liberation, a period when women realised that while gaining the vote was a great achievement it did nothing to change social and cultural inequalities in ordinary life. At first in Hobart and then in Melbourne Eilean Giblin sought roles in which she could advance feminist aspirations.

In the small, insular society of Hobart in the 1920s, she campaigned for the feminist goal of 'equal citizenship'. This did not have the ringing tone of a suffragette slogan and nothing approaching its publicity appeal. It aimed at small, incremental victories that gradually chipped away at the overwhelming male dominance in public life. It was an unspectacular period of consolidation as feminists sought reforms that required endless and constant lobbying of male politicians. These could be as mundane as the appointment of a few women as justices of the peace or a sole female member

---

[11] MS366/1, Letters L.F. Giblin to Eilean Giblin, 29 September 1937.

to a government board or as far reaching as motherhood endowment or encouraging women to stand for parliament. In the international sphere it meant lobbying national governments for major reforms on fundamental issues such as allowing women to retain their nationality after marriage. As I researched Eilean Giblin's life I discovered she was involved in these and many similar campaigns. She represented Australian women on an international committee on the Nationality of Married Women, she was the first woman to be appointed to a hospital board in Tasmania and she put a case for child endowment at the 1928 Royal Commission. Two decades after she began campaigning in Hobart, she was a witness in her diary to the realisation of one of the goals she had pursued in Hobart with the election of the first women to the Australian Parliament in 1943: Enid Lyons to the House of Representatives for the Liberal Party and Dorothy Tangney to the Senate for the ALP.[12] Her achievements become apparent only after lengthy searching through old newspapers, records of the Federation of Australian Women Voters and other sources including her husband's letters, in which there is some incidental mention of her activities.

In the much larger and more complex society of Melbourne in the 1930s she worked to extend educational opportunities for women. After years when no progress had been made on the building of a non-denominational women's college at the University of Melbourne, in the space of a few years under her leadership a site was secured, a college built, a principal found and the college opened to pupils. Again, discovering her role in the establishment of the college required detailed searching through newspaper records and archives. When Lady Gowrie opened University Women's College in 1937, Eilean Giblin as Chair of the College Council presented her with a copy of Virginia Woolf's famous work, *A Room of One's Own*. The book's theme was appropriate to the opening of a women's college but its feminist consciousness had a deeper resonance reflecting aspects of Eilean Giblin's own life. She noted Virginia Woolf's death in 1941 in her diary.[13] It was symbolic of the end of an era, a mark of the change caused by war when social, political and feminist goals, so important in the pre-war years, were overtaken by a more momentous struggle.

Eilean Giblin was 55 when the Second World War began and for the third time in as many decades she faced life in a new city and new environment. Had she stayed in Melbourne she could have looked forward

---

[12] MS366/6/2, 1 September 1943.
[13] MS366/6/1, 5 April 1941.

to continuing to oversee the further development of University Women's College. Her new home Canberra was a small, immature city lacking the framework for feminist activism of older cities. In the place of active participation she decided to observe and record. The diaries she kept from her base in Canberra are a unique social record and a powerful witness to the immense human suffering and futility of war. While she recorded the war raging around the world and her agonised concern for the loss of life and the double standard applied to Allied and enemy actions, she became a more private person, although still stirred to action by injustice. She found respite from the war in establishing a studio pottery which she saw as a creative act, a temporary defence in blotting out the horrors of the war and the destruction she saw around the world. Although her days of feminist activism were behind her, the diaries she kept in Canberra are important not only for their record of a country at war but because it is possible from them to gauge something of her character, interests, opinions, her moral outlook and her marriage.

This book aims to document and place in historical context a woman's pursuit of feminist goals entwined in the mosaic of the history of the first half of the twentieth century. The invisibility I initially found in researching Eilean Giblin's life was eerily echoed in the invisibility of much of the essential but often barely noted initiatives of the women's movement in this seemingly fallow period between first and second wave feminism.

As I researched more of her background I discovered a life shaped not only by the cataclysmic events of the first half of the twentieth century – the two world wars and the Great Depression – but by many of the ideological and social movements of the late Victorian and Edwardian eras in England: the widening of educational opportunities for women; the militant suffrage movement; the idealism of the socialist vision in the early Fabian movement; the sexually liberating bohemian influences of the Bloomsbury Group, the intellectual and artistic circle centred on Virginia Woolf and her sister Vanessa Bell; the social inclusion of the arts and crafts movement; and later, the growing anti-war sentiment during the First World War. She met her future husband through their individual connections to the Bloomsbury Group.

Her story began in London in the late Victorian era.

Chapter 1

Radical waves in a sea of conformity

London 1884–1912

Eilean Burton was born in 1884 into an affluent London family. Her childhood and youth were spent in the last decades of the reign of Victoria in a patriarchal society in which the talents of many women were buried in domestic pursuits. Her parents, Edward and Ada Burton, epitomised the increasing wealth and social standing of the more successful members of the middle-class in late Victorian England. Soon after they married, they moved to East Molesey on the outskirts of London, typical of a trend for moving far from the overcrowded slum tenements and factories of the inner city that provided much of the wealth of the middle classes. Their home was large and they employed indoor and outdoor servants. They chose a public school for their sons, not the small private establishments where they had been educated. They took up the fashionable pursuit of boating on the Thames. And they were frequent visitors to the Continent. Eilean's father, Edward Pritchard Burton, was joint owner of a large tobacco factory in London, and her mother, formerly Ada MacRae, came from a family of Scottish descent, branches of which had been leather manufacturers and educationists. Both families had risen to affluence, although temporary in the case of the MacRaes, as a result of the Industrial Revolution.[1]

The comfortable wealth of the Burton family began with Eilean's grandfather, Alfred Burton, born at Twyford near Reading, the son of a farrier. In 1846, when he was 14, Alfred was apprenticed to Edward Pritchard, a cigar and snuff manufacturer in King Street, Snow Hill, in the City of London. Pritchard and his wife, Jane, a middle-aged childless couple,

---

[1] Clive Mence Burton, 'Burton Family History', typescript, 1978, copy with author. Most subsequent information on the Burton and MacRae families originates from this unpublished typescript.

took the young apprentice into their home at Canonbury, north London and at the age of 21 he married their niece, Mary Dennis. A few years later he became a partner in the prosperous tobacco manufacturing business and the firm became Pritchard and Burton. On Pritchard's death in 1869, Alfred Burton became sole proprietor. The original business established by Edward Pritchard in the early nineteenth century traded in snuff and cigars but by the time Alfred Burton became a partner snuff was going out of fashion. The firm's main business was the manufacture of shredded tobacco for pipe smoking and hand-rolled cigars made from raw dried leaf tobacco imported principally from Virginia. Soon after Alfred became a partner he made a fortunate buy of a cargo of raw tobacco from the East Indies, sold as salvage. The tobacco proved to be only superficially damaged but very different from Virginia tobacco, being extremely dark in colour and of very strong flavour. To use this bulk buy Alfred Burton blended small quantities into the firm's regular mixture. This new mixture, marketed under the name of 'Boar's Head Shag', became very popular among London workers, particularly in the East End. The brand was still being sold in London into the 1970s, long after the firm of Pritchard and Burton was taken over in 1954 by the international tobacco firm of Philip Morris Inc. The name of this tobacco is the unlikely and unconventional origin of the boar's head segment in the coat of arms of University College, Melbourne. In honour of her association with the founding of the College in the 1930s, Eilean (Burton) Giblin, when asked to suggest a segment for the College's coat of arms, nominated a boar's head.

In the early 1870s when the Pritchard and Burton factory in King Street, London, was compulsorily acquired for the construction of the Metropolitan Railway Company's underground railway, Alfred Burton was offered a new site at No. 1 Farringdon Road, near Smithfield Market. On this site he built a five-storey factory incorporating the latest ideas in Victorian industrial technology and employed a large workforce either hand-rolling the more expensive products or operating machinery. Charlie Chaplin, later the famous film star and director, was briefly an employee in his youth, in the early twentieth century. Products of the factory were sold direct to retail outlets, mainly pubs and coffee stalls throughout the London area. Pritchard and Burton owned their own horse-drawn two-wheeled gigs driven by liveried coachmen in which their bowler-hatted salesmen did their rounds. During the First World War one of the first aerial bombs dropped on England by German Zeppelins fell in 1915 on the Pritchard and Burton stables which were near St Bartholomew's Church, the main target. The Pritchard and Burton horses were cut loose and escaped unharmed but a

Ford motor van, the firm's first investment in motor transport, was hit and burst into flames, setting the yard alight.

As a prominent London manufacturer, Eilean's grandfather Alfred Burton became a Freeman of the City of London and a member of the prestigious Vintners' Company, one of the city's 12 great livery companies dating from medieval times, when they were powerful in economic, social, political and religious life. In the mid-1880s his name was put forward as a future Lord Mayor of London but he declined nomination because of the considerable cost involved in carrying out the duties of the office. In 1905 he was elected Master of the Vintners' Company.

At the age of 21, Alfred's eldest son, Edward Pritchard Burton, stepped into this business and social world as a junior partner, and a few years later his brother, Frank, also became a partner. At about the time Edward became a junior partner, Alfred Burton moved his family of five from Canonbury to a much larger residence, Hereford House, Park Hill Rise, in Croydon, Surrey, where the family lived in substantial comfort with a large staff of servants including a butler and coachman. While living in Croydon Edward became friendly with the MacRae family who lived at Homefield, Beddington Lane, between Croydon and Mitcham. In 1880, when he was 23, he married Ada Maude MacRae, aged 21. Ada was the second of the eight daughters of James MacRae and his wife, formerly Georgiana Roberts, a daughter of Welsh-born Dr Daniel Roberts, proprietor of Eagle House boys' school at Mitcham where Edward Burton had been educated. James MacRae was descended from a branch of the MacRae family that had left the Scottish Highlands early in the nineteenth century and begun a leather tanning business on the River Wandle near Mitcham in Surrey. The business was successful for many years – James MacRae employed just over 100 workers at the 1871 census and 75 at the 1881 census – but later became engulfed in financial difficulties. The unusual spelling of Eilean's first name reflects her MacRae ancestry. It is not a variant of the well-known girl's name, Eileen, but comes from Eilean Donan (Island of Donan), site of an ancient castle in the Scottish western Highlands, connected to the MacRaes.

Edward and Ada lived at first with Ada's parents in Beddington Lane, until they set up home in Arnison Road, East Molesey, a rapidly expanding rural village that was becoming a popular residential area for business executives working in the city following the opening of the railway to nearby Hampton Court station. They had a particular reason for choosing to live at East Molesey: it was close to the River Thames with its facilities for boating. Edward Burton was enthusiastic about this popular summer recreation and owned a skiff that he kept at Thomas Tagg's boatyard on Tagg Island near Molesey Lock. In their early married life Edward and Ada sometimes left their family of young children in the care of Ada's sisters, while they made boat trips up the Thames from Kingston to Oxford and back. The popularity of these jaunts was immortalised in Jerome K. Jerome's classic humorous novel, *Three Men in a Boat*, published in 1889. Jerome described the crowded, festive scene of fashionably dressed women and men at Molesey Lock as 'a brilliant tangle of bright blazers, and gay caps, and saucy hats, and many-coloured parasols, and silken rugs, and cloaks, and streaming ribbons, and dainty whites'.[2] Unlike the three in the novel, who had a camping tent and slept in their boat, the Burtons stayed overnight at guesthouses and hotels on their boating trips.

Between 1881 and 1887, Ada and Edward Burton had five children, Kenneth MacRae born on 1 June 1882, Colin on 3 July 1883, Eilean Mary on 6 August 1884, Esmond on 5 October 1885 and Geoffrey Edward on 19 July 1888. The arrival of a sixth child, Clive Mence, born on 15 October 1904 after a gap of 16 years, was greeted with surprise by the then grown-up older sons, who are reputed to have remarked when they became aware of their mother's pregnancy, 'Mother, what have you done!' Eilean, born in the middle of a group of brothers, shared with them a childhood typical of a late Victorian upper middle-class family, although her parents were more adventurous and travelled than many others. Apart from their boating trips on the Thames and bicycling to the local Anglican church on Sundays (their mode of transport was a scandal to more conformist members of the congregation), the parents took holidays in England or Europe at least twice a year. Their trips to Europe included visits to Ada's aunt, Amy Roberts, whose home, following her marriage to a German mill owner, Albert Heucke, was at Parchim, near the Baltic coast.

In the 1890s the Burtons moved from Arnison Road a short distance around the corner to a recently built larger house at 22 Spencer Road, East Molesey, which they named Homefield (the name of Ada's parents' house at Mitcham). Built on a one-acre block formerly part of Molesey Park, containing many magnificent old trees, Homefield had eight bedrooms and a grass tennis court. Eilean's older brothers Kenneth and Colin, and her younger brother Esmond were sent to Marlborough College. Originally founded in 1843 to educate the sons of Anglican clergy, Marlborough came under the influence of two early headmasters who introduced the educational

---

[2] Jerome K. Jerome, *Three Men in a Boat*, J. W. Arrowsmith, Bristol, 1889, p. 95.

reforms that Dr Thomas Arnold had initiated at Rugby. By the time the Burton boys went to Marlborough it had a reputation for scholarship, preparing students for the professions, the armed services, the church and the colonial service. Kenneth entered Marlborough in April 1895 and stayed until July 1897, Colin was enrolled from January 1896 to July 1900 and Esmond entered the College in May 1899.[3]

While Marlborough was a conservative choice for their sons, the Burtons made a much more adventurous choice of school for their only daughter. In 1899 Eilean became a boarder at Wycombe Abbey at High Wycombe in the Chiltern Hills about 50 kilometres north-west of London, a school founded only four years before by Dame Frances Dove, the famous educationist who had advanced views on the education of young women.[4] This choice suggests the Burtons were either quite enlightened on the education they wanted for their daughter, that they had some now unknown personal connection with Wycombe Abbey or, perhaps, that they were influenced by the progressive views of Ada MacRae's suffragette sisters. The founding headmistress, Frances Dove, was described by the School Archivist as an 'active suffragette [who] had a big influence on her pupils'.[5]

Dame Frances Dove's educational ideals and philosophy reveal the background to many of the traits that stayed with Eilean to the end of her life, notably her independence, her public spirit, her developed but austere taste, her practical bent and the abstemious quality of her life. Frances Dove saw education as 'the preparation for a life of service and a sense of public duty'.[6] Her fostering of independence and service to others was a challenging philosophy at a time when a prevailing aim in the education of many girls of middle and upper class families was the acquisition of accomplishments such as French, music and painting, as a preparation for marriage to a suitable husband of similar social standing. This idea of education was anathema to Frances Dove. 'My whole soul revolted at this degradation of womanhood,' she wrote.[7] The furnishing of the school reflected Miss Dove's eye for elegance combined with the simplicity that she expected her staff and students to

---

[3] Dr Terry Rogers, Honorary Archivist, Marlborough College, to author, 10, 12, 16 November 2007.
[4] Elsie Bowerman, *Stands There a School: Memories of Dame Frances Dove DBE*, Wycombe Abbey School, High Wycombe, Bucks, [1966].
[5] Alison Heath, Archivist, Wycombe Abbey, to author, 22 May 2006.
[6] Bowerman, p. 57.
[7] Frances Dove, 'The Modern Girl, how far are we fitting her for her varied duties in life?' *Wycombe Abbey Gazette*, Vol. III, No. 9, November, 1907; Bowerman, p. 48.

follow. The blue Rouen china was elegantly shaped; the dormitory curtains were of Liberty material with Morris designs; chairs were simple but well-proportioned and in the entrance there were tapestries and antique furniture. In the midst of this sparse elegance, the routine was spartan. A daily cold bath was part of the regime as were cold unheated dormitories, music rooms and passages. The cold baths were apparently alleviated by maids adding small cans of hot water to the cold water in the small individual hip bath which each girl stored under her bed when not in use.

The curriculum included some subjects very unusual at the time. A trained gardener encouraged the students to cultivate their own small plots; a Scotswoman, Miss Jane Foulis, who had trained at the Edinburgh School of Art, was employed to teach carpentry, and Swedish drill (gymnasium) classes were important in the timetable. The curriculum excluded cooking, dressmaking, domestic economy, sick nursing and hygiene, as Frances Dove believed these subjects were better acquired, if required, in short courses after school. She also abandoned the prevailing educational ideas of constant supervision and restriction, in the running of Wycombe Abbey. Girls were taught to take responsibility and to learn to direct and control others. Senior students, not mistresses, were in charge of dormitories and supervised study away from formal classes and sports were controlled by school and house captains. There was little emphasis on dress, leading some mothers to deplore the lack of interest in clothes and personal appearance. Girls wore dark blue gym suits most of the time and shoes of thick black leather with heavy rubber soles suitable for games.[8]

The English relatives of famous Australian radical feminist, Jessie Street (then Jessie Lillingston), who was a student at Wycombe Abbey in the 1900s, wanted her taken away from the school as they were afraid she was not being taught to behave as a lady. But when her parents visited and found happy, healthy girls in classes, in the gym and at games, they decided she should remain. In her autobiography, Jessie Street acknowledged Frances Dove's influence on her development. 'She had no affectations, a great sense of humour, a great ambition for girls to develop their capacities and she exuded a self-confidence I found most stimulating,' she wrote. And 'She always liked those girls who were not self-conscious and who expressed their opinions.'[9]

---

[8] Lorna Flint, *Wycombe Abbey School 1896–1986*, Wycombe Abbey School, 1989.
[9] *Jessie Street: A Revised Autobiography*, ed. Lenore Coltheart, Federation Press, Annandale, NSW, 2004, p. 11.

By the end of 1899, the year Eilean Burton enrolled, the school had reached its then capacity of 210 pupils. It was already a school with a growing reputation and unlike many other girls' schools it prepared students for entry to Oxford and Cambridge universities. It was to become one of the leading girls' schools in the United Kingdom. Eilean entered the school in the year she turned 15 and stayed until she was 18. She was listed in school records as a member of the boating committee in 1900. In 1901 she played lacrosse and hockey and in 1902 she was in the hockey team. The school paper, the *Wycombe Abbey Gazette*, recorded in the spring term of 1902: 'Eilean Burton, left outer, is not quite as fast as the rest of the forwards. Dribbles well, and when in form shoots very hard and straight, but is variable in her play.' She was assigned to Cloister House, one of six houses, under house mistress Anne W. Whitelaw, a New Zealand-born Cambridge-educated teacher who joined Wycombe Abbey immediately after leaving Girton College. In 1905 she became headmistress of Auckland Girls' Grammar and in 1910 returned to Wycombe Abbey to succeed Frances Dove as headmistress.

During her final two years at school, Eilean was house editor, an early indication of her interest in writing, probably an interest inherited from her mother who kept detailed diaries for considerable parts of her life. Eilean also learnt carpentry at school and it became a skill she used all her life. On one of their visits to the school, inspectors from the United Kingdom Board of Education remarked that it was 'an exceptional thing' for girls to undertake carpentry and also to turn out such 'presentable' work. The inspectors recorded that several girls were making bookcases and one a full-sized punt.[10] Jessie Street wrote in her autobiography of her carpentry efforts, ambitiously attempting to make a two-level revolving bookcase for her father. It ended up as a one-level stationary model but her father was very proud of his daughter's effort and always kept it on his desk.[11] Many decades after she left the school Eilean still made pieces of simple furniture for her homes in Australia.

After Eilean left Wycombe Abbey school records state that she studied in Paris,[12] a city familiar to her MacRae aunts, two of whom ran a private hotel there for students. Although not stated in her record, Eilean appears to have studied art, for which she had inherited some interest and talent.

---

[10] United Kingdom. Board of Education, *Report of First Inspection of Wycombe Abbey School, High Wycombe, Buckinghamshire, 3–5 June, 1908*, p. 13.

[11] Street, p. 13.

[12] Wycombe Abbey School Register, p. 45.

Figure 1.1 Wycombe Abbey hockey team 1902. Eilean Burton is kneeling far left. (Wycombe Abbey School)

Her maternal grandmother, Georgiana Mence MacRae (nee Roberts), had been a scholar and artist who had studied at the University of Louvain and the youngest of Eilean's MacRae aunts, Mary, was a landscape artist. It is likely that Eilean joined Mary in Paris where she had resumed her painting career after leaving her husband, James Martin White, a former member of United Kingdom parliament. A wealthy Dundee jute merchant and importer, White had been briefly a Liberal Member for the Scottish electorate of Forfarshire but had resigned following publicity concerning a breach of promise case brought against him by the daughter of a Scottish clergyman. A few years later, in 1898, he married Mary MacRae, then aged 24, and they set up house at Cumberland Terrace, Hanover Square, London, and had two children, Joan and Oliver. They separated in the early 1900s. At the divorce hearing in 1912 Mary described White as a persistent womaniser but the divorce was granted to him on the grounds of Mary's desertion when she stated she refused to 'live under the roof of any house' owned by her husband.[13] Mary, known as Molly, only ten years older than Eilean and sharing similar interests, remained her closest friend throughout her life.

---

[13] *Times* (London), 18 November 1896.

Figure 1.2 Cloister House Group, July 1901. Eilean Burton is sitting in the boat holding the pole. (Wycombe Abbey School)

At intervals throughout her life Eilean painted – several of her paintings are among treasured possessions of family connections and friends – but the inculcation of Frances Dove's ideals at Wycombe Abbey had a lasting influence. She left Paris to return to London to train as a social worker at the United Girls' Schools Settlement at Camberwell, one of the poorest parts of south London. Later known as the Peckham Settlement, this was part of a movement to alleviate the social problems caused by the huge influx of people into the cities of Great Britain following the industrial revolution. The movement was begun by an Anglican clergyman, Canon Samuel Barnett, who proposed that 'settlements of university men' should volunteer to live in the poor areas of overcrowded cities to experience themselves the appalling poverty and tenement housing and to bring education and material help to the people living there. Barnett's vicarage in the East End of London became the first settlement, Toynbee Hall, where well-known workers included Clement Atlee, later British Prime Minister, and Lord Beveridge, the architect of Britain's welfare state.

Women followed this lead and in 1896 representatives of a group of girls' schools, including Frances Dove of Wycombe Abbey, set up the United Girls' Schools Settlement. Former students of Wycombe Abbey were

Figure 1.3 Carpentry workshop Wycombe Abbey. (Wycombe Abbey School)

encouraged to take part in the work of this Settlement which fitted in well with Miss Dove's educational aims.[14] For some young women work at the Peckham Settlement was a temporary phase, but for those like Eilean who took up social work as a career it was a long-term commitment. The training in Eilean's time appears to have been work-based but a few years later the London School of Economics became associated with the education of social workers at the Settlement. Eilean's work at the Settlement was with the Apprenticeship Committee and the Children's Care Committee. Her example evidently influenced her painter aunt, Mary MacRae White, who after the First World War taught art at the Greenwich Settlement House in New York. The House aimed to ameliorate the living conditions of Greenwich's then mostly poor immigrant population and to offer cultural enrichment through exposure to the arts.

The Peckham Children's Care Committee was later taken over by the London County Council and Eilean worked for the Council as Assistant Organiser of Children's Care.[15] She shared a flat in London with her

---

[14] Jennifer Stephens, *The Peckham Settlement 1896–2000*, Stephens Press, Bickton, Hants, 2002.

[15] Wycombe Abbey School Register, p. 45.

brother Esmond, who had trained as a wood carver. At the 1911 Census she is listed as the sole occupant of a five-roomed dwelling at 30 Bedford Way, Camden, but this appears to have been when Esmond was on a visit to his parents. Eilean and Esmond were the least conformist children of the Burton family. The eldest son, Kenneth, after leaving Marlborough College and spending some time in Germany, joined the family firm of Pritchard and Burton as a junior partner and he and his cousin Guy Burton eventually succeeded their fathers, Edward and Frank, as owners of the firm. The second brother, Colin, joined the East Surrey Rifles and served with the Royal Warwickshire Regiment at the Boer War. He was commissioned in the Royal Army Service Corps in 1905 and remained in the Army all his life, rising to the rank of Brigadier and being awarded Commander of the British Empire and the Distinguished Service Order. A younger brother, Geoffrey, went to Stubbington House School at Fareham, which coached students for naval cadetships. At 13 he joined the Royal Naval training ship *Britannia* at Dartmouth and later transferred to the newly formed submarine branch. He was commissioned Lieutenant in April 1911 and commanded a submarine during the First World War.

Unlike his older brothers, Esmond did not fit into the mould of Marlborough College and he did not share their more conventional ambitions. He left Marlborough soon after he turned 16, explaining to an interviewer later in life that he could not pass examinations, he loved working with his hands and he was much more at home in a carpenter's shop than in a classroom. His passion was studying medieval carvings in village churches. With no encouragement or financial assistance from his father, Esmond became articled in London to Lawrence Turner, a well-known carver in wood and stone, and attended night classes in life drawing. In 1908, when he was only 22, he was commissioned by Mervyn Macartney, architect to St Paul's Cathedral, to work on the reredos (screens behind the altar) in St George's Chapel. Macartney was influenced by the arts and crafts movement, a major aim of which was collaboration of architects with artists and craft workers. In 1883 Macartney had joined William Lethaby and other architects in forming a group to debate and voice concern about the increasing separation of architecture and art. The following year they joined with another group to form the Art Workers' Guild, which aimed to promote the creative marriage of architecture, painting and sculpture on equal terms.[16]

---

[16] Rosalind P. Blakesley, *The Arts and Crafts Movement*, Phaidon Press, London, 2006, pp. 58–60.

Esmond Burton was elected to the Art Workers' Guild in 1919 as a carver and he was later president of the Master Carvers' Association.[17] His first solo commission was a memorial to industrialist, parliamentarian and friend of Gladstone, Lord Rendel, a marble altar tomb with a stone canopy and figures on either side erected in East Clandon Church, Surrey.[18] In later life he was a highly regarded architectural sculptor who was commissioned to do major carvings in many cathedrals and for many national memorials erected in Britain after each of the world wars. Through Esmond, Eilean came in contact with the ideas of the arts and crafts movement which was inspired by concern for social reform and social inclusion and challenged the tastes associated with the Victoria era. Her taste in furnishing her homes and her choice of architect for her Tasmanian house reflected the influence of the arts and crafts movement.

Already radicalised by her work with severely deprived children living in acute poverty in overcrowded slums at the Peckham Settlement and with the London County Council, Eilean also came under the influence of another of the great movements for social change in the Edwardian era, the fight for woman suffrage. Two of her MacRae aunts were deeply involved in this struggle. The unmarried MacRae sisters, partly through their straitened circumstances due to their father's bankruptcy and partly through their upbringing in a family where education and scholarship were valued, became, unlike many others of their era, very independent women. Elizabeth (Betty) MacRae trained at University College London and served as a sister at the Boer War in Queen Alexandra's Imperial Military Nursing Service. Two others, Georgina and Helen MacRae, after their venture in running a private hotel in Paris, established a boarding house in Vernon Place, Bloomsbury. There they became part of the intellectual, political and social world of the pioneers of the Fabian Society and the radical arm of the suffrage movement, as well as friendly with members of the Bloomsbury set, the intellectual and artistic circle of writers and artists centred on Leonard and Virginia Woolf and Virginia's sister Vanessa Bell. The MacRaes' nephew, Clive Burton, described the MacRaes' boarding house:

> In London many of their guests were members of the so-called "Bloomsbury Intelligentsia" and the sisters met many people associated with the recently formed Fabian Society and others

---

[17] Philip Ward-Jackson, *Public Sculpture of the City of London*, Liverpool University Press, Liverpool, 2003, p. 453.

[18] Sir Henry Bashford, 'The Sculpture of Esmond Burton', *Country Life*, 27 January 1950.

who were advanced thinkers, some of eccentric habits, all of them against the accepted conventions of the period and the economic conditions then prevailing. Amongst these persons whose names later became famous were H.G. Wells, Constance Garnett and Sylvia Pankhurst (the latter a well-known Suffragette).[19]

The MacRae sisters' association with Constance Garnett (nee Black), who became renowned as a pioneer translator of Russian classics into English, was to play an important part in Eilean's life as a conduit for her meeting with her future husband. Georgina and Helen MacRae knew Constance and her sister Clementine Black through the early Fabian Society in which the Blacks were both active members, Clementine serving a term on the Executive Committee. Before her marriage to writer and literary editor Edward Garnett, Constance Black worked as a librarian at the People's Palace, an organisation that aimed to bring culture and recreation to the people of the East End of London. It was called originally the 'People's Palace of Delights for Eastenders'. The Palace library, modelled on the reading room at the British Museum, is now Queen's Building at the University of London.

Through their friendship with Sylvia Pankhurst Georgina and Helen MacRae became militant suffragettes. They joined the Women's Social and Political Union, formed by Emmeline Pankhurst and her two daughters Christabel and Sylvia, and became active supporters of their militant 'Votes for Women' campaign. The Pankhursts had begun the WSPU because they believed existing organisations fighting for women's suffrage by conventional methods had achieved little over many years of peaceful campaigning and they determined to use tactics that would gain public attention and force Parliament to grant women the vote. During the years of the militant suffragette campaign, from the mid-1900s to the start of the First World War, thousands of women went to prison for their involvement in WSPU's campaigns. In prison, very few suffragettes were given the political status they demanded, which would have made them eligible for the privileges available to political prisoners. In protest they went on hunger strike, refusing all food. Many suffragettes were force fed by prison doctors under instruction from a Government that was afraid the women would starve to death and become martyrs.[20]

---

[19] Clive Burton, 'Burton Family History'.
[20] Antonia Raeburn, *The Militant Suffragettes*, Michael Joseph, London, 1973; Diane Atkinson, *The Suffragettes in Pictures*, Museum of London, Stroud, Glos., 1996.

Militant suffragettes were supported by the weekly paper *Votes for Women*, which portrayed their struggle in military terms. They were described as 'holy warriors', their fundraising was for the 'war chest', and specially struck medals, the 'Prison Medal' and the 'Holloway Medal', were awarded to those who served prison terms. There was an additional 'For Valour' medal for hunger strikers. Those who had been imprisoned wore proudly the convict's arrow in processions. Whenever suffragettes were in prison loyal members of the WSPU and sympathisers stood outside the prison walls singing suffragette songs to try to keep up their morale and to remind them they had not been forgotten. Breakfast parties were held to welcome released prisoners.

Both Georgina and Helen MacRae, who by 1910 had moved to the rural village of Edenbridge, Kent, south of London, joined violent WSPU demonstrations. Georgina was arrested following demonstrations on 18 November 1910, known as 'Black Friday'. Violence developed after the Prime Minister Herbert Asquith refused to see a deputation from the WSPU. Suffragettes who attempted to reach the House of Commons to see the Prime Minister were stopped by police, and several women were thrown to the ground; some were seriously injured and there were allegations that some were sexually assaulted.[21] Women demonstrated against this treatment during the following week, mainly by attacking the homes of politicians; Georgina was arrested for taking part in one of these demonstrations. By then aged about 50, she came before Sir Albert de Rutzen at Bow Street court charged with throwing stones at the home of Winston Churchill, Home Secretary in the Asquith Liberal Government, in Eccleston Square. In her defence, she stated that the demonstrators had no option but to resort to militant measures after the police action against the peaceful women's deputation the previous Friday. A fellow defendant, Miss Fison, added: 'We were forced to make a protest. I want you to know I am a law-abiding woman, but I have had to do this for political reasons. I am not in the habit of throwing stones through windows.'[22] All the defendants charged with attacking Winston Churchill's home were sentenced to 14 days' imprisonment in default of paying a fine of £2. Other women who were charged with throwing stones at the home of Sir Edward Grey, Foreign Secretary in the Asquith Government, at Queen

---

[21] *Votes for Women*, 25 November 1910.
[22] *Votes for Women*, 2 December 1910; Beverley Cook, Museum of London, to author, 8 October 2007.

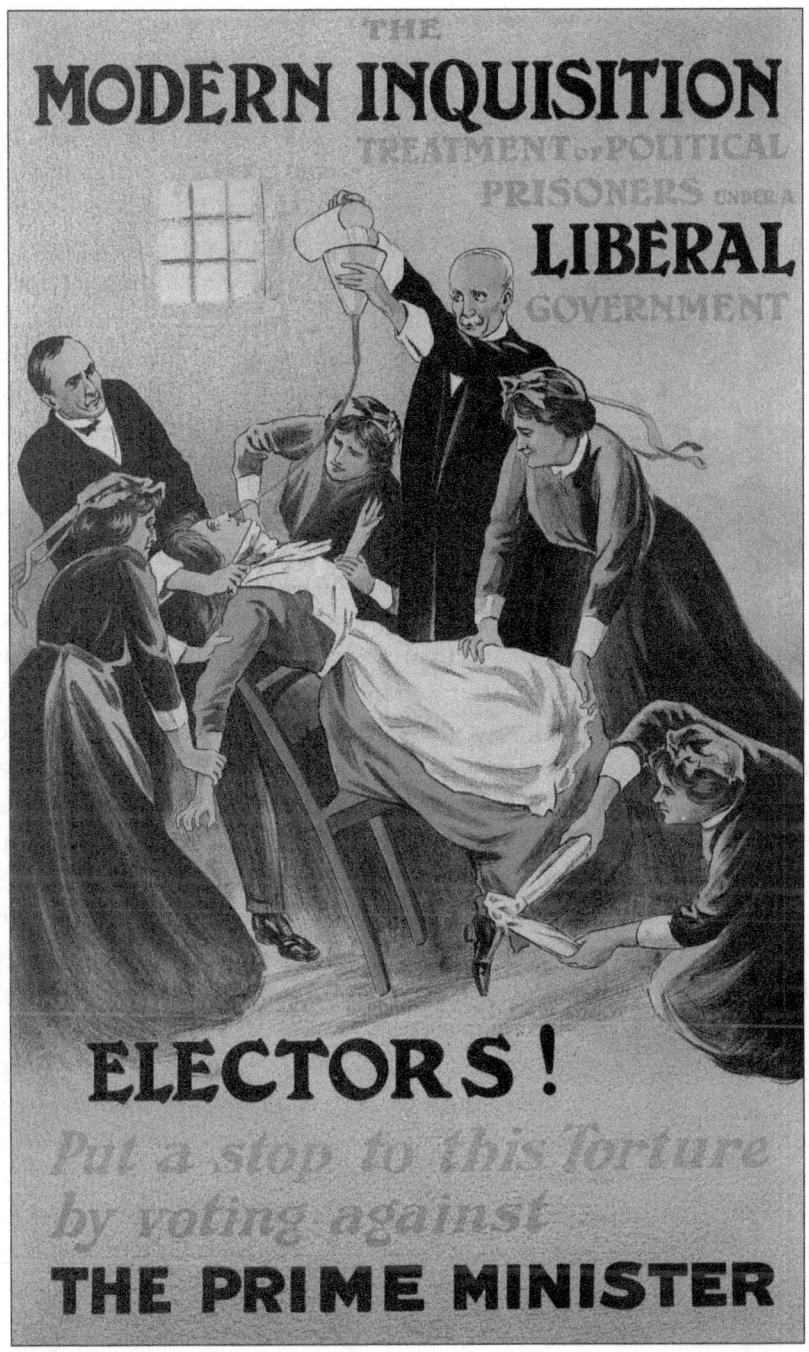

Figure 1.4 Eilean's aunt, suffragette Helen MacRae, was force fed while imprisoned in Holloway Goal in 1912. (Election propaganda poster issued by the Women's Social and Political Union denouncing the Government's treatment of suffragette prisoners. c. 1910. ID No. 50.82/1115. Museum of London)

Anne's Gate, were sentenced to imprisonment for one month on refusing to pay a fine of £5. Georgina MacRae, in line with the suffragettes' policy, chose to go to prison rather than pay a fine.[23]

The WSPU's periodical, *Votes for Women*, carried detailed reports of the event, including graphic pictures of the women thrown to the ground by police during the 'Black Friday' deputation, and detailed accounts of the court proceedings and sentences. Once in prison the paper published the names of the women in 'For Valour' lists and they were mentioned again when the paper announced plans for their welcome after their release on 7 December 1910, at 8 am. The notice read: 'A special breakfast will be held in their honour at the Criterion Restaurant at 9 am. Tickets, from 2s. 6d. can be obtained from the Ticket Secretary WSPU, 4 Clements Inn, WC.'[24] Unlike some other suffragettes who served several prison sentences, Georgina MacRae does not appear to have become a repeat offender. Perhaps she took part in only one violent demonstration or she may have taken part in others and been fortunate not to have been among those charged.

Two years after Georgina's imprisonment Helen MacRae was arrested on 1 March 1912 for taking part in a window smashing campaign that involved hundreds of suffragettes running through the streets of London's West End, breaking shop and office windows with toffee hammers and stones. This campaign of violent action was adopted by Emmeline Pankhurst after repeated failures to get a political response to the adoption of female suffrage but it alienated many other suffragists who supported peaceful, legal methods of gaining their objective. When Helen MacRae was tried with 125 other women before Mr Robert Wallace KC at Newington Sessions, on 26 March 1912, the prosecutor, Mr Travers Humphreys, said the women were charged with the wanton destruction of property worth £4000. In addition the damage committed by other women who were dealt with summarily and by others who were unknown amounted to £8000. *Votes for Women* described the scene in the courthouse when the women's cases were heard as like a busy railway station at the height of the holiday season. Most of the women came prepared for imprisonment and their heaps of luggage were piled against the walls. The public hall was packed with the women and their friends, the police witnesses and the general public. In the street outside crowds of people gathered and watched the arrivals.[25]

---

[23] *Votes for Women*, 2 December 1910.

[24] *Votes for Women*, 9 December 1910.

[25] *Votes for Women*, 29 March 1912; Beverley Cook.

Helen MacRae, like most of the other defendants, was sentenced to four months' imprisonment in Holloway Gaol. In prison the suffragettes were stripped and made to wear coarse prison dresses and were confined to their tiny cells, furnished only with bare wooden benches, for 23 hours each day. No visits or letters were allowed for the first four weeks. During her term in prison Helen MacRae joined her fellow suffragettes in a hunger strike, protesting against their treatment as common criminals instead of their claimed right to have the advantage of being classified as political prisoners. She is listed in *Votes for Women* under the heading, 'The Imprisoned Rank and File'. Several women were released before being force fed because of ill health, some others were released after being force fed because of their deteriorating condition, but Helen MacRae was listed among those who continued to be force fed.[26] This procedure involved being held down by force by up to six warders while a doctor inserted a steel instrument to attempt to force the prisoner's jaw open and push a tube down her throat as she struggled to keep it closed. If this failed a tube was inserted through the nostrils.

After their release from prison, *Votes for Women* published the names of the women in a 'Roll of Honour' alongside descriptions by several of the women of the horrors of the procedure of force feeding. They described being held down and tied to chairs or iron bedsteads while a tube was forced up their nostrils if the attendant was unable to open the prisoner's mouth.[27] As soon as she was released, Helen was involved in another suffrage demonstration in London where more windows were broken. Imprisoned for a second time, MacRae and 65 other suffragettes embroidered their names on a handkerchief that is displayed at the Priest House, a small museum at West Hoathly near East Grimstead in West Sussex.[28]

The militancy of Georgina and Helen MacRae spilled over into the Burton household. Eilean's mother, Ada Burton, did not join her sisters in any London demonstrations but she volunteered at the Kingston-on-Thames WSPU office, addressing hundreds of circular letters. Her father, Edward Burton, described by his son Clive as 'a good stolid citizen, very law abiding, with little sense of humour, a staunch follower of the Church of England, and in politics a strong Conservative', strongly disapproved of the suffragettes and their activities. A rift developed between the Burton parents over the

---

[26] *Votes for Women*, 28 June 1912.
[27] *Votes for Women*, 5 July 1912.
[28] http://www.spartacus.schoolnet.co.uk/SUwspu.htm

militant suffragette activities of Ada's sisters and this was not healed for some years. When Helen MacRae was imprisoned, Clive Burton recorded that his mother instructed the cook at Homefield to bake a special cake and to insert a secret container with a message. Ada took the cake to London but was dismayed to find that prison guards inspected all gifts. The cake was cut open, the message disclosed, and Ada was severely reprimanded by the prison authorities and, according to her son, was lucky not to be charged. This episode was kept from Edward Burton until some months later when Helen was staying at Molesey after her release from Holloway.[29]

Eilean, who was to devote a considerable part of her life in Australia to the women's movement, undoubtedly shared her aunts' views on the pressing need for women to have the vote and was affected by their ordeal. There is no record, however, of her taking an active part in suffrage demonstrations and it is possible that like Virginia Woolf and many other suffragists she chose to support a more moderate organisation. She was a consistent reader of the *Nation*, the liberal radical weekly begun in 1907, which was opposed to the militant suffragette campaign and its 'tactics of violence', which it believed had lost the suffrage movement most of its parliamentary support. Its editor, H.W. Massingham, although moved by the plight of women subjected to forcible feeding, believed that 'bad tactics prejudice a good cause'.[30] Years later in Australia, where the situation was radically different, with women having the vote since the beginning of the twentieth century, Eilean was active in suffrage organisations, but their activities were legal and peaceful and directed towards a broader expansion of women's rights.

---

[29] Clive Burton, 'Burton Family History'.
[30] *Nation*, 23 October 1909, quoted in Alfred F. Havighurst, *Radical journalist: H.W. Massingham 1860–1924*, Cambridge University Press, London, 1974, p. 196.

Chapter 2

Searching for the unknown

Australia 1913–1916

By the end of first decade of the twentieth century, Eilean Burton was at a turning point in her life. She had experienced at first hand the intractable social problems in the poverty-stricken, overcrowded London slums. She was acutely aware of the antagonism that faced reform movements through the gaoling of her suffragette aunts. She had come in contact with many of the new waves of social and political thought in Edwardian London. By contrast, despite her mother's support for her suffragette sisters, her family home remained a bastion of middle-class conservatism. Photographs of the era may have limitations due to the sitters having to remain motionless for some time but to the extent that they can be seen as portrayers of degrees of happiness and contentment, Eilean appears rather remote and disengaged in Burton family images. A hint of suppressed antagonism to the conformist views in the family perhaps? Her father was a staunchly conservative man who led a very ordered life. Each morning a servant brought his polished bicycle to the front door of the residence and Edward Burton rode to Hampton Court railway station where he caught the train to his factory in the city of London. Eilean's eldest brother, Kenneth, heir to his father in the business, followed the same routine. At the five-storey factory, rows of workers operated machinery on the lower floors producing the popular plugs of tobacco while on the highest floor longer-serving, often elderly, workers sat at long tables rolling cigars.[1]

This ordered life was very different from Eilean's experiences at the Peckham Settlement working among some of the most deprived people in London living in crowded tenements in acute poverty in an era when there were no old age pensions, no unemployment pay, and very few public health

---

[1] Clive Burton, 'Burton Family History'.

Figure 2.1 The Burton family at Homefield, East Molesey. Eilean Burton is seated far right. Seated beside her are her parents Edward and Ada Burton and on the left her brother Colin and his wife Gladys. From left (standing) Nanny; Geoffrey; Kenneth; nurse with child; Esmond. The boy in front is Eilean's youngest brother, Clive, and the baby held by a nurse is Nancy, first child of Colin and Gladys Burton. (Gillian Pole-Carew)

services. It was also out of sympathy with the ferment of ideas raging through the circles she had come to know in London: the struggle for equality and expanded opportunities for women, the socialism and idealism of the Fabian Society and the young Labour Party, the sexually liberating influences of the Bloomsbury Group and the social inclusiveness of the arts and crafts movement.

Eilean appears to have had no romantic ties and through the attitudes she had developed she had moved away from the more conventional social circles and the predictable routine of her home. Many of her contemporaries at school had married. She was at, if not past, the age when young women of her generation commonly married. It was a juncture in her life when she was ready for a new challenge. She decided to travel and to write a book about her experiences, following a track pioneered by many 'lady' travellers in the preceding century. To most, travel brought adventure and personal fulfillment, to some like Gertrude Bell and Isabella Bird Bishop it brought notoriety and fame, through their published travel writing. To a professional like journalist Flora Shaw it was a career move. Shaw's dispatches to the London *Times* from South Africa, Australia, New Zealand and Canada were so highly regarded some were published later in book form.[2] Eilean evidently saw herself as a working woman with a mission rather than a 'lady traveller'. It was an occupation that gave purpose, even professional status, to travel; it could be a means of becoming independent and it could lead to a vocation.

She chose to travel to Australia, a country of interest to women in the early part of the twentieth century not as it may have been in the previous century – because of the exotic strangeness of its landscape and flora and fauna – but because female suffrage had been achieved so early. The contrast with England could not have been more striking. At the time Eilean left England her aunt Helen MacRae was still in prison being force fed as a warrior in the fight for female suffrage. Australian women had achieved this goal at the beginning of the twentieth century when they gained the vote federally and became eligible to be elected to the Federal Parliament under one of the first Acts of the Commonwealth of Australia. The right to vote for the lower houses of some of the states had been won earlier: in South Australia in 1895 and Western Australia in 1900. New South Wales followed in 1902, Tasmania in 1904, Queensland in 1907 and Victoria in 1909, although the right to be elected to these parliaments varied from state to state.

Eilean had sufficient family support to finance some basic expenses in Australia but she planned to take a variety of jobs as she travelled to supplement her income and to give her the experiences she hoped would make interesting reading. Like Flora Shaw she went first to South Africa, travelling to Cape Town in September 1912 on the *Tainui* and the following year she joined the White Star line steamship *Afric* in Liverpool to travel to Australia. She arrived in Melbourne on 23 June 1913 and made the Overseas Club in Flinders Street her base. The imperialist orientation of this club – 'the Patriotic League of Britons Overseas' was added to its title during the First World War – makes it appear an unlikely headquarters for a young woman with feminist and radical views but perhaps convenience overcame other considerations. The Overseas Club, founded in 1910, aimed to establish meeting places for British travellers and to provide introductions and offers of accommodation in members' homes. Eilean used the Melbourne branch of the Overseas Club as her postal address during the time she was in Australia.

---

[2] [Flora Shaw], *Letters from Queensland*, Macmillan, London, 1893.

She arrived in Australia with references to a number of people. The names of two – Arthur Garnett in Tasmania and Harold Roberts at 'Shirley' station in western Queensland – are known as their names appear in later letters but she almost certainly had letters of introduction to many other people. Her Tasmanian contact, Arthur Garnett, a son of Dr Richard Garnett, former Keeper of Printed Books at the British Museum, was the youngest brother of Edward Garnett, the well-known writer and critic, influential literary editor and publisher's reader, renowned as a nurturer of writing talent. Joseph Conrad, D.H. Lawrence, John Galsworthy, Ford Madox Ford and Stephen Crane were among the notable writers whose work he promoted; Ford Madox Ford called him the 'Non-Conformist Pope of the literary world'.[3] Eilean's letter of introduction to Arthur Garnett came through her acquaintance with the Garnetts, particularly Edward's wife, Constance, an early member of the Fabian Society where she was a friend of the young, then unknown Bernard Shaw. Constance Black had learnt Russian while studying at Newnham College, Cambridge, and had begun translating Russian literature after meeting Leo Tolstoy while visiting Russia in 1893. She was one of the first English translators of Tolstoy, Dostoevsky and Chekhov, introducing them and other Russian writers to a wide readership.[4] The Garnetts' only child, the writer David Garnett, was intimately connected with the Bloomsbury Group. At one time a lover of the painter Duncan Grant, he later married Angelica Bell, Grant's daughter with Vanessa Bell and a niece of Virginia Woolf.

At the time Eilean visited Australia, Arthur Garnett, a horticultural journalist who had been on the staff of Kew Gardens, was in Tasmania staying with a close family friend, Lyndhurst Falkiner Giblin, a member of a well-known Tasmanian family. Giblin had led an extremely colourful life – as a student at Cambridge, a rugby international for England, a gold-digger and lumberjack on the Yukon and a plantation manager in the Solomon Islands. In the 1890s, during the time when he was studying at University College, London and at King's College, Cambridge, and again after his return to London from his adventurous search for gold on the Yukon, he had often stayed with Edward and Constance Garnett, at their temporary London homes and from 1896 at the Cearne (named Cearne because it was encircled by a forest), the house they built near Edenbridge on the Kent/Surrey border. The Garnetts' home, approached by a rough track through

---

[3] Frances Spalding, *Duncan Grant*, Chatto & Windus, London, 1997, p. 160.
[4] Richard Garnett, *Constance Garnett: A Heroic Life*, Sinclair-Stevenson, London, 1991.

magnificent beech trees, was in an area of the north Downs around the villages of Crockham Hill, Froghole and Limpsfield, within commuting distance of London, that attracted many Fabians. It had become identified as 'a close-knit community of radicals and writers' and had acquired such a reputation one family had to buy a house through an intermediary because the landowners around were uneasy about the influx of 'rebellious eccentrics into what came to be nicknamed "Dostoevsky Corner"'.[5]

In his book of reminiscences, *The Golden Echo*, David Garnett wrote of the visits in the 1890s by 'a young man from Tasmania' – the student Lyndhurst Giblin – to the Garnett home. The acquaintance between Giblin and the Garnetts that developed into a close friendship began because of a distant connection through the relationship of both families to Felix Wanostrocht, a noted Kent cricketer and a member of the All England Eleven. Giblin, moreover, had been named Lyndhurst after Lord Lyndhurst, Lord Chancellor intermittently from 1827 to the 1840s, who was related to the Garnetts through an ancestor on the maternal side. Although they met through these distant connections, Giblin was already a famous man to Arthur Garnett, then a schoolboy, who regarded him with awe as a rugby international who had played for England. Later he became a hero to David Garnett, always known to his family and friends as Bunny, who credited Giblin with helping him when he dreaded school because of constant tormenting by fellow students at University College School in London. Giblin, just returned from the Klondike, met the schoolboy Garnett in London, greeted him with what Garnett described as his 'slow look and friendly smile', took him out for a meal, bought him a rump steak and a shandy and established that he had been at Cambridge with one of Garnett's masters. He then took Garnett to the wrestling gymnasium he had established in London, got a Japanese wrestler champion to give him a lesson and a few weeks later arranged a demonstration of Japanese wrestling for the assembled school at which Garnett was singled out as a friend by the wrestler. Garnett wrote that Giblin's kindness did 'a lot to restore my morale at a time when it was pretty shaky'.[6]

In 1913 when Eilean Burton arrived in Tasmania, Lyndhurst Giblin was 41 years of age and an apple orchardist at Seven Mile Beach near Hobart. In January that year he had been elected to the Tasmanian House of Assembly

---

[5] Norman and Jeanne MacKenzie, *The First Fabians*, Weidenfeld and Nicholson, London, 1917, p. 99.

[6] David Garnett, *The Golden Echo*, Chatto & Windus, London, 1953, pp. 32, 111.

as a Labor member for the seat of Denison,[7] a radical political affiliation for a member of a long-established and distinguished Tasmanian family. Lyndhurst Falkiner Giblin was born on 29 November 1872 into a family that had been in Tasmania for three generations. His father, William R. Giblin, the first native-born Premier of the colony, held office briefly in 1878 and then from 1879 to 1884. He was regarded at the time as the most effective of the colony's premiers, being credited with re-organising the colony's finances and ensuring the stability of his government despite continuing disputes with the extremely unrepresentative Legislative Council.[8]

Lyndhurst Giblin was a brilliant student at The Hutchins School winning the Tasmanian Council of Education's Gold Medal in 1889 and being awarded a State Government scholarship to study at an English university. He went first to University College, London, then to King's College, Cambridge. In vacations he wandered over much of Britain and Europe as far as Iceland, where he studied medieval sagas and translated some into English. After completing his degree at Cambridge in 1896 – he graduated Senior Optime (second highest) in mathematics and science and was an outstanding sportsman – he set off with a Cambridge friend Martin Grainger for North America to seek gold and adventure at the Klondike gold rush. The pair walked 750 kilometres over snow-covered mountains from the Alaskan coast to reach the Klondike River over the Canadian border. Their search for gold was unsuccessful and for the next three years they worked along the Yukon River, the major means of transport for the goldfields, as lumber-jacks and hunters and transporters of supplies by river-boat and dog-sled, sometimes in temperatures below 50 degrees Fahrenheit. Giblin returned to Australia from Vancouver by working his way on a sailing ship, ending the voyage by navigating the vessel through Port Phillip heads to the port of Melbourne. Still seeking adventure he went to the Solomon Islands to report on enterprises for an English company. There he sailed around the islands in a small chartered steamer, tramped through the jungles with a retinue of head-hunters, discovered a gold mine and contracted fever. Reporting back to London, he rejoined Grainger, who was introducing the art of Japanese jiu-jitsu

---

[7] L. F. Giblin was elected on 23 January 1913 and sworn in on 22 April 1913.
[8] Lloyd Robson, *A Short History of Tasmania*, updated by Michael Roe, Oxford University Press, Melbourne, 1985, p. 43; E. M. Dollery, 'Giblin, William Robert (1840–1887)', *Australian Dictionary of Biography*, Vol. 4, Melbourne University Press, 1972, pp. 243–4.

into England, and together they ran a wrestling studio and edited a manual on the art.⁹

Back in Tasmania he taught for a while at his old school, tried poultry farming without success and then cleared some land for the apple orchard that he was to keep until the end of his life. His first foray into Tasmanian politics, when he stood in the 1909 election for the small Liberal-Democrat League, a recently formed party that aimed to reform the State's finances, was a failure. It established him, however, as a person of independence and courage in a state where 'xenophobia, sectarian hatreds and class antagonisms' were rife before the First World War and were to become extreme during the war.¹⁰ During his campaign he was accused of disloyalty to the British Empire and heckled and yelled at during a public meeting at the Hobart Town Hall, when he questioned the popularly accepted idea that Australia should finance a dreadnought warship for the British Navy. Instead Giblin proposed that Australia should undertake to defend its own coast and adjacent seas out of its own revenue. Only he and his seconder supported his motion.¹¹

Soon after, Giblin joined the Australian Labor Party and became an active member, arranging a series of Sunday evening lectures to party branches mainly on elementary economics and the history of wages and working conditions. He was a delegate to the annual state conference in 1912 and was elected to the Party's State Executive. He was also a delegate to the 1912 federal ALP conference but his proposal for a national insurance scheme was overwhelmingly defeated. After a campaign in which he stressed Tasmania's grave financial situation he was elected a Labor Member of the House of Assembly in 1913, a time when the State was experiencing the results of a long-running economic depression with high unemployment and the loss of thousands of young people to the mainland each year in search of work. When a minority Labor Government took office in 1914, with J. A. Lyons, later Prime Minister of Australia, the Minister in charge of Treasury, Education and Railways, he called on his friend, the highly qualified Giblin, for his expertise in statistics and finance. According to Ross McMullin in

---

⁹ Charles Camsell, 'Giblin in North British Columbia 1898–99', in Douglas Copland, ed., *Giblin, The Scholar and The Man: Papers in Memory of Lyndhurst Falkiner Giblin*, Cheshire, Melbourne, 1960, pp.21–28; F.C. Green, 'Lyndhurst Falkiner Giblin', *Stand-to*, August–September 1952, p. 2.

¹⁰ Marilyn Lake, *A Divided Society: Tasmania during the First World War*, Melbourne University Press, Carlton Vic., 1975, p. 195.

¹¹ Frank C. Green, *Servant of the House*, Heinemann, Melbourne, 1969, pp. 9–10.

his history of the Labor Party, 'together they began to renovate the state's financial system'. Lyons and Giblin had been friends since 1909 when they began a Fabian discussion group in Hobart.[12] In 1915 Giblin was elected a foundation member of the first ALP Federal executive.

At about the time he was elected to Parliament Giblin also became a very active member of the University of Tasmania Council, joining the University Extension Board, the Board of Studies (later Professorial Board) and the Council's Standing Committee, all positions of considerable influence in the University. Always on the side of freedom of expression, in 1915 he sided with university lecturer Herbert Heaton who in an atmosphere of war hysteria came under extraordinary attack in parliament and the press following a university extension lecture he gave at Scottsdale. He was reported as saying that, as there had been atrocities on both sides in the war, a draw would be the best result. The University Council supported Heaton but he resigned in 1916 under pressure of sustained attacks. His place was filled the following year by Douglas B. Copland who was appointed lecturer in economics and history and tutor with the Workers' Education Association, the beginning of Copland's distinguished career as an economist and academic. Heaton was later the author of important economic works including an economic history of Europe.[13]

To this point in his life, Giblin's friends appear to have been almost exclusively male. Some of his friends from Cambridge were ruggedly physical and adventurous like Martin Grainger, with whom he spent the best part of a decade in England and Canada, some were homosexual such as historian G. Lowes Dickinson, novelist E.M. Forster and some members of the Bloomsbury Group. In Tasmania he devoted a great deal of time and energy to schoolboy relatives, either taking them camping or having them to stay at his seaside orchard, and he maintained an attachment to boys' own adventure-style books all his life. David Garnett remembered Giblin reading Richard Jefferies' novel *Bevis*, regarded as one of the best books written for boys, 'with profound attention for the fourth time' before going off to the Klondike goldfields.[14]

There are several stories about Eilean Burton's initial meeting with Lyndhurst Giblin while she was in Tasmania as part of her plan to travel

---

[12] Ross McMullin, *The Light on the Hill: The Australian Labor Party 1891–1991*, Oxford University Press, South Melbourne, 1991, p. 89.

[13] Herbert Heaton, *Economic History of Europe*, Harper & Bros., London, 1936.

[14] David Garnett, p. 32.

around Australia, seeking work and adventure as she went. According to her brother Kenneth, who relayed a story told by a fellow student of his sister's at Wycombe Abbey, Eilean had a job in Hobart and, not being able to 'stand foolish folk and their chatter' used to go off on her own at weekends and camp in 'some wild part of Tasmania'. 'There,' Kenneth wrote, 'she met a bloke who also got bored with silly people and their idle talk, and he also used to go away alone and go camping. And that was that.'[15] According to another story told by a Giblin relative, the romantic aspect of their meeting was more explicit. She believed they had met when Eilean was camping near Giblin's apple orchard, that they became lovers in the sand dunes and Eilean decided he was the man she wanted to marry. A more prosaic explanation would be that they met when Eilean turned up at Giblin's home, a two-room shack he had built himself on the beach-side edge of his 100-acre block, and which he had named 'Cobblers End' after his rooms at Cambridge, with her letter of introduction searching for Arthur Garnett. It may have been merely a meeting of two people with compatible views.

However it occurred, it was a meeting of two unusual and unconventional people, both with radical left-wing social and political views and both with a desire for intellectual and political discussion rather than social exchange. As she travelled Eilean kept in touch with progressive thought in England through the British weekly, the *Nation*, begun in 1907 as a Liberal supporting publication but edited by the radical journalist H.W. Massingham. Neither she nor Giblin had much regard for comfort and none for luxury and neither cared for appearance or dress but each had a developed appreciation of the natural world and a desire for a simple, uncluttered life. Giblin, according to his friend Frank Green, was already known as an 'unusual personality'.[16] He had a black beard and when dressed for public occasions wore a homemade red neck-tie, a suit of unusual cut without lapels, and heavy boots greased with dubbin rather than polished. He had adopted these unusual if not eccentric habits of dress at Cambridge, where he first made a red flannel tie, a distinguishing mark he kept all his life.

It is apparent from Giblin's later letters that Eilean became part of his life at Seven Mile Beach. She knew of Arthur Garnett's problems – he had a very pronounced stammer and may have suffered from bouts of depressive illness. She was aware too of Lyndhurst Giblin's attachment to his sisters, his unmarried sister Ella, Edith, married to Hobart ornithologist Robert

---

[15] Kenneth Burton to Mr and Mrs Desmond Giblin [1955].
[16] F.C. Green, *Stand-to*, p. 2.

Hall, and 'Cush' (Muriel Kathleen), married to Reverend Ashley Teece, Minister of Clayton Congregational Church, Norwood, Adelaide.[17] They may have become lovers, as one of the stories went. They shared what were then unconventional social attitudes and were secure enough in their own views to disregard the mores of a very conservative society. But just as they may have entered a relationship unconventionally, any relationship that may have developed appears to have been without commitment.

Whether the start of the First World War in August 1914 influenced their separation is debatable. It seems just as likely to have been Eilean's determination to continue her travels in Australia, writing as she went. Giblin spent the first two years of the war as a part-time citizen soldier in Hobart in the Australian Intelligence Corps that he had joined as a lieutenant in 1909. The role of the Corps, which undertook rough mapping and exploration in the bush, suited him. When war broke out he was in charge of a small intelligence unit in Hobart and was ordered to investigate a report that German warships were hiding near Port Davey in the uninhabited south-west of the state. Tracking through largely unexplored bush, he and his companion made the 225 kilometre journey in the extraordinary time of six days. They reported by carrier pigeons that no enemy was at Port Davey.[18] This was an enterprise that suited his adventurous nature but it appears to have been an isolated event. His army involvement was part-time, his main occupations until 1916 remaining his parliamentary duties in the House of Assembly and his apple orchard.

At the end of 1915, with a Tasmanian battalion being raised, he was called up as a company commander in the 40th Battalion. At this point with the war dragging on he decided not to re-contest the forthcoming state election and in March 1916 volunteered to join the AIF. At the age of 43, just two years below the enlistment age limit, he joined as a captain in the 40th Battalion, all of whose officers were Tasmanians. Although he had an operation to re-set a wrist injured in an accident to make it possible to volunteer, Giblin was far from an enthusiastic supporter of the First World War. Many of his friends in England were conscientious objectors and his later extraordinary bravery on the Western Front came in the face of a consistent belief that the war was a great tragedy that should be ended by negotiation.

---

[17] Adelaide *Advertiser*, 30 August 1909.
[18] L.F. Giblin, 'Port Davey in Wartime', in Copland, *Giblin, The scholar and The Man*, pp. 121–127.

The start of the war does not seem to have altered Eilean's plans and by the latter part of 1915, if not well before, she was in north Queensland. Although most of her movements in Australia are now untraceable, it is possible to pinpoint her in western Queensland for a brief period in late October and early November 1915 because of the fortunate discovery of four of her letters.[19] These four are a very small remnant of what must have been more than 150 letters she wrote at weekly intervals to her parents as she travelled for about three years in Australia. Apart from keeping in touch with her parents her letters were probably intended to form the basis of the book she intended writing. Letters were an established literary form for women travellers. While these four letters are a great discovery, locating her for a short time and giving some insight into what interested her and from what vantage point and what cultural background she interpreted what she saw, those missing would have been an invaluable resource.

What did she tell her parents about meeting Lyndhurst Giblin? Where else did she go and who else did she meet? These are questions that are largely unanswered in her few surviving letters. From information in one of the four letters, it is apparent she spent some time in the Cairns area. She informed her parents that when she told Harold and Grace Roberts, at the outback station from which she wrote the letters, about her experiences in Cairns they 'simply shrieked', as they knew the people she had to deal with. What were these experiences and where else was she in 1914 and 1915 before she turned up at Harold Roberts' station in western Queensland? The first of the letters, dated 20 October 1915, detailed her recent movements. After spending some time around Cairns she had taken a coastal steamer south to Townsville, planning to catch a train to go west. In Townsville she walked a few kilometres to visit John Oliver Feetham, the recently installed Anglican bishop of North Queensland, in his 'large straggling bungalow on the spur of a hill overlooking the sea and the broken coast and islands'.[20] Their connection was their interest in the Settlement Movement. Feetham had worked in a parish at Bethnal Green in the slums of the East End of London until he left for Australia in 1907.

The next morning Eilean left Townsville on the line west to Hughenden for a 12-hour rail journey through Charters Towers and Torrens Creek to Prairie, a railway station about 335 kilometres distant. Her destination was

---

[19] Letters in possession of Eilean's nephew, Peter Burton, Addo, Cape, South Africa; copies with author.

[20] Eilean Burton to Ada Burton, 26 October 1915.

Harold Roberts' sheep station, 'Shirley', in the Barcoo country south-west of Charters Towers, just south of the Tropic of Capricorn. 'Shirley' station now forms the Moorrinya National Park and its remoteness is apparent from its description as an area of dry, flat plains in the heart of an area known as the 'desert uplands'. Tourists are warned that the park, about 90 kilometres south of Torrens Creek railway station on the west side of the road to Aramac a further 180 kilometres south, is 'remote and undeveloped'. It is accessible only by four wheel drive vehicles and not at all after wet weather.[21] Eilean had apparently been advised to continue on the railway past Torrens Creek to the next station at Prairie, the start of a mail run that meandered south through isolated stations to Muttaburra. At Prairie she found no one to meet her as she had arrived before her letter to Harold Roberts could be delivered via the weekly mail run.

Harold Griffydd Roberts was a distant but perfectly situated relative for Eilean's purpose. He provided a route into the heart of the outback and a means of furthering her aim of writing about Australia. Although she was meeting him for the first time, his place in the family tree was well known to her as her mother's cousin. He and his eldest brother Arthur, two of the many children of Dr George Roberts, a Doctor of Divinity and a schoolmaster of Croydon, Surrey, had migrated to Australia while Eilean was a child. Although Eilean was meeting him for the first time, her mother's family maintained close ties with numerous far-flung members whether living in the home counties or in Australia, in Germany or the United States. After Eilean and Harold met, one of their first conversations was about family members.

'Shirley' originally had been part of two huge squatting cattle stations, Lammermoor to the north and Aberfoyle to the east, covering large areas of the semi-desert country west of the Great Dividing Range. The major waterway, Torrens Creek, was often dry but when it flooded it drained south to the Thomson and Barcoo rivers and into Coopers Creek, joining the water system that fed into Lake Eyre. Gradually, under the provisions of successive Queensland Lands Acts the original stations had been reduced in size and 100,000 acre lots put up for auction. 'Shirley' was one of these lots and Harold Roberts had run a sheep station there since the end of the 1890s. In 1908, aged 39, Harold married Grace Adelaide Allen, 34, the Mackay-born daughter of an accountant, at St John's Anglican Church, Cairns. They

---

[21] Queensland, Department of Environment, *Moorrinya National Park: Management Plan*, Brisbane, [c.1998].

had two children, Alan Griffydd, born in 1909, and Shirley Desiree, born in 1911. In the Roberts' time the station with its large, comfortable homestead was a social hub; the first race meeting in the district was held at Nooracoo, a waterhole on 'Shirley'.[22]

When Eilean arrived at Prairie railway station in the evening there was no one to meet her and she had a further shock when she discovered 'Shirley' was 70 miles (about 112 kilometres) from Prairie, not seven miles, as she had believed. She stayed the night at the hotel and left early next morning on the mail run. After travelling over mile after mile of spinifex and gidgee scrub, past country she described as 'absolutely flat and partly covered with thin shrub', Harold Roberts met her and she transferred to his car for the last part of her journey.[23] It is obvious from her letters to her parents from 'Shirley' that Eilean did not have in mind the more usual role of a female relative visiting an outback station. The idle visitor, the worthy governess or nursery help, the 'new chums' often despised for their ignorance and for not immersing themselves in station life, are familiar figures in Australian fiction. Though she liked the Roberts' children, the most Eilean did was observe them sympathetically, walk out in the bush with the boy, Alan, searching for goannas, and attempt to resist their constant entreaties that she come out and play with them in the shade of the poinciana tree.

She was sympathetic with Grace Roberts' life and appreciated that her companionship was valuable for a woman who, although capable and well adapted, still felt the loneliness and isolation of outback life. When the weather got unbearably hot, Eilean was glad to share the hottest hours from 10 to 4 with Grace, both lying about in a minimum of clothes and taking frequent baths even though the water came hot from the artesian bore. But she was critical of the restricted outlook and conversation of the women on the neighbouring stations. 'I think the station people around here are the deadliest I have ever met,' she wrote. 'The babies, the sheep and the weather are the only topics of conversation.'[24] She was struck by the ubiquitous use of the telephone in these vast distances. In the midst of a drought, the merest hint of rain set the telephones ringing, 'everybody is wanting to know who has had rain and whether there are any likely clouds about! Then when it does fall the people with motors go out and "Look for Rain", that is look where

---

[22] Queensland Racing, Oakley Amateur Picnic Race Club, http://www.queenslandracing.com.au/raceclubs/show.asp?id+52792.

[23] Eilean Burton to Edward Burton, 20 October 1915.

[24] Eilean Burton to Ada Burton, 26 October 1915.

it has fallen and then shift the sheep.' When the Roberts' children became ill in the hot weather – at times the temperature reached 114°F [46°C] – neighbours rang to give 'all sorts of advice'. Nevertheless the Roberts family drove 160 kilometres to the nearest town, Hughenden, a major journey in a T model Ford on bush tracks, to seek medical help. When they had car trouble on the way back they had to camp out overnight. 'Motors and telephones have revolutionised the bush,' Eilean wrote.[25]

Although she was sympathetic about domestic problems it is obvious from Eilean's letters that she had arrived with a purpose. She wanted to find out how the station worked and to help with the station activities. From the time she arrived she wanted a horse to ride and Harold was happy to give her one and she was soon in the saddle. She began by accompanying Harold when he checked the sub-artesian bores or looked for signs of the scanty bursts of rain and she watched at an almost dry waterhole while Harold set a pumping engine in motion to fill a long trough with water. Then she watched as the long lines of sheep walked up from different directions, while native companions stalked about and galahs and white cockatoos whirled overhead. Harold has 'pumping engines and boring plant, blacksmiths' shop and a small shearing plant', she reported. Then she went out with one of the men mustering sheep. 'The horses are trained for this work and swing round and turn on their back legs as though they were pivots,' she wrote. Eilean came off twice, once on her forehead, but was not badly hurt.[26]

Everywhere she went she saw signs of the pervading drought, 'the odd sheep lying in the glaring sun too weak to get up, and the dead carcasses of horses, cattle and sheep lying about in the paddocks'. At night she listened to Harold as they sat outside and he talked of the days of the vast stations, enormous herds of cattle and journeys lasting months, when he first arrived in Queensland. As she rode over the station or travelled by car she recorded the landscape – 'curious' to her eyes, 'in some places called desert, which means there are trees and scrub, with patches of bare earth and long waving straw-like grass – in other places there are downs and miles of flat open country with no trees, only queer coarse hefty grass'. Elsewhere she found that 'brown and silver trees grow on brown bare soil with shining stones lying about'.[27]

---

[25] Eilean Burton to Edward Burton, 2 November 1915.
[26] Eilean Burton, 26 October, 2 November 1915.
[27] Eilean Burton, 26 October 1915.

The shearing shed and shearers' quarters, 16 kilometres from the 'Shirley' homestead, remain a prominent landmark even today, the station name painted on the shearing shed roof in letters large enough to be seen from an aeroplane. It is an often-repeated family story that Eilean worked as a shearers' cook during her travels around Australia and this is likely to have been at 'Shirley'. When Harold Roberts was running 'Shirley' as a sheep station, the influx of shearers was a major event and there would have been work for even such an inexperienced cook as Eilean. Giblin relatives who relay the story of her work as a shearers' cook usually add that they felt sorry for the shearers as she was 'no cook'. Nevertheless she must have been proud of her work in this proletarian atmosphere, as her cooking for shearers became a fairly widespread story. As she cooked she probably heard stories of the 1890s shearers' strikes, defining events in Australian history and still, in 1915, a vivid memory to many shearers. Barcaldine to the south of 'Shirley' and Clermont to the south-east had been major strike camps for the shearers while some of the detachments of police and military sent to protect strikebreakers were stationed at Hughenden to the north-west. Even at the small settlement of Torrens Creek to the north of 'Shirley' there had been a clash between squatters and shearers. Aberfoyle, the property to the east of 'Shirley', was a setting in fictional disguise for two novels written by Queensland-born expatriate novelist, Rosa Praed, *Mrs Tregaskiss* (1895) and *Lady Bridget in the Never-Never Land* (1915), that portray the bitterness and high drama of the shearers' strikes. Praed's information on the strikes came from her sister Lizzie Jardine, who lived on Aberfoyle.[28] Eilean also worked as a cook in a mining camp during her travels, an experience that 'gave her a breath of outlook she might not otherwise have attained'.[29]

There are occasional references to the First World War in Eilean's four letters from 'Shirley' but war news was hard to come by, a problem for someone as interested as she was in current events and opinion. Throughout her travels, her parents sent her copies of the London *Times* and the periodical the *Nation* but they were months old by the time they arrived and even the Australian weekly papers, to which Harold Roberts subscribed, could be well out of date by the time they arrived by the mail run. The telephone was the best source of up to date news but the news that came that way Eilean found exasperating. 'One wants to know so much and can

---

[28] Patricia Clarke, 'The Queensland Shearers' Strikes in Rosa Praed's Fiction', *Queensland Review*, May 2002, pp. 67–87.

[29] Eveline Syme, 'Tribute', UC Archives.

only get scraps of information,' she wrote. 'The various stations ring up after the Postmaster has rung off and try to find out if anyone has gathered any other interesting point.'[30] 'Last night we heard by telephone that Roumania is probably coming in on the side of the Allies but that Greece is still shilly shallying,' she wrote. A few weeks later she heard, again by telephone, of a change in the Greek Cabinet with the hope that Greece would join the Allies. She added, 'Serbia seems to be having an appalling time. It is ghastly that a second nation should suffer the fate of Belgium.'[31] By the time her letters reached her parents the war had moved far beyond these concerns. It was via letters from her parents that arrived at 'Shirley' early in November that she heard that the Pritchard & Burton stables had been burned as a result of one of the first German Zeppelin air raids on London a few months before.

Apart from mustering and cooking for shearers and miners there is no record of what else Eilean did during her travels on the mainland, but when she arrived back in England early in 1917, she had with her the manuscript of her travels. The few extant letters from 'Shirley' station indicate that it would have contained descriptions of life in the outback, the isolation, the heat, the drought, the overwhelming importance of the weather, and the subtle colours of the vegetation in the Australian bush. The manuscript would also have contained her experiences and adventures in other parts of Australia including Tasmania and her meeting with an unusual Labor parliamentarian.

It has been claimed that Eilean returned to England via the 'New Australia' settlement, the socialist experiment begun in the 1890s by William Lane in Paraguay, South America, but there does not appear to be evidence of this. The visit is mentioned in Gibbney's *Canberra 1913–1953* in a short description of Eilean, as a preliminary to quoting from her Second World War diary.[32] Eilean's supposed Paraguayan visit has been repeated in other contexts and has an appealing resonance. She would have heard of the 'New Australia' venture during her visit to Australia and as a socialist experiment it would have interested her. It is also possible that with international shipping in turmoil during the First World War a ship travelling via South America may have been an alternative for a traveller with no travel priority wishing

---

[30] Eilean Burton to Ada Burton, 9 November 1915.
[31] Eilean Burton, 9 November 1915
[32] Jim Gibbney, *Canberra 1913–1953*, AGPS, Canberra, 1988, p. 209. The reference is to a letter from C. F. Giblin to Gibbney, 10 July 1986, but the letter contains no mention of Paraguay. Gibbney Papers, NLA MS 3131.

to return to England. Although the settlement itself, rent by division and clashes of personalities, had deteriorated drastically from its idealistic beginnings, when it had attracted such people as poet Mary Gilmore and her husband, even in 1916 it was an experiment that remained of interest. Shipping records, however, indicate that Eilean returned to England from New Zealand sailing on RMS *Maitai* from Wellington via Rarotonga in the Cook Islands and Papeete in Tahiti to San Francisco. She arrived in San Francisco in December 1916 and made her way from there to London by early 1917. She listed her occupation as teacher, on the passenger list, presumably referring to some temporary position she took in Australia or while in New Zealand waiting for a passage to England.[33]

Eilean returned to England with high hopes of getting her manuscript published. When she re-established contact with Lyndhurst Giblin, by then on the Western Front, one of his first questions was, 'How is the book? Are you still putting stuff together?' Later, when he read Eilean's manuscript, he particularly liked the Queensland part. It 'went very well – full of meat', he wrote. 'It will be very stupid if no publisher here will take it.' He suggested she try his friend from his University College days, Edward Verrell Lucas, essayist and writer for the satirical periodical *Punch*, who was a director of the publishing house Methuen. Lucas was also a friend of Edward Garnett's and lived at Froghole only a few miles from the Cearne. 'I expect it's rather out of Methuen's line – their game is very much safety,' Giblin wrote, 'but I am sure Lucas personally would appreciate it. ... If you do try Lucas with a sample, you might say I advised it.'[34]

When Eilean rejected the idea of sending a section to Lucas, apparently because a literary agent advised against it, Giblin suggested another publisher, Herbert Jenkins. Through 1917 he inquired regularly about the fate of the manuscript. 'No further news of ms?' he wrote on 14 October.[35] When he heard it had been knocked back by an unspecified publisher, he again suggested trying Lucas but Eilean sent the manuscript to America. 'Sorry to hear about the ms,' he wrote in November 1917. 'Good luck with it in America! If not let us try Lucas with it.'[36]

---

[33] List of Passengers, *RMS Maitai*, on arrival in San Francisco, December 1916.
[34] Giblin Papers, NLA MS366/1, 13 August 1917.
[35] MS366/1, 14 October 1917.
[36] MS366/1, 6 November 1917.

Chapter 3

Love in wartime

England 1917–1919

In March 1917 Captain Lyndhurst F. Giblin wrote to Eilean Burton from the Western Front after hearing that she was back in England. He had arrived in England in the late summer of 1916 after sailing from Hobart on the *Berrima* at the beginning of July, in command of D Company of the 40th Battalion, Australian Imperial Force. By the time the 40th Battalion reached the front line on the Western Front, the First World War had settled into a stalemate with the opposing armies facing each other across Belgium and north-eastern France. The Tasmanians spent the winter bogged down in trench warfare near Armentières and it was from there that Lyndhurst Giblin wrote to Eilean.

She kept this letter and more than 400 other letters he wrote to her over more than 30 years, including some hundred or more he wrote during the First World War. None of Eilean's letters in reply has survived but it is sometimes possible to follow what was happening to her and to gauge her views, from Giblin's letters. They are not usual 'love' letters. Apart from the first one, which began 'Dear Wanderer', none has a salutation and none has an ending except the initials LFG. They portray a comfortable relationship between two compatible people united by similar views on national and international events and by common scepticism and fury about the political and military conduct of the war. There is no indication in this first letter that they had been lovers in Tasmania but there is also no indication in Giblin's subsequent letters of the developing relationship that culminated in their marriage. Perhaps their intimacy may have been so accepted that it required no expression. With no beginning and no end, the letters read like snatches of a continuing, sometimes laconic, one-sided conversation.

Giblin often mentions news from Tasmania, how Arthur Garnett was getting on at Cobblers End, or what his sisters, Ella Giblin and Edith Hall, were doing, references that implied that Eilean knew the people well and was quite familiar with the shack and orchard at Seven Mile Beach. Absent, however, is any hint of the sexual attraction that presumably existed between this 33-year-old woman and 45-year-old man. If this was expressed in some letters, they are not among those that have survived and so many have survived that it hardly seems likely that any others would have been markedly different in tone. The letters are casually intimate but they give no sense of a developing love affair. Several opportunities for meetings during Giblin's leaves appear to slide by with, at the most, fleeting encounters, although the exigencies of life in wartime aborted some arrangements. The letters contain many close glimpses of life in the trenches and in battle, in which there is an underlying but unstated sense of Giblin's courage. He does not mention winning the Military Cross in the Battle of Messines or being awarded the Distinguished Service Order after the Third Battle of Ypres but he frequently expresses concern for his troops. On one occasion, on a long three-day march during which even tough bushmen suffered severely from feet complaints after months in the wet and mud of the trenches, he 'got rid' of his horse and took his pack 'to keep more in touch with how things were going' among his troops.[1] From other accounts this was a feature of his war service – his troops, mostly a generation younger than he was, often referred to him as 'Dad'.

Eilean was at her parents' home, Homefield, East Molesey when she received Lyndhurst Giblin's first letter beginning, 'Dear Wanderer':[2]

> It was a good deed to send me a line. I have been separated from some of my papers & had not your English address. You expected to be in England early in the year but I did not feel sure you would not loiter a good deal on the way – if you struck anything of interest.
>
> I have been here since end of November; leave is a distant prospect – too distant to think of at present. Things are livening up & there is not much chance of any more generous allowance coming into practice. But should like to hear what you can tell me by letters. I know you are a noble writer of letters, and you will be kind to my infirmity that way. Tell me something of what you did after

---

[1] MS366/1, Letters L.F. Giblin to Eilean, 23 March 1917.
[2] MS366/1, 4 March 1917.

leaving Tasmania, & particularly what you are doing now. How is the book? Are you still putting stuff together? I have an idea you sent some copy from Tasmania, but I'm not sure.

Things are going pretty fairly for our Battalion here. We have been hit rather hard for stationary trench warfare; we've lost with others the two men in the battn I could least afford personally to lose – I have come through myself without damage & am generally very fit.

Letter from Arthur [Garnett] last week full of news of Cobblers End – chiefly devastations caused by the floods. Your letter dated Febr 7 delivered an hour ago; March 4th mail closing now so you will see how long it takes home the other way. Mails are very slow. The runner grows restless.

    LFG

This letter was the start of a correspondence that reveals Giblin as a man out of sympathy with British and Allied political conduct of the war and with military leadership and it is obvious that Eilean shared these views. She sent him copies of the American progressive paper, the *New Republic* (often unobtainable in England – Eilean got copies from a relative in New York) and the English radical periodical, the *Nation*, which under the editor H.W. Massingham changed during the First World War from a Liberal to a Labour supporting journal advocating a negotiated peace. Massingham regarded military conscription introduced by the British Government early in 1916 as 'this historic reversal of Liberalism and democracy'.[3] In his letters, Giblin discusses the alternative policies advocated in these publications as well as in others to which he subscribed. These included the *Cambridge Magazine*, the No Conscription Fellowship's publication the *Tribunal* which was supported by Bertrand Russell, and the left-wing periodical the *New Statesman*, begun in 1913 (although Giblin found even the latter 'more jingo every week'). They also read and discussed books by left-wing writers. These included *The Choice Before Us* by G. Lowes Dickinson, a pacifist associated with the Bloomsbury Group whom Giblin had known at Cambridge where

---

[3] Thomas C. Kennedy, *The Hound of Conscience: A History of the No Conscription Fellowship 1914–1919*, The University of Arkansas Press, Fayetville, 1981, p. 238.

Dickinson was a fellow of King's and a member of the Apostles, the elite discussion group of Cambridge intellectuals, and *The War of Steel and Gold* by journalist H. N. Brailsford, who wrote editorials for the *Nation* and some of whose publications were impounded because of his criticism of government policies.

When Eilean wrote of the hatred for Germans expressed in British newspapers, Giblin replied 'you won't of course find much of that here. There's a good deal of fellow feeling with Fritz as the victims of the same sort of higher command – which is apparently callous and unreasonable and quite evidently makes a muddle of nearly everything it touches'. He attributed 'the big anti-conscription vote from the Somme' in the first conscription referendum held in Australia in December 1916 to the 'feeling of being fooled about by people who do not know their job'.[4] He believed the overthrow of the Czar and the takeover by the Provisional Government in Russia, was 'too good to be true', he couldn't believe it had been carried out 'so easily & quickly'. He hoped it would lead to a change in Russian policy towards Finland and Poland and the abandonment of the 'incubus' of Constantinople as a Russian war aim, which would be as good as the wiping out of three German armies. Most of all he longed that England would get back 'a little liberty of speech' so that 'one might fairly well hold up one's head again'. He added, 'I am rather wondering how much of this will reach you. From recent experience, it is very difficult to keep a sufficiently high note of optimism & rather irrational patriotism to pass some of the gentlemen who look at letters at the Base.'[5] In another letter he asked, 'By the way do you know of a decent & sober minded MP who carries a little weight. I am tempted to try & put one on to certain points.'[6]

The appointment of influential newspaper publisher and strident proponent of a punitive war settlement against Germany, Lord Northcliffe, as the British Government's Director of Propaganda provoked him to exclaim, 'My God! Fancy having the country's reputation built upon accordance with Northcliffe's views.'[7] He was incensed when British philosopher, mathematician and pacifist, Bertrand Russell, was sentenced to six months' imprisonment for what Giblin described as a 'only a bit of a slightly ill-tempered sling off' at America while 'hundreds of things, 20

---

[4] MS366/1, 23 March 1917.
[5] MS366/1, 23 March 1917.
[6] MS366/1, 5 November 1917.
[7] MS366/1, 22 February 1918.

times stronger', were 'slung off' at Russia with 'never a hint of disapproval'.[8] Russell in the course of an editorial in the *Tribunal* had warned trade unionists of plans Allied governments might be hatching to intimidate them by the use of American troops as strikebreakers, 'an occupation to which the American Army is accustomed when at home'.[9] Interviewed by two detectives while at home in his bath, Russell was charged with writing material concerning the use of American troops as strikebreakers that the prosecution claimed could have a 'diabolical effect' on the morale of Allied armies. Within a week he was put on trial at Bow Street magistrates' court and convicted and sentenced to six months as a second division or ordinary prisoner without the option of a fine. His appeal against the sentence was dismissed but following intervention by Arthur Balfour, Foreign Secretary in the Lloyd George Government and a former Conservative Prime Minister, he served his sentence in the first division where he was treated as a political prisoner and allowed his own clothes, furniture, books and writing material.[10]

On an earlier occasion Russell, the most prominent member of the No Conscription Fellowship, had been found guilty under the Defence of the Realm Act for 'statements likely to prejudice the recruiting and discipline of His Majesty's Forces' and fined £110. On that occasion when Russell refused to pay the Government did not imprison him but instead sold his goods at Trinity College, Cambridge, at auction. The Trinity College Council voted unanimously to remove him from his lectureship and he was also refused permission to leave Britain to take up a position at Harvard.[11]

In these same letters, interspersed with his deep antipathy to the prosecution of the war, Eilean read of Giblin being wounded in horrendous battles. As the war dragged on she must have wondered whether he could possibly survive the desperate battles being fought on the Western Front. When, however, after he had been wounded twice, she suggested that he try to get a staff or base job away from the front line, he replied that there were other officers who 'mentally & physically' needed relief much more and most were married and had young children. 'You see I can hardly put in a claim for preference,' he wrote.[12]

---

[8] MS366/1, 22 February 1918.
[9] *Tribunal*, 3 January 1918, quoted in Kennedy, pp. 243–5.
[10] Kennedy, pp. 243–5.
[11] Kennedy, pp. 128–30.
[12] MS366/1, 14 August 1918.

Eilean heard of Giblin's first wound when he wrote from a field hospital that he had 'got mixed up with a shell'. He was tempted to 'take a Blighty', he wrote, but felt he couldn't be away from his troops for long.[13] Giblin was wounded on 14 April 1917 during a German bombardment preparatory to a raid near Armentières but managed to avoid being evacuated to a hospital in England. He returned to his unit in time for the Battle of Messines in Flanders in June 1917, a major offensive that was a prelude to the Third Battle of Ypres the following month. As he led his troops during the Battle of Messines through a constant stream of gas shells and mine explosions and was within two hundred yards (183 metres) of the objective, Giblin was shot through the thigh by a machine gun bullet. Although badly wounded, he remained with his men, rallying them and supervising the consolidation of the position they had captured. He was awarded the Military Cross for his 'conspicuous gallantry and devotion to duty' leading his men 'with great dash and determination' and setting 'a magnificent example of personal courage and devotion to duty throughout'.[14] He was promoted to Major soon after the battle. After he was taken from the casualty clearing station to No 3 General Hospital, France, he wrote to Eilean, 'in hospital again you see'.[15]

After about two weeks, Giblin was transferred to the 3rd General Army Hospital at Wandsworth, south-west of London. The day after he arrived he wrote to Eilean, hoping that if she was not too much immersed in her war job, she would visit him. He gave directions about train and bus routes but added 'it's an awful way to drag anyone'.[16] Eilean visited the hospital but missed Giblin, who was temporarily absent for a medical examination, and it is unclear whether they met at all during his time at Wandsworth. They probably met later during his convalescence when Giblin visited Constance Garnett at the Cearne, which was only about six kilometres from where Eilean was staying at Comforts Cottage, the home of her aunts Georgina and Helen MacRae, at Oxted, in the Surrey/Kent border district near Edenbridge.

The Garnetts' home where Giblin spent part of his convalescence from his wound was an unconventional household. For some years Edward and

---

[13] MS366/1, 27 May 1917.
[14] F.C. Green, 'Giblin in Politics and War', in Copland, *Giblin, The Scholar and the Man*, pp. 33–34; *London Gazette*, 24 August 1917; NAA WWI records L.F. Giblin, B2455, 5029591, recommendation, 16 June 1917.
[15] MS366/1, 13 June 1917.
[16] MS366/1, 24 June 1917.

Constance Garnett had led largely separate lives either at the Cearne or at their flat in Hampstead. Edward Garnett had a long-standing relationship with the painter Ellen Maurice (Nellie) Heath, a daughter of Richard Heath, an engraver, unorthodox religious thinker and writer on agrarian socialism, who leased a cottage owned by Constance's sister, Grace, about half a mile from the Cearne. Nellie Heath had trained in Paris and was influenced by the prominent but unconventional British impressionist painter Walter Sickert, whose most famous works included a Camden Town series of paintings portraying the grim, seedy side of urban life. Nellie became, as David Garnett remarked, 'almost one of our family', the relationship adding to the district's reputation as a hotbed of libertarians and radicals and to the Cearne as a centre of unconventional attitudes to love and marriage. Even H.W. Massingham, editor of the radical *Nation*, was wary of Garnett's 'militant anti-puritanism, particularly on matters of sex', wishing that he would be a little more tolerant of conventional attitudes when reviewing fiction for the periodical.[17] When D.H. Lawrence visited the Cearne in 1911 he wrote that Edward and Constance 'consent to live together or apart as it pleases them'.[18] Garnett had begun his relationship with Nellie Heath when Constance was a lover of the Russian exile and anarchist Sergei Stepniak, who had fled Russia after assassinating the head of the Tsarist security police. When Stepniak died after being hit by a train on a level crossing, David Garnett wrote that it was a blow from which Constance took 'long to recover'.[19]

During his convalescence Giblin also visited the young David Garnett who was living at Charleston at Firle in East Sussex, the legendary country meeting place of the artists, writers and intellectuals in the Bloomsbury Group. Vanessa Bell had recently acquired the farmhouse and garden and in August 1917 when Giblin visited she was living there with her two young sons and with David Garnett and the artist Duncan Grant who was a lover of both David Garnett and Vanessa Bell. Garnett and Grant had been classified as conscientious objectors and instead of being conscripted into the army were assigned to work on surrounding farms as agricultural labourers. Garnett describes Giblin arriving 'full of warmth and friendliness, to reassure himself that I was not having too bad a time

---

[17] Kennedy, pp. 147–8.

[18] James Boulton ed., *The Letters of D.H. Lawrence, Vol. I, 1901–1913*, Cambridge University Press, Cambridge, 1979, p. 16.

[19] David Garnett, *The Golden Echo*, Chatto & Windus, London, 1953, pp. 19–20.

as a conscientious objector!' The irony of Giblin's concern about his life as a conscientious objector was apparent to Garnett who was well aware that Giblin, convalescing from the serious wound he had received at Messines, was about to return to France to the horrors of the Ypres offensive and Passchendaele where 'his future did not seem likely to be a long one'. His visit, Garnett wrote, 'helped to make me see the world impartially and to restore my confidence'.[20]

Garnett described Giblin as very large, with close-cropped hair, rugged features tanned to pale mahogany, very slow in speech and untidy in unbuttoned tunic and badly wound puttees. Giblin sat in the Garden Room at Charleston, 'pulling at his pipe and taking small sips of beer', talking to Vanessa Bell with, as Garnett wrote, 'a sure instinct' about his old friends at Cambridge. All were fellows of his old college King's, the historian, political activist and pacifist, G. Lowes Dickinson who was closely associated with the Bloomsbury Group, Nathaniel Wedd, a noted scholar in classics who was an influential lecturer at King's, and the economist historian, Sir John Clapham, a professor at King's. Giblin also wanted to know, Garnett wrote, all they could tell him about the economist, Maynard Keynes, who had been at King's some years after Giblin. Keynes had visited Charleston shortly before,[21] one of the many famous names associated with the farmhouse including Virginia and Leonard Woolf, Roger Fry, Lytton Strachey, T.S. Eliot, Desmond McCarthy and E.M. Forster, all of whom were at intervals visitors or residents.

While he was recovering from his wound and during his later posting to Perham Downs, a re-training camp on Salisbury Plain, and in between visits to friends and strenuous walking on the Sussex Downs with his friend Dr Charles Goring, to strengthen his leg, Giblin read Eilean's Australian manuscript. He encouraged her efforts to find a publisher and several times offered to help promote it to his friend from University College London, E.V. Lucas, a prolific novelist and essayist, and with Edward Garnett. Both had been influential supporters of Australia's Henry Lawson during his ill-fated visit to London in the early 1900s,[22] promoting him to Blackwood which published two of his collections, *Joe Wilson and His Mates* in 1901 and *Child of the Bush* in 1902. Although his two years in London are often

---

[20] David Garnett, *The Flowers of the Forest*, Chatto & Windus, London, 1955, pp. 158–9.
[21] Garnett, *The Flowers of the Forest*, p. 159.
[22] George Jefferson, *Edward Garnett: A Life in Literature*, Jonathon Cape, London, 1982, p. 91.

regarded as a disaster, Henry Lawson's 'Joe Wilson' stories are some of his best work.

Soon after Giblin returned to the Western Front, the 40th Battalion was in action again in the Third battle of Ypres, a major British offensive in Flanders fought over several months with the final objective of Passchendaele. After the first gains in battles at Menin Road and Polygon Wood, the 40th Battalion joined the attack on Broodseinde Ridge which, although successful, resulted in huge Australian casualties. Giblin, still convalescent, took part in the battle only from the distance of divisional headquarters, a very different experience from his usual position in the thick of the battle, as he explained to Eilean:

> War is a very attractive game from the point of view of div. Hqrs ... You do late hours & irregular meals & give the impression of being very strenuous & important, but the cooking is good & supplies plentiful & varied. More important you think of casualties as thousands (not as Dick Hall & Jack Bourke)[23] & glow with the virtue of the life-saver, when they are 7000 and not, as you expected, ten thousand.[24]

The 40th Battalion lost so many men in the battle of Broodseinde Ridge that Giblin, although still not recovered from the wound he had received at Messines, went back to command of his company for the attack on Passchendaele a few days later. After this battle he wrote to Eilean: 'I don't know what the papers are telling you about it, but it was a failure on a big scale. ... My luck was in & I came through unscathed. But there were not many of us left between the two affairs – in fact the whole division is out of action for some time.'[25] The 40th Battalion, which had entered the Third Battle of Ypres with 944 men, came out with 120. In the morass of mud on the battlefield, British and Dominion casualties totalled a quarter of a million.[26] Following the Battle of Ypres, Sir John Monash, in command of the Third Australian Division, recommended that Major L. F. Giblin receive the Distinguished Service Order, a higher decoration

---

[23] F.C. Green, *The Fortieth: A Record of the 40th Battalion, AIF*, 40th Battalion Association, Hobart, 1922, pp. 222, 229. (John Thomas Bourke killed in action Broodseinde, 5 October 1917; John Hall killed in action 13 October 1917 at Passchendaele.)

[24] MS366/1, 14 October 1917.

[25] MS366/1, 14 October 1917.

[26] F.C. Green, 'Lyndhurst Falkiner Giblin', *Stand-To*, August–September 1952, p. 5.

than the Military Cross, for 'great ability, courage and initiative'.[27] Giblin did not mention his bravery awards in his letters to Eilean but she may have read of them in the *London Gazette* or in newspaper reports. The 40th spent the next few months out of action and training reinforcement troops before returning to the Western Front.

The next opportunity for Eilean and Lyndhurst to meet came between 8 to 18 December 1917 when Giblin was suddenly given leave. Eilean had moved from Edenbridge where she had been involved in 'rural pursuits', presumably farm work, to a new war job with the Ministry of Labour which had been established the previous year to take over the Board of Trade's responsibilities for conciliation, labour exchanges and industrial relations.[28] At this time she was briefly in Manchester. According to Eilean's brother, Kenneth Burton, Giblin went to Liverpool and tried to arrange for them to marry there but time and circumstances were against them and it seems from Giblin's letters that they may not even have met during his leave. At the end of his leave Giblin wrote, 'I missed you after all. – I got your note of course, saying you would be away last week. I came back from the North last Wednesday & was in London the next two days, – & was due for the Cearne on Saturday. So I reckoned to find you Monday midday. They may have told you I called just after you had gone out.'[29] That night Giblin was on his way back to the Western Front.

His leave took place at a time when disaffection with the British conduct of the war reached a crescendo. The huge cost of the offensive at Ypres and Passchendaele was the last straw for many in England who criticised the 'wanton prolongation' of the war. A letter questioning the British Government's direction of the war and supporting peace by negotiation, by Lord Lansdowne, a Conservative peer, a former Governor General of Canada, Viceroy of India, Foreign Secretary and leader of the Conservative Party in the House of Lords, published in the *Daily Telegraph* on 27 November 1917, became a catalyst for these views. At the same time the British Government issued a new regulation, 27c, under the Defence of the Realm Act (DORA), further tightening censorship. When he returned to his battalion, Giblin told Eilean:

> I felt very rebellious during my stay, & felt very like a row. I was rather hoping there might have been a call for volunteers to sell

---

[27] NAA L F Giblin, WWI records, B2455, 5029591.
[28] www.nationalarchives.gov.uk, Administrative history.
[29] MS366/1, 18 December 1917.

Lansdowne's letter or some other pamphlet in defiance of 27c. – If I had been in Hyde Park on Sunday or any other spouting place, I think I should have succumbed to the temptation to hold forth. – I have always rather hated elections. But I think I should really enjoy backing someone agin [sic] the Government in England at present.[30]

Figure 3.1   Officers of the 40th Battalion AIF. Western Front, Neuve Eglise, Messines Area, Belgium, 26 January 1918. Major Lyndhurst Falkiner Giblin DSO MC is third from right front row (Australian War Memorial ID No.: E01610).

During the winter of 1917–18, the 40th Battalion was in the Somme valley in a forward area of the line but at times there was almost an unofficial truce between the opposing sides. Giblin's letters from this period reached Eilean in Birmingham where, after moving from Manchester, she spent two to three months from January to March 1918 in her job with the Ministry of Labour. Following the passing of new legislation the Ministry had acquired further responsibility for enforcing minimum wages in industries that had sprung up during the war, particularly munitions factories employing

---

[30]   MS366/1, 18 December 1917.

many thousands of women who had joined the workforce for the first time. When she first returned to England Eilean had considered taking a job in a munitions factory, a suggestion that led to a discussion in her correspondence with Giblin on the position of newly independent women, who had entered the workforce for the first time during the war and were unlikely to be willing to return to their pre-war status.[31] This was to become a live issue after the war ended when the Ministry of Labour instituted classes in domestic work in an attempt to retrain female munitions workers to return to their former lives as housewives or domestic servants.[32]

On 21 March 1918 a great German offensive began and the 40th Battalion, with Giblin second in command, was sent to the gap east of Amiens between the River Ancre and the Somme. Their orders were to push forward against the enemy's advance troops and to secure the high ground west of Morlancourt. Immediately the battalion came under heavy machine gun and artillery fire and suffered heavy casualties including the commanding officer leaving Giblin in command. When his men were finally held up by enemy resistance, Giblin dug in and held on despite having no artillery or machine gun support and few reserve troops. This action at Morlancourt helped end the great German Spring Offensive, the last major enemy advance of the war. Giblin was mentioned in Sir Douglas Haig's dispatch of 7 April 1918.[33] His unhappiness at the conduct of the war continued, however. 'I get the impression of unlimited incompetence running right through the whole show,' he wrote to Eilean.[34] The frank criticism of the conduct of the war in both his and Eilean's letters and the dispatch of banned periodicals – overseas circulation of the *Nation* had been prohibited under war regulations since March 1917 on the ground that certain statements had been used as enemy propaganda[35] – eventually attracted the attention of the censors and Eilean was questioned. Giblin wrote:

> I'm rather amazed at the amount of work that must have been put in – because they must have combined a letter of mine with one of yours to get the full plot ... it seems as though they have used one of those letters of mine to give some basis for the absurd business.

---

[31] MS366/1, 27 May 1917.
[32] Angela Woollacott, *On Her Their Lives Depend: Munitions Workers in the Great War*, University of California Press, Berkeley, 1994, pp. 154–5.
[33] *London Gazette*, 28 May 1918.
[34] MS366/1, 14 April 1918.
[35] Kennedy, p. 250.

However I am sorry you have been worried by it. And I hope it won't make any difference to what you write or send. The thing is too ridiculous to take any notice of – I don't think they are the least likely to worry me over it – rather wish they would. I should rather like to have a row on such a point.[36]

* * *

This is the last letter in the collection before the marriage of Major Lyndhurst Falkiner Giblin, DSO, MC to Eilean Mary Burton at the registry office Kingston-on-Thames, Surrey, by licence on Monday, 29 July 1918. This was the first weekday after the start of Giblin's leave that began on the previous Friday. Nothing in the sequence of his letters to Eilean prepares the reader for this marriage and the letters continue after their marriage in the same tone of casual intimacy and trust with no salutation or ending except the signature 'LFG' and no expressions of love. To Eilean's eldest brother, Kenneth, the marriage was 'very "sudden" to say the least'[37] but it evidently had the approval and support of the Burton family. Eilean's parents, Edward and Ada Burton, and her brother, Esmond, a Captain in the Royal Army Service Corps, were witnesses. The other witness was Dr E.G.L. (Leopold) Goffe, who practised at Kingston-on-Thames and had been a fellow student and rugby player with Giblin at University College, London in the early 1890s.

When his leave began Giblin had gone straight from France to Homefield and both Eilean and he gave the Burton home in Spencer Road, East Molesey, as their address. Eilean noted their marriage in a few words at the top of the first letter he wrote to her after his brief leave but there is no other reference to it. On their honeymoon they spent a few days in Cornwall then to test Giblin's wounded thigh they went on a walking tour on the South Downs, calling at Charleston, the haven of the artists, writers and intellectuals of the Bloomsbury Group, where Giblin talked with the renowned economist John Maynard Keynes, who was often a visitor.[38] Then they collected David Garnett from Charleston where he was living with Vanessa Bell and Duncan Grant and he walked with Giblin

---

[36] MS366/1, 8 June 1918.
[37] Kenneth Burton to Mr and Mrs Desmond Giblin, [1955].
[38] L. F. Giblin, 'John Maynard Keynes', *Economic Record*, Vol. XXII, June 1946, pp. 1–2.

and Eilean to Alfriston[39] where two of Eilean's aunts, Elizabeth (Betty) MacRae and Mary (Molly) MacRae White, lived.

Giblin arrived back at the battalion just in time for the great Allied offensive that began in August 1918 and culminated in the end of the war. 'Just back in time for this push,' he wrote.[40] Not long after Eilean received this letter, the war was over for Lyndhurst Giblin. He was wounded for the third time in a battle to drive the German Army back through the Hindenburg Line over the heavily fortified Somme battlefields. The 40th Battalion's task was to take the town of Bray-sur-Somme. Although it was successful, the company suffered heavy casualties including Giblin who was badly wounded by shrapnel early on 24 August 1918. From No. 2 Red Cross Hospital in Rouen, France, he wrote to Eilean, less than a month after their marriage:

> You observe I am here, a lump of shrapnel in my thigh early yesterday morning during taking of Bray at fairly early stage. Had to lie in a hole for an hour during heavy shelling & then was carried out. At the CCS [Casualty Clearing Station] they operated & got a fine big chunk out, so that's first rate. Don't know yet what the prospects of coming to Blighty are – think it probable sooner or later. I don't want to move for a few days – always feel anaesthetics badly, & am only fit to be hidden for the next week and nobody can help me.[41]

This letter and several that followed were written in pencil as Giblin lay on his back. They were so faint and difficult to read, Eilean made legible copies of them, after her husband's death in 1951, before she gave the originals to the National Library of Australia. A letter he wrote a few days after he was shot made it clear that he was more badly hurt than he at first thought – the wound had to be reopened – although, he wrote, 'nothing of importance has been cut or touched by shrapnel'. He added: 'When I feel like smoking again, I will know I have got to the end of this stupid sickness.'[42] A few days later he reported that he was 'taking an interest in food & tobacco', but he was dismayed by the attitude to the war as the Allied advance continued.

---

[39] Garnett, *The Flowers of the Forest*, p. 159.
[40] MS366/1, 9 August 1918.
[41] MS366/1, 25 August 1918.
[42] MS366/1, 28 August 1918.

'The yelp for blood is getting almost triumphant; I don't like the look of the *Times*. You can see the foul slaver on their jaws,' he wrote.[43]

By the first week in September 1918, Giblin was back in England at Wandsworth Hospital and when the war ended on 11 November 1918, he was convalescing in England. He did not return to his battalion, stationed at Tours-en-Vimeu, near Amiens, until mid-December where his first task was an interview with the Australian war historian Charles Bean, 'the correspondent collecting data for history'.[44] For the next six months he was anchored in a frustrating role in command of troops who, with the war over, just wanted to go home but who had to wait month after month until berths could be found for their return voyage. At first at Tours-en-Vimeu and later in England, he tried to keep his troops occupied with sport, dramatic entertainments and the educational sessions that the Army authorities encouraged. 'Have started a trigonometry class,' he told Eilean in one letter.[45] But circumstances were against him; educational courses were held under extreme difficulties, some in open cow sheds in the depths of winter without text books, notebooks, pencils, paper or blackboards.[46] He appealed to Eilean to send songbooks that he had left at Homefield for community singing and later he asked her to send plays suitable for staging on a small, primitive stage – he suggested Irish playwright, J. M. Synge's two-act play, *The Tinker's Wedding*.[47]

Giblin's letters written during the first few months of 1919 reached Eilean at the Cearne on the Surrey/Kent border where she was staying with Constance Garnett, a visit arranged by Giblin which did not turn out well. Eilean had influenza, one of the many who caught the disease in the pandemic that spread across the world from the trenches in 1918–19, causing many millions of deaths including a quarter of a million in Britain. Her illness lingered and she did not recover fully for some months. Additionally, she found living with Constance Garnett a challenge. Although she had experienced some rough living during her pre-war visit to Australia, she was accustomed at Homefield to a well-run household with servants, unlike the Cearne where she had to do many domestic chores in a household that appears to have been chaotic. When she complained

---

[43] MS366/1, 31 August 1918.
[44] MS366/1, 21 December 1918.
[45] MS366/1, 16 January 1919.
[46] MS366/1, 25 December 1918.
[47] MS366/1, 6 February 1919.

to her husband about the dangers of chopping wood, however, he did not see any need for sympathy. 'There shouldn't be a danger splitting logs,' he told her, 'use the weight and swing of the axe don't force it.' By the time Eilean returned to Homefield he seems belatedly to have become aware that he had encouraged her into a difficult situation. Early in March 1919 he wrote:

> I am afraid you have had rather a time at the Cearne. I realised that the mess of the place would be a worry, but I rather light-heartedly hoped that it would clean itself up more or less automatically if you were there – that it was a slackness due to much living alone & bad eyesight – not allowing for the obstinacy of old habit. That Connie herself would be at times not easy I hadn't thought of, my ideas that way were more concerned with Edward, to whom I am probably never quite fair.[48]

At one stage Giblin seems to have entertained the idea that he and Eilean would be able to travel to Australia together, perhaps via Canada, but after he became commanding officer of the 40th Battalion he was committed to travelling home with one of the last drafts of his troops. Although the first quotas began leaving on the first stage of their trip to Australia in February and March, it was several months before there was any prospect that Giblin could leave and Eilean's departure was equally uncertain. As a war bride she also was in a long queue waiting for transport.

When Giblin had a few days off in March he spent the time returning to the scenes of old Somme battles with his friend, Frank Green, also a major in the 40th Battalion. As they inspected Bray, the town the 40th Battalion had retaken, they found a café with a fire, food and red wine. After the meal they walked around in the snow observing how the cellars and basements had been fortified and why it had been so difficult to take. At the church, the roof of which had been destroyed by shelling, they found the old curé directing a gang of German prisoners who were erecting a temporary roof. With the snow falling and the curé and the enemy prisoners looking down on them, Giblin and Green sang 'The Vicar of Bray' in the street.[49]

In April 1919 Giblin received orders to attend an investiture ceremony by King George V in London for his Distinguished Service Order and Military Cross, but his leave was only long enough to cover travel time and he was

---

[48] MS366/1, 6 March 1919.
[49] Green, *Stand-to*, p. 5.

back in camp at Tours-en-Vimeu the day after the ceremony. It was not an event Giblin looked forward to – he had dodged it so far, he told Eilean, but couldn't any longer. Eilean may have attended this ceremony at Buckingham Palace but there is no mention of this in Giblin's letters and she shared her husband's abhorrence of public occasions. Giblin was the only man on that day who failed to obey the injunction to wear gloves. This did not seem to faze King George V who, after shaking Giblin's ungloved hand, held a long conversation with him on war in the trenches.[50]

By the beginning of May 1919, Giblin and the remainder of the 40th Battalion were back in England at Camp Codford in Wiltshire and he was planning how to fit in all the things he wanted to do before he returned to Australia. With leave limited some of his plans remained distant dreams, including a trip to Ireland with Eilean. Whether they got to the ballet, the opera or the pictures in London as he hoped is unclear. His troops were more unsettled than ever – he attempted to keep them occupied with long, instructive walks on the Downs but, he told Eilean, he had a 'portentous list' of AWLs [Absent Without Leave] to deal with. In June he was able to get to London for the Vintners' annual dinner, a very important occasion for the male members of the Burton family. In 1918, Eilean's father, Edward Pritchard Burton, had followed his father in being elected Master of the Vintners' Company and he was the host for the 1919 ceremonial annual dinner. The family connection continued when Eilean's brother, Esmond Burton, was elected Master in 1948.

Before he left England for Australia on 4 July 1919, on *SS Wiltshire*, Giblin heard that Eilean had been booked to go to Australia on HMAT *Katoomba*, with a party of war brides who would be accompanied by their children and soldier husbands. He told her that 'demob' was 'sorry about it being a family ship but say it is the only one available for a long time'. He thought it might be better than a troopship. He had hoped for a ship with cabins rather later when the regular quotas had all departed but that did not seem likely. Giblin arrived in Tasmania in August 1919 with 'the pitiful remainder'[51] of the men who had served under him in France. He went back to his apple orchard and he also very quickly re-established his connection with the Labor Party, as he indicates in a letter to Eilean as she was nearing Australia.

---

[50] Sir Roland Wilson, 'L.F. Giblin – A Man for all Seasons', *47th ANZAAS Congress Papers*, Hobart, 12 May 1976, p. 12.

[51] Wilson, p. 13.

Eilean sailed from England on 8 August 1919 on the *Katoomba*, a lone figure in the midst of family groups of AIF soldiers travelling with the wives they had married overseas and children born to them. She did not fit the description of the young women on the ship depicted in the *Katoomba News*, a shipboard journal published at Durban as a souvenir of the voyage from England to Australia. It described the ship as not only a troopship returning veterans to Australia but a 'family ship' 'conveying hundreds of young English, Scottish, and Irish girls from the lands of their birth, from their family associations, to be soon thrust into unknown adventures of life in a foreign land'.[52]

Eilean was almost certainly unique among war brides in being offered a week at a Labor Party conference as her introduction to Australia. As the *Katoomba* was nearing Fremantle, Giblin wrote that he would meet her in Melbourne but he was due to go to Sydney on 2 October 1919 for the Labor Party Federal conference. He suggested they could go straight from Melbourne to Sydney 'put in a week or so there (with the conference)' and then go on to Hobart. If, however, Eilean was 'weary of moving' and preferred to go straight to Tasmania they would do that and he would go alone to Sydney a week later. 'It can be just what you like,' he told her.[53] The ALP had called a special federal conference in Sydney in October to review Labor's policy on land taxation, following the severe disruption to the Federal Conference held in June 1919 caused by the influenza pandemic when some delegates had been too ill to attend.

The *Katoomba* docked in Melbourne on 22 September 1919 but it is unclear whether Eilean went to Sydney or straight to Tasmania. In Hobart she met Lyndhurst's elderly mother who was shocked that she was not wearing a wedding ring. She had refused to accept a ring for the marriage ceremony – believing both husband and wife, or neither, should have rings – but in the small conformist society of Hobart and to appease her husband's family she bought and wore a wedding ring. It was a pointed indication that she had left a huge metropolis for a small parochial town in which members of her husband's family were well-known citizens and where she would be noticed.

Soon after Eilean's arrival in Hobart, Lyndhurst Giblin was appointed Tasmanian Government Statistician and adviser to the government on financial and economic matters. In 1924 his title but not his duties changed

---

[52] *Katoomba News*, August–September 1919, p. 1.
[53] MS366/1, 12 [September] 1919.

when the Tasmanian Statistical Office became part of the Commonwealth Bureau of Census and Statistics and he became Deputy Commonwealth Statistician for Tasmania. By late in 1919 he was also back on the Tasmanian University Council where he was more influential than ever. Soon he was promoting the establishment of a chair of Economics and the appointment of Douglas B. Copland to the chair. He continued in these roles in the economic, financial and academic affairs of Tasmania during the following decade. At the same time, he maintained his orchard at Seven Mile Beach, supplying not only the local market but exporting to England.

Eilean faced a new life as a resident of Hobart, not as a visitor as she had been in 1913.

Chapter 4
─────────

'A Woman's Place is in the World'

Hobart 1920s

Eilean Giblin's new home was a town of about 50,000. As she remarked after being in Hobart a few years, 'there are very few progressive people to be found in such a town'.[1] It was a town in which many of the high hopes for a brighter post-war world were fading. According to one observer the old exclusive social class still set the fashion in thinking and the University and religious and other bodies paid deference to them,[2] a situation exacerbated by economic malaise. The early and mid-1920s were a boom period in other parts of Australia but not in Tasmania where the State's finances were in crisis, business stagnated and large numbers of young people left for the mainland.[3] It was also a period when, in the aftermath of the terrible losses in the war and the divisions in society following the conscription campaigns, Australia, from being 'one of the most democratic and progressive of countries', was becoming 'one of the most conservative'.[4]

Into this 'gloomy atmosphere' Lyndhurst Giblin, back from the War, appeared to progressives 'like a brilliant meteor quick to challenge every out-of-date attitude'. He was at the centre of much that happened in the intellectual life of the State, always to the fore in battles against 'prejudice and stupidity' exercising 'a wide influence upon his generation'.[5] He was

───────

[1] E. M. Giblin, 'Tasmania: News of the Woman's Movement', *International Woman Suffrage News*, July 1923.
[2] John Reynolds, 'L.F. Giblin: A plea for an Adequate Biography', Ingamells Collection, Flinders University Library.
[3] (Sir) Roland Wilson, 'L.F.Giblin – A Man for all Seasons'. The Giblin Memorial Lecture, *47th ANZAAS Congress Papers*, Section 24, Hobart, 12 May 1976, p. 12.
[4] Marilyn Lake, *A Divided Society: Tasmania during World War I*, Melbourne University Press, Carlton Vic., 1975, pp. 195–6.
[5] Reynolds, p. 3.

soon back on the Tasmanian University Council and influential as a leading member of the dominant block. According to Roland Wilson, a student from 1922 to 1925, 'everything at the University more or less revolved around Giblin',[6] but his independent, anti-establishment views often came under conservative attack. In 1924 he was criticised by the *Mercury* for defending students who were widely attacked for 'disgusting and vulgar displays' in the University's Commemoration Day procession. In a letter to the editor he stated there was 'nothing morally undesirable' about the displays which were no coarser than Shakespeare or what could be heard in smoking rooms or clubs.[7] The following year he was attacked when the Selection Committee he chaired chose Roland Wilson as the State's Rhodes scholar. Wilson had been educated at a State high school unlike all previous Rhodes scholars who had been to prestigious public schools, and he had studied economics not Latin and Greek. There was an attempt to rescind this choice of the first student from such a non-establishment background but Giblin and his ally on the Council, classicist Professor R.L. Dunbabin, had the support of some other members, economists Professor Douglas Copland and J.B. Brigden. According to Tasmanian author John Reynolds, Giblin was from that time 'a target for abuse by the snobs and the opponents of progress and fair dealing in social affairs'.[8] Ironically at this time, a Giblin relative, Lt Colonel Wilfrid Wanostrocht Giblin, CB, was president of the prestigious, exclusive Tasmanian Club, and he held the position again for two terms during the 1930s.[9]

Eilean Giblin, an unknown, an interloper, a feminist, sought a role in this socially conservative and economically depressed society where she faced the prospect of being permanently cast in the shadow of her controversial husband. Not surprisingly, it took her some time to find an independent role. She discovered that although women had been voters in Australia for about two decades they had made little progress in politics. When she looked around in Tasmania she found a variety of feminist organisations working towards achieving some limited goals that the vote had put within reach. The Women's Health Association and the Child Welfare Association worked for health and welfare reforms; the Women's Association for the Reform of

---

[6] Richard Davis, *Open to Talent: The Centenary History of the University of Tasmania 1890–1990*, University of Tasmania, Hobart, 1990, p. 87.
[7] *Mercury*, 15 May 1924, pp. 5, 6.
[8] Reynolds, p. 4.
[9] Frank C. Green, *The Tasmanian Club 1861–1961*, Tasmanian Club, Hobart Tas., 1961. W. W. Giblin was president 1922–4, 1934–5 and 1938–9.

the Criminal Law aimed at greater representation of women in the criminal justice system as lawyers, policewomen, justices of the peace and on juries; other women's organisations concentrated on temperance and moral issues.[10]

Eilean looked for a broader canvas. She found the organisation that suited her when early in 1922 a group of Hobart women formed the Women's Non-Party Political League in response to a change in the law that for the first time allowed women to stand for the Tasmanian Parliament. Tasmanian women had been entitled to vote and to stand for election to the Commonwealth Parliament since the passing of the Commonwealth Franchise Act in 1902 and in 1904 had gained the right to vote for the Tasmanian House of Assembly, but not the right to stand for election to the Tasmanian Parliament until the passing of the Constitution (Women) Bill in January 1922. The Tasmanian Women's Non-Party Political League (WNPPL) adopted 'equal citizenship' between men and women in all spheres as its main aim and encouraged women to stand for parliament. It set out to educate women about the responsibilities of citizenship and make them aware of the opportunities the vote had made available to them. It aimed to educate women to use their vote, to obtain full civic rights for women and children and to have women appointed to government boards and as justices of the peace.[11] Equal citizenship did not have the ringing tone of a suffragette slogan and none of its ability to attract publicity. It was not 'a big, elemental, simple reform'[12] like gaining the vote but a long-drawn out struggle to achieve incremental, unspectacular but important gains in changing the society in which women lived. It involved the recognition of the right to economic independence through equal pay and motherhood endowment; the right of women who married men of a different nationality to retain their nationality and the right to an equal moral standard applied to men and women.[13]

Eilean became Honorary Secretary of the new organisation, a breakthrough for a newcomer, as many of the women holding office were well-

---

[10] Stefan Petrow, 'Boiling Over: Edith Waterworth and Criminal Law Reform in Tasmania 1912–1924', *Tasmanian Historical Studies*, 4.2, 1994, p. 9.

[11] Australia. Royal Commission on Child Endowment or Family Allowances, *Minutes of Evidence*, Government Printer, Canberra, 1928–29. Eilean Giblin's statement on the role of the Tasmanian WNPPL, p. 704.

[12] Barbara Caine, *English Feminism 1780–1980*, Oxford University Press, Oxford, 1997, p. 174.

[13] Barbara Caine, *Australian Feminism: A Companion*, Oxford University Press, Melbourne, 1998, p. 137.

known activists who had been prominent in other causes promoting women's interests. Mrs Edith Waterworth had been one of the founders of the Women's Association for Reform of the Criminal Law and was extraordinarily active through the 1920s and 1930s in campaigning on many issues affecting women's political, civil and legal rights. She was the first woman to be endorsed by the WNPPL when she stood for parliament as an Independent candidate for the seat of Denison at the first Tasmanian election open to women candidates. Mrs Frances Edwards, also a founder of the Criminal Law Reform Association, was later a children's court magistrate and one of the first women to be appointed a justice of the peace in Tasmania, and Mrs Lesley Murdoch was the first woman elected to the Tasmanian University Council. All were later presidents of the Tasmanian WNPPL.

Soon after it was formed, the WNPPL joined the Australian Federation of Women's Societies for Equal Citizenship (later the Australian Federation of Women Voters), a body set up on the initiative of Mrs Bessie Rischbieth, an energetic Perth resident who was president of the Women's Service Guilds of Western Australia and editor of their monthly paper the *Dawn*. Mrs Rischbieth attracted women's organisations from other states to the Federation and gained affiliation with the International Woman Suffrage Alliance. She was Federation President from 1921 to 1942 and publicised the news of constituent bodies in the *Dawn*.

Late in 1922, in her role as Honorary Secretary of the Tasmanian WNPPL, Eilean received a letter from Bessie Rischbieth asking affiliated societies to nominate representative women to form delegations from each State to attend the Ninth Congress of the International Woman Suffrage Alliance to be held in Rome from 12 to 19 May 1923. 'Do you know of any suitable women likely to be visiting the old country from Tasmania at that time?' Bessie Rischbieth asked in a letter dated 8 November 1922.[14] Her query reflected the fact that few if any women's organisations had the financial resources to pay the fares and expenses of delegates to international conferences. Some attempted to raise money to finance delegates' travel but generally delegates had to be able to finance their own travel and expenses. Edith Waterworth raised funds to finance her overseas trips on behalf of women's organisations by part-time journalism.[15]

---

[14] Bessie Rischbieth Papers, NLA MS2004/ 5/158.
[15] Marilyn Lake, *Getting Equal: The History of Australian Feminism*, Allen & Unwin, St Leonards, 1999, p. 140.

The invitation for a delegate to represent Tasmania in 1923 suited Eilean. She had the financial resources to pay for her travel and this would give her the opportunity to take part in an important international feminist conference and, as well, visit her family in England. She joined the largest delegation ever to represent Australia at an international suffrage conference. Although Victoria and Queensland were unable to send delegates, New South Wales sent four: Mrs Jamieson-Williams JP, Dr Ethel Renfry Morris, Mrs Emily Bennett JP and Miss Stella George; Western Australia three: Mrs Bessie Rischbieth JP, Mrs A.E. Joyner JP and Councillor Elizabeth Clapham, and South Australia two: Dr Eleanor Allen and Miss Constance Davey, who joined the delegation in London where she was studying on a Catherine Helen Spence scholarship for a PhD at the University of London. Eilean Giblin represented Tasmania and Harriet Newcomb, an Australian feminist living in London, also joined the delegation as an observer from the British Commonwealth League.

Figure 4.1   Australian delegation to the International Woman Suffrage Alliance Conference, 1923. Eilean Giblin is standing second from left. The leader of the delegation, Bessie Rischbieth is seated centre. (National Library of Australia. BibID: 3279316)

The leader of the delegation Bessie Rischbieth became a friend of Eilean's. For decades afterwards she was always ready to welcome her to Perth when she was passing through on a ship to or from England and she always noted her visit with a news item in the *Dawn*. In these notices she usually referred to Eilean's status as a member of the 1923 Australian delegation to the Rome Congress and she regularly published Eilean's dispatches on the activities of the Tasmanian WNPPL. Superficially they were very different people. In contrast to Eilean's drably unfashionable appearance, Bessie Rischbieth was described by feminist Julia Rapke, who wrote impressions of many Australian women activists, as 'the exact opposite of the once popular conception of a militant suffragette'. She had a 'fondness for frothy clothes' and 'all the little accessories that spell charm & chic', Rapke wrote.[16]

Bessie Rischbieth and Eilean had in common a strong belief in the need for equality of status and opportunity between men and women in law and in practice and a deep knowledge of the suffrage movement in England. Bessie Rischbieth, during her marriage to wealthy merchant, Henry W. Rischbieth, lived in London for several periods at the height of the suffrage campaigns. Her papers in the National Library of Australia document in considerable detail the militant suffragette movement led by Emmeline Pankhurst. Her archive includes a pictorial volume of the movement from 1906 to 1913, pamphlets, copies of the suffrage periodicals *Votes for Women* and the *Suffragette*, court orders for the appearance of suffragettes who were charged with various offences, biographical notes on suffragettes and mementos of suffragette struggles.[17] She knew intimately of the militant struggle, the violence, the hunger strikes, forcible feeding and the history of broken pledges over more than 60 years of struggle, as Eilean did through the experiences of her MacRae aunts, although neither favoured militant methods. Bessie Rischbieth admired the fearlessness of militant speakers she observed in London in 1913 and did not think women suffragists who favoured different methods should be critical of each others' organisations.[18]

In Rome Eilean Giblin joined one thousand delegates from 43 countries, 18 of the countries still without female suffrage, who met under the motto of the International Woman Suffrage Alliance Congress, 'A Woman's Place is in the World'. The Alliance had been formed at a meeting organised by

---

[16] Rapke Papers, NLA MS 842/12.
[17] Rischbieth Papers, NLA MS 2004, Series 3.
[18] Kate White, 'Bessie Rischbieth: The Feminist', in *Westralian Portraits*, ed. Lyall Hunt, University of Western Australia Press, Nedlands, WA, 1979, p. 217.

American suffragists in Washington DC in February 1902 at which 11 countries were represented. Australian feminist and suffragist, Vida Goldstein, who represented Australia, was a prominent figure at the meeting particularly as it coincided with the passing of legislation giving Australian women the right to vote and to stand for election to the Commonwealth Parliament. Goldstein was elected secretary of the Alliance and was called to give evidence on woman suffrage to committees of the United States Congress; she also attended the International Council of Women Conference. The Alliance was formally constituted as the International Woman Suffrage Alliance at a second meeting in Berlin in 1904 and continued to meet regularly until the outbreak of war in 1914. The 1923 Congress was the second to be held since the end of the First World War.

The Ninth International Woman Suffrage Alliance Congress was held in Rome at the invitation of Benito Mussolini, who became president of the congress at his own request. His presence – he had only recently come to power and had just begun to dismantle constitutional restraints and establish himself as a dictator – did not appear to inhibit the wide-ranging discussions at the congress. Apart from the major issue of suffrage, delegates discussed equal pay and the right to work, sex education, the incidence of venereal disease, the trafficking of women and children, married women's nationality rights, the economic status of wives and mothers, slavery, child marriage and the excessive use of narcotics. They also expressed strong support for the League of Nations. Eilean's main contribution was in the work of the committee on the Nationality of Married Women[19] and this became a long-standing cause. The following year at the First Triennial Conference of the Australian Federation of Women's Societies, held in Adelaide from 26–29 March 1924, she was nominated as Australian representative on the IWSA's Nationality of Married Women standing committee.[20]

When Eilean returned from Europe to Tasmania late in 1923, the *Mercury* carried a column-long interview and photograph in which she cited as the Congress's most notable outcomes, resolutions on equal pay for equal work and the nationality of married women. She told the interviewer she supported the Congress view that in order to achieve equal pay for equal work the same educational training in the professions and trades should be available to women as was available to men. She hailed the Congress

---

[19] *International Woman Suffrage News*, July 1923, p. 151.
[20] Bessie Rischbieth, *March of Australian Women: A Record of Fifty Years' Struggle for Equal Citizenship*, Paterson Brokensha, Perth, 1964, p. 71.

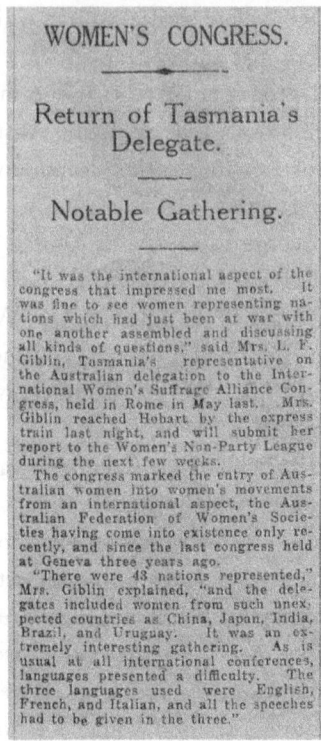

Figure 4.2 Eilean Giblin interviewed in the Hobart *Mercury* (27 October 1923) after her return from the International Woman Suffrage Alliance conference in Rome.

resolution that women who married men of a different nationality should not be obliged to change their nationality.[21] She made similar comments in a speech at a welcome home afternoon tea hosted by the Mayoress of Hobart.[22]

The Tasmanian WNPPL built on the publicity gained from Eilean's attendance at the international gathering. In December 1923, she was a member of a WNPPL delegation to the new Labor Premier, J.A. Lyons, which raised several issues affecting women, particularly the plight of deserted wives left without support for themselves and their children,[23] an important issue in Tasmania where many men moved to the mainland. She was also a member of several other deputations to ministers in the new

---

[21] *Mercury*, 27 October 1923, p. 7. Eilean had disembarked in Hobart the previous day from the *Port Melbourne* which left London on 8 September 1923.

[22] *Mercury*, 8 November 1923, p. 11.

[23] *Dawn*, 12 December 1923.

State Labor Government requesting among other matters that women be appointed to public boards and as justices of the peace. When she reported to the 1924 annual general meeting of the WNPPL held at the Hobart Town Hall, she pointed to considerable success. As a result of representations to the Tasmanian Government seven women were appointed justices of the peace in March and April 1924: Mrs Amelia Piesse, Mrs Lucie Evelyn Hurst, Mrs Alice Gordon Elliott and Mrs Frances Edwards in Hobart; Mrs Ella Louisa Smith and Mrs Ida Mary Tynan in Launceston and Mrs Eliza Burnell (Enid Lyons's mother and the Premier's mother-in-law) in Burnie. Eilean was appointed to the Board of the Hobart Public Hospitals.[24] Optimistically, she hoped that in future 'public appointments may be filled equally by men and by women' pointing out the importance of this aim to the organisation:

> The chief aim of the League, which is shortly expressed by "equal citizenship" i.e. equality of opportunity between men and women, has thus received much encouragement. No other body of women in Tasmania has this aim for the chief plank of their programme, and the special work we are doing is, we feel, of value to all the women of Tasmania.[25]

Eilean's appointment to the Hobart Public Hospitals Board was a signal achievement, the first appointment of a woman to a hospital board in Tasmania. She immediately became a member of the Board's Finance Committee and the following year moved to the more senior House Committee.[26] She remained on the Board through the 1920s when there was a long-running crisis in hospital administration following a dispute with the British Medical Association on the qualifications of the Board-appointed Surgeon Superintendent, Dr Victor Ratten.[27] She resigned only when the Giblins left Hobart.

During the 1920s Eilean remained active in the WNPPL, representing the League at several interstate conferences. At the Second Triennial Conference of the Australian Federation of Women Voters, held in Sydney 17–20 May 1927, she became a member of the Federation's board.[28] She

---

[24] *Walch's Tasmanian Almanac*, 1925, pp. 88, 90, 93.
[25] *Dawn*, 22 April 1924; *International Woman Suffrage News*, June 1924.
[26] *Public Hospital Hobart Annual Report 1924–25*.
[27] *Public Hospital Hobart Annual Report 1925–26*.
[28] *Dawn*, 14 June 1927.

was also active as Honorary Secretary of the Tasmanian branch of the League of Nations Union and in 1926 she was a member of the Australian delegation to the British Commonwealth League's conference on 'Migration and Government' held in London.[29] The conference, entitled 'Women and Oversea Settlement and some Problems of Government', was mainly concerned with the migration of women from Britain to the Commonwealth countries and only towards the end of the two-day conference discussed the nationality of married women. The conference supported a declaration of the British Parliament on 18 February 1925, and a similar declaration by the Australian Parliament on 25 February 1926 which read: 'That a British woman shall not lose her nationality by act of marriage with an alien but that it should be open to her to make a declaration of alienage'.[30]

By far Eilean's most important role for the WNPPL came in 1928 when she gave evidence at the Hobart sittings of the Commonwealth Government's Royal Commission on Child Endowment or Family Allowances. Child endowment paid to the mother, sometimes referred to as motherhood endowment, was an important aim of feminist organisations as a step towards women achieving economic equality and independence. Nominally the Tasmanian League was represented at the Royal Commission by the president Lesley Murdoch, vice president Eilean Giblin and Honorary Secretary Edith Waterworth, but it was Eilean who presented the League's case and who faced intense questioning by the commissioners. The Commission had been set up the previous year by the Bruce-Page Nationalist-Country Party Government to report on the possible introduction of child endowment with particular reference to its social and economic effects. Eilean argued strongly for child endowment financed by the Federal Government through taxation with all payments to be made to the mother, although she canvassed the advisability of making part of the payment in kind. She also raised general questions including the high rate of maternal mortality and the plight of widows and deserted wives with dependent children as well as some issues, current at the time, such as the eugenic concern at the propagation of children by 'mentally deficient' people, the need for training girls in home-making and the low standard of health of Australian school children.

---

[29] *Dawn*, 11 May 1926; 14 July 1926, p. 3.

[30] British Commonwealth League, *Women and Oversea Settlement and Some Problems of Government, Report of the Conference*, 22, 23 June 1926.

The commissioners interrogated her with 126 questions and in the course of her replies she was led into some counter-productive byways, including eugenic discussions – she favoured segregation of 'mentally deficient' people rather than sterilisation as a means of preventing their having children but she agreed problems of diagnosis could arise. She also became bogged down in explaining the League's view that some part of child endowment should be paid in kind if there was evidence that the payment was not being used on children's food and clothing. When she returned to the League's core case, however, that the most important immediate issue was support for necessitous widows and deserted wives with dependent children and for families with more than two children, she argued strongly.[31]

Giving evidence was an ordeal and the result of the Royal Commission was a disappointment for all advocates of child endowment. The majority report by T.S. O'Halloran, KC, President of the South Australian Law Society and Chairman of the South Australian National Football League, Ivor Evans, a Victorian businessman, managing director of a firm of hardware merchants, and Stephen Mills, CMG, a former Comptroller-General of Customs, recommended against a system of child endowment mainly on the grounds that it had not been established that wages were insufficient to support a family with children and that the additional taxation necessary would cause disastrous consequences. The minority report by John Curtin, editor of the *Westralian Worker*, Perth, soon to begin his parliamentary career as a Labor member of the House of Representatives and later to become Prime Minister of Australia, and Mrs Mildred Muscio, feminist, Federal President of the National Council of Women, supported the main points Eilean Giblin put in the League's submission. Curtin and Muscio believed the country could afford a moderate system of family allowances. They recommended payment for widows and single mothers with dependent children, a means-tested payment to the mother of a family for each child excluding the first two children and an allowance for each child in families where the income was below the basic wage.[32]

The Government accepted the majority report that child endowment would be too costly. It was not introduced into Australia until 1941, well over a decade later when, ironically, as Eilean pointed out in an entry in her

---

[31] Australia. Royal Commission on Child Endowment or Family Allowances, *Minutes of Evidence*, Government Printer, Canberra, 1928–29, pp. 703–08.

[32] Australia. Royal Commission on Child Endowment or Family Allowances, *Report of the Royal Commission*, Government Printer, Canberra, 1929, pp. 103–25.

diary, with the demands of a world war to be financed and taxation higher than it had ever been and likely to go higher, the cost of child endowment could be swallowed 'like a jujube'. 'It seems as though money can be found when it is really wanted, but it takes a war to move politicians to bring about such a desirable reform,' she wrote.[33]

* * *

In July 1924 Eilean heard news of her father's sudden death after he became ill while touring the Western Highlands of Scotland. When a train bringing him from Scotland arrived at Kings Cross station in London, Edward Burton was so ill his wife summoned a taxi to take him to St Pancras Hospital but he died on the journey. The Deputy Coroner's inquest recorded that Edward Pritchard Burton died on 25 July 1924 in Grays Inn Road, St Pancras, in a taxicab. He was aged 67 and the cause of death was given as syncope rupture of the heart muscle and artheroma arteries.[34] The Burton sons were summoned by telegram to Homefield. Kenneth had resumed his career as a director in the Pritchard and Burton family business after his service in the First World War, first as a private and later as a second lieutenant in the Royal Army Service Corps (RASC). Colin, a Lieutenant Colonel in the RASC in the permanent army, married to Gladys Astley Cooper the father of two daughters, Nancy, aged 15, and Sheila, 13, and a son Lovick, aged 3, was stationed at Aldershot. Esmond, a Captain in the RASC during the War, was re-establishing his career as an architectural sculptor in London. Geoffrey had returned to civilian life after he was moved to the retired list as a Lieutenant Commander in the Navy at the end of the First World War and was soon to marry his cousin Alfreda Mary Burton, whose father Frank was a partner in Pritchard and Burton. The youngest son, Clive, was at Wye College where he was studying for a career in agriculture.

In distant Tasmania Eilean had no opportunity to return for her father's funeral but his death was to have an effect on her life. Under her father's will she received a lump sum and an annuity of £300 a year, a considerable sum making her a person of independent means. The lump sum enabled her to partly finance the building of a new home in Hobart on a block of

---

[33] Giblin Papers, Eilean Giblin Diary, NLA MS366/6/1, 12 February 1941.
[34] Death certificate, St Pancras, County of London, 1924/569206.

Figure 4.3 The Giblins' Lynton Avenue house (centre), designed by architect Bernard Walker and built in 1925. (Courtesy Elaine Ross)

land at 12 Lynton Lane (later Avenue) on the side of a steep hill bordering a quarry site, south of the city, for which the Giblins paid £200. Eilean wrote many years later when she was considering selling the house: 'I put up £1000 (from my Father's estate) & L.F. raised £500'.[35] They engaged a leading Hobart architect, Bernard Walker, whose ideas were attuned to Eilean's interest in the Arts and Crafts style of architectural design. Walker had studied and worked in London and travelled in Britain and Europe before the First World War where he was influenced by the arts and crafts movement and the new Garden City ideas. His first domestic architecture after he returned to Hobart was described as 'a skilful adaptation' of these themes. Later as the English arts and crafts style became less fashionable he moved to a Mediterranean approach.[36] He designed a modest, rather Italianate looking house for the Giblins. Originally named 'Hillside', a name

---

[35] Eilean Giblin to 'Copper' Giblin, Polegate, 28 October 1954.
[36] Barry McNeill and Leigh Woolley, *Architecture from the Edge*, Montpelier Press, North Hobart, 2002, pp. 27–8; Alison Alexander ed., *The Companion to Tasmanian History*, Centre for Tasmanian Historical Studies, University of Tasmania, Hobart, 2005, p. 378.

the Giblins discarded because there were too many Hillsides in Hobart, it was later named 'The Jungle' by Lyndhurst Giblin after he had struggled with the overgrown garden. He put this name on a temporary sign only, however, until he heard Eilean's views and its long-term name became 'The Side'. Although built to be the Giblins' permanent home in Hobart and Eilean's first opportunity to design and furnish a home to her own taste, they lived in it for only short periods during the next 20 years.

Eilean visited England in 1926 when her mother was seriously ill and she left again for England in November 1928 at a time when she had been in her new home in Hobart only about 18 months. During her 1928–29 visit, she proposed bringing her mother to Hobart but it is unclear whether for a visit or permanently. If she had followed her pattern of three-yearly visits she would not have begun this trip until about February or March of 1929, but her early departure was because of concern for her health. At about this time she developed an illness that appears to have been undiagnosed in Hobart and which was not easily diagnosed even by London specialists – it was eventually described as 'muscular heart trouble'. It may have been a condition aggravated by the upheaval she could see ahead following the offer to Lyndhurst Giblin of the position of Ritchie Professor of Economic Research at the University of Melbourne.[37]

Moving would involve leaving their new home built and furnished to her design. It would mean moving from a small city where as a newcomer and an outsider she had had some success in advancing on the painstaking path towards the goal of equal citizenship and had forged a satisfying and productive life, achieving an enviable status in Hobart in less than a decade. There are several indirect references to this esteem in her husband's letters. On one crossing to Tasmania by boat from Melbourne, he reported a woman fellow traveller asking after Eilean: 'Tell her the police-woman was asking. We owe her so much,' the traveller said.[38] The appointment of policewomen was a key goal of feminists, not particularly as an advance in equal opportunity in employment, but so that they would be available as guardians of women and children[39] entangled in the legal and prison systems. At this time only one had been appointed in Tasmania; both Victoria and New South Wales had four. In another letter, Giblin wrote, 'Some of the Hospital Board sent

---

[37] MS366/1, 20 November 1928.
[38] MS366/1, 12 August 1929.
[39] Lake, *Getting Equal*, p. 61.

greetings and how much they missed you.'⁴⁰ In Melbourne Eilean would have to start a new life in a much more formidable environment.

Soon after she arrived in England Eilean saw a heart specialist and had radiographs taken but her husband complained that he did not hear the result and was disturbed when Eilean decided to make no further reports on her health. 'No doubt you are tired of it as a subject,' he wrote, 'but that is hardly sufficient ground'.⁴¹ In the first months she was in England her health was overshadowed by a tragic and unexpected event in the Burton family. Soon after leaving Wye College, Eilean's youngest brother, Clive, had been employed in Seville, Spain as an agricultural adviser for a British Government agency. Early in 1928 he had married Phyllis Petrococino and their son, Peter, was born late that year but Phyllis died soon after the baby's birth. This left the Burton family to work out how to care for the young baby. The first plan appeared to be for Ada Burton, by then a woman of nearly 70, to care for her grandson at Homefield, immediately putting a stop to plans for her to accompany Eilean back to Hobart. Then Eilean contemplated bringing the baby to Australia but this was soon dismissed as impossible because it would mean separating him from his father. Giblin raised the possibility of making inquiries about getting a job for Clive in Australia – his agricultural and managerial experience would make him very employable, he believed. These possibilities raised by Eilean and to which Giblin responded remain unresolved in his letters and none eventuated. The baby's great-aunt, Elizabeth MacRae, a nursing sister, rescued Peter from Spain and cared for him for the first few years of his life at the thatched cottage she shared with her sister, Mary MacRae White, at Alfriston, near Polegate on the Sussex Downs. When he was a few years old he moved to live with his grandmother, Ada Burton, his bachelor uncle Kenneth Burton, and his widowed great-aunt, Edith (MacRae) Mollison, at Homefield. In the late 1930s, he went to live with his father, Clive Burton, by then remarried with a young daughter, Gillian, and living at Farnborough.

The crisis over the death of Clive's wife and arranging for the care of his baby son coincided with Eilean's disturbing visits to a Harley Street heart specialist who warned that it could take six months for her to recover. Another specialist, however, decided her problem was her teeth and she had all her teeth extracted – by coincidence Lyndhurst Giblin had all his teeth extracted in Melbourne at about the same time. When Eilean's symptoms persisted yet

---

40 MS366/1, 12 June 1929.
41 MS366/1, 10 February 1929.

another specialist told her she had to diet, avoiding all nitrogenous products. Lyndhurst Giblin found her letters about these treatments 'very disturbing'. 'Is there no end to these discoveries?' he wrote. 'It seems necessary that you should close up the thing in some way, harmonise the various experts into some reasonable plan of treatment – before you leave for Australia.'[42] This long, never completely diagnosed illness, which contributed to Eilean's absence from Australia for about nine months, invites speculation about the state of her marriage. It coincided with a time when any prospect of having children – assumed by Giblin relatives to have been their wish – had faded as Eilean moved beyond child-bearing age.

Several times her husband suggested she take trips to the Continent – the Alps, the Royat baths, a Mediterranean fishing village. Then, realising that Eilean needed intellectual stimulus as well as a change of scene, he wrote: 'There ought to be some place that offers climate & air with some inspiration to them, with occupations on which you could get really keen.' Among his suggestions were places with political interest, 'Ireland might offer something or Sicily and study the Mussolini effect.' 'Find something worth doing within your physical power under good climatic conditions. Let me know if money will be helpful I am fairly low with settling expenses here but shall be ahead in another couple of months.'[43] Before she returned to Australia Eilean visited Geneva sending her husband news of the League of Nations and the International Labour Office. She sailed for Australia on the *Orsova* from Toulon to a new home in Melbourne.

* * *

'There must be many women, feminists at heart, in a place the size of Melbourne'

Melbourne, Canberra 1929–1932

Eilean Giblin arrived in Melbourne from Europe on 23 September 1929 a little more than a month before the Wall Street stock market crash that

---

[42] MS366/1, 12 June 1929.
[43] MS366/1, 21 April 1929.

heralded the start of the Great Depression. Her husband had been living in the city since taking up his post as Ritchie Professor of Economics at the University of Melbourne early in the year. He left Hobart amid a storm of protests directed at remarks he made at a farewell dinner held in February 1929 at the Royal Society of Tasmania and presided over by the Governor, Sir James O'Grady. In his speech, Giblin disturbed Tasmanians by challenging the view that the state possessed vast untapped economic potential. Instead he categorised it as a 'poor country' that would never be 'a very rich community'. Presciently, in view of present-day opinion, he suggested that Tasmania, instead of seeking eminence in material wealth, should put its energies into research and knowledge particularly a study of its natural environment, citing country still unexplored and mountains only recently mapped. A few years before, after several failed attempts, Giblin had been the first white man to climb Mount Anne, the highest peak in south-west Tasmania. His views were attacked as heretical by politicians and business leaders and the *Mercury* ran a leading article, 'Major Giblin and the State', in which the editorialist stated he 'leaves his country for his country's good'.[44]

In Melbourne, once it became clear Eilean would be away for the best part of 1929, he began searching for temporary accommodation, at first for a 'balcony' room near the University then around Parliament House in the city, but he finally settled on a 'queer little cottage' in South Yarra. 'A cottage sounds pretentious but it costs not more than a single room,' he wrote in March 1929. The cottage was at 142 Domain Street, a side street running off the prestigious Domain Road. The playing fields of Melbourne Grammar were opposite the house, a tramline to the University was a few steps away in Domain Road and just over Domain Road were the extensive Botanic Gardens. At first Giblin promoted the house to Eilean only as a temporary home:

> It has a shed at the back open and suitable for sleeping in. I don't suppose you would consider the cottage possible as a place to live in but I think it will make a reasonable bed & breakfast & evening place putting into it the barest minimum, had to take it for 6 months, on your present prospects not a serious objection.[45]

---

[44] *Mercury*, 13 February 1929.
[45] MS366/1, 16 March 1929.

In his next letter, however, he implicitly assumed that this small, leaky, neglected, cold house with a bathroom reached via a verandah at the back and a lavatory at the bottom of the backyard would become at least a semi-permanent residence. He listed some minimal purchases he had made, seeking her approval and deferring to her taste in furnishings. His sister had found some 'red and dark blue and green' china during a visit to Melbourne that he thought Eilean would approve and which he thought would go with her 'prospective hangings'. He had bought some strips of matting 'like the big mat in Hobart' – essential as the floors were so awful – some second hand chairs, two tables, a cedar chest of drawers and a Coolgardie safe, but was still looking for some bookshelves and a table with its legs cut off to make a bed. 'You should look out for a gay enamel coffee pot without a spout,' he told Eilean.[46]

When it rained and leaks appeared in his sleep-out and water poured into the kitchen, and he discovered that the cottage would get no sun in winter and the southerly winds beat in, Giblin decided he had been hasty in taking the place and that it needed a new roof. His letter describing 142 Domain Street contains a plan of the house that gives some idea of the curious blend of taste and spartan abstemiousness that marked the Giblins' life. Named 'Mulberry Cottage' – there was a big mulberry tree in the backyard – this unpromising but well-situated house remained the Giblins' home for the decade they lived in Melbourne. Being a few minutes' walk from the famed Melbourne Botanic Gardens compensated for many discomforts.[47]

By the time Eilean arrived back from England, Lyndhurst Giblin had checked out some of the advantages of life in Melbourne. He was appreciative of the standard of music in contrast to his view of the theatre – 'very poor', only one decent play in four months. He reported the recently published *All Quiet on the Western Front* by E.M. Remarque was selling well but he did not think it was a true representation of the war. He suggested books for her voyage back to Australia – Andre Maurois' *Disraeli* and Dorothy Gardiner's *English Girlhood at School: A study of women's education through twelve centuries* – and he reported that Cambridge University was 'excited' about Radclyffe Hall's recently published lesbian novel, *The Well of Loneliness*.[48]

Soon after he settled in Melbourne Lyndhurst Giblin was in the news when a Melbourne *Herald* journalist interviewed him as he washed up

---

[46] MS366/1, 26 March 1929.
[47] MS366/1, 26 March 1929.
[48] MS366/1, 14 July 1929.

accumulated dishes at Domain Street. He was a newsworthy subject as a joint author with J.B. Brigden, D.B. Copland, E.C. Dyason and C.H. Wickens of an inquiry into the Australian tariff set up by Prime Minister S.M. Bruce because of concerns about growing trends towards increased protection. *The Australian Tariff: An Economic Enquiry* proved to be popular seller, the first 3000 copies going quickly when it was published in July 1929. He sent a copy of the publication to Eilean to catch the *Orsova* at Port Said, advising her to give it to the ship's library when she had finished.[49]

In September while Eilean was still travelling back to Australia, Lyndhurst Giblin was at a Statistical Conference in Canberra staying with his old friend from the 40th Battalion, Frank Green, then clerk-assistant in the House of Representatives. His visit coincided with the night of 10 September 1929 when the Bruce Government was defeated by one vote in the House of Representatives on its industrial relations legislation. Giblin believed Bruce had made a mistake getting into 'this Arbitration business' as otherwise he had been doing very well. He told Eilean he expected Labor to get a small majority at the forthcoming election and that the general run of Labor ministers were likely to be better than 'the present average'. The night Bruce was defeated Giblin dined at the Hotel Canberra and walked home around Capital Hill to Green's house in Forrest, a walk that took him an hour in the centre of a city that was still largely undeveloped bush. He passed the Prime Minister's house, the Lodge, but met no one on his entire walk. Earlier on the way to dinner and in daylight he had walked across the bush on Capital Hill, the future site of Parliament House, cutting the journey to half an hour.[50]

At the election held on 12 October 1929, the Bruce-Page Government was defeated by the Labor Party, under James Scullin, the Prime Minister Stanley Melbourne Bruce losing his seat of Flinders. Just over two weeks later the spectacular crash of the United States share market marked the start of the Great Depression that was to dominate politics for years to come. By the time Bruce was defeated Eilean had arrived back in Australia, 'pretty fit', as Giblin told his sister, Edith, but still having 'to go slow for some time'. Eilean brought back a small gramophone that was to give pleasure to the Giblins for many years and she had plans to buy a car. Contemplating their return to Tasmania for the summer holidays, Giblin wrote that the gramophone 'with Eilean's car, when she gets one, will mean we do not

---

[49] MS366/1, 27 July 1929.
[50] MS366/1, 10 September 1929.

travel light; not to mention a formidable case of books & papers that I shall want'.⁵¹

When Eilean Giblin arrived in Melbourne in September 1929 believing it was to be her permanent home she could little foresee the disruptive effects of the unfolding disaster of the Great Depression. Inevitably Lyndhurst Giblin as a leading economist was soon called on to advise the new and inexperienced Federal Labor government on ways to tackle the economic crisis. In the time between settling in Melbourne and her husband's summons to Canberra, Eilean approached her life in the new city in a similar way to her arrival in Hobart a decade earlier. Her first move, however, joining the Victorian Women's Citizenship Movement, the state organisation affiliated with the Australian Federation of Women Voters, turned out to be a false start. Her reputation as an effective feminist representative in Hobart evidently preceded her as she was almost immediately elected a member of the VWCM executive at its annual general meeting late in 1929.⁵² Professor L.F. Giblin was listed as the guest speaker at a lunchtime meeting on 31 July 1930 to speak on 'The Fight for Prosperity'. It was not long, however, before Eilean became aware of criticism of the way the Victorian organisation was run by its president, Britomarte James.

Mrs Elizabeth Britomarte James had jointly founded the VWCM in 1922 and was a dominating figure in the organisation. She was president from 1929 to 1932 and represented the Movement on the Australian Federation of Women Voters; she was also extraordinarily active in many other organisations some of which she had founded. She was regarded by her admirers as a 'born administrator'⁵³ but her critics believed that under her presidency the VWCM had become little more than a fortnightly social luncheon club. Her distinctive, showy personality and her penchant for social events was not what Eilean looked for in a serious feminist organisation. The VWCM secretary, Julia Rapke, described Britomarte James as a large, well-dressed woman who carried off her entrances with an 'air of hauteur' aided by her props of a lorgnette and ebony stick and her striking 'un-Australian Oxford-like accent'. She had acquired this accent although she had been born on the Ballarat goldfields and had spent her childhood and youth in the slums of Port Melbourne and at Williamstown where her father was a chaplain to seamen. She was regarded by some as 'a humbug, a

---

[51] MS366/3, LFG to Edith Hall, 1 October 1929.
[52] *Dawn*, 18 December 1929. Report of Annual General Meeting of VWCM.
[53] Julia Rapke Papers, NLA MS 824/7.

clever publicist, or a social climber' but she had also gained much feminist admiration. As one of the first women justices of the peace in Melbourne, she had refused to leave a South Melbourne court when requested to do so while details regarded as 'unsavoury' were heard in an assault case. Her stand made headlines and was a subject of newspaper controversy. Feminists applauded her for upholding the right of women to play a full role in positions to which they were appointed.[54]

As a newcomer Eilean may have been seen by Britomarte James's critics as the most likely person to change the VWCM's direction. Even Britomarte James herself admitted that the organisation was dysfunctional. 'I am doubtful if I can pull together the disintegrated threads of the Victorian Women's Citizens Movement,' she wrote to Bessie Rischbieth.[55] Apparently reflecting a groundswell of opposition and with the backing of some members including the influential Kathleen Gilman Jones, headmistress of Merton Hall (Melbourne Church of England Girls Grammar School), Eilean decided in 1931 to stand for president. She wrote to Bessie Rischbieth:

> I do this unwillingly as I am by temperament unsuited for such a position, but there is a most extraordinary dearth of women in Melbourne who could take on the position. There must be many women, feminists at heart, in a place the size of Melbourne who have not yet been touched by the feminist movement, & I suppose only time will show if we can reach them.
>
> I have been very worried for some time at the state of the VWCM, but it is only this year that it quite clearly came to me that the President is at the bottom of this state of affairs. How often our first impressions are correct. I first met the President at the Sydney conference in 1927 & my impressions were not favourable. Later on when I saw more of her I thought I had been unfair – but now I know my first impressions were right.
>
> I quite agree with you of the importance of affiliated societies existing in all the States, & it is one of the reasons for my agreeing

---

[54] Julia Rapke Papers NLA MS824/7; Judith Smart, 'James, Elizabeth Britomarte (1867–1943)', *Australian Dictionary of Biography*, Supplementary Volume, Melbourne University Press, 2005, pp. 198–99.
[55] Rischbieth MS2004/5/698.

to stand for election, hoping that we shall be able to pull the Victorian society together.

I am glad to say I am in better health than I was a year ago, but I still have to be careful how much I do.[56]

Bessie Rischbieth invited Eilean to Sydney to represent the VWCM at a Board meeting of the Australian Federation of Women Voters[57] during which they apparently discussed the problems of leadership in the Victorian organisation – Julia Rapke had resigned as secretary in August – and Eilean's uncertainty about her future. Her letter to Bessie Rischbieth had been written from Canberra where she was living temporarily following the Government's call for her husband's advice in the economic crisis of the Depression. Subsequently she withdrew her nomination for VWCM president, apparently because she was uncertain about where she would be living and she intended to visit England again in 1932. As it turned out Eilean was to find a much more satisfying role when she returned to Melbourne in 1933.

As the full horrors of the Depression unfolded with the collapse of trade and business, an explosion in the numbers of unemployed workers and many families close to starvation, Giblin's role as government adviser escalated. When the Commonwealth Statistician, C.H. Wickens, collapsed in February 1931, Giblin became Acting Commonwealth Statistician, ensuring he was on hand to advise the Government on economic and financial matters. He joined with other economists in preparing the drastic recommendations for reductions in expenditure and increases in taxation that became part of the Premiers' Plan. He remained Acting Commonwealth Statistician for nearly two years until December 1932, through the upheaval of the landslide defeat of the Scullin Labor Government at the end of 1931 and the success of J.A. Lyons, who left the Labor Party to lead the United Australian Party (UAP) to victory.

By the middle of 1931, Eilean and her husband were living in the Canberra suburb of Barton where they temporarily rented a house owned by the Melbourne *Herald* and ordinarily occupied by the *Herald* journalist, Joe Alexander. The development of Canberra, then a small scattered community of about 7000 residents, had ceased with the onset of the Depression when

---

[56] Rischbieth, MS2004/5/1253, 17 July 1931, Macquarie St, Canberra.
[57] *Dawn*, 23 September 1931.

workers building the city's infrastructure and housing were sacked and many public servants were retrenched. Long after, Eilean remembered her 'most desolate' impression of the shopping centre at Manuka with all the shops bordering the Lawns and in the Arcade empty.[58]

At the beginning of 1932 Eilean left on another trip to England, coinciding with the change of government from Labor to UAP and some uncertainty about the time her husband would remain in Canberra. When her ship stopped in Fremantle, Bessie Rischbieth arranged a lunch at the Karrakatta Club to welcome her in Perth. In her speech Eilean stressed the importance of the Disarmament Conference to begin in Geneva in February and the Conference on Reparation and Debts in Lausanne in June. She believed there was no use in inaugurating new systems of banking unless peace was to become universal, she told guests.[59] Bessie Rischbieth had requested the inclusion of women in the Australian delegation to the Disarmament Conference but the change of government left this unresolved.[60] The VWCM vice president, Kathleen Gilman Jones, suggested Eilean as a delegate to the conference. 'Mrs Giblin will be in Europe and we consider she would be excellent – also we approve of Dr Osborne's name, but we are not very enthusiastic about Mrs Jamieson-Williams and distinctly cold about Miss Ruby Rich,' she wrote to Bessie Rischbieth.[61] Eilean may have been an observer at the conference but there is no record of her being a delegate.

When Eilean left Canberra her husband was uncertain about his future following the change of government, but he continued to be in demand by the new government led by his early associate from Tasmania, Joe Lyons. Soon after Eilean arrived in England, she heard that her husband was in hospital in Canberra with shingles and she contemplated returning early but then heard that he was recovering. After convalescing at the Hotel Canberra for some time he moved to a small room with a fireplace – and an adjoining porch where he could sleep – in the home of his protégée, Roland Wilson, and his American wife Valeska, at 64 Empire Circuit in the Canberra suburb of Forrest. Following his usual eccentric sleeping pattern, he made a bed on the floor of the porch and refused electric light

---

[58] MS366/6/1, 6 March 1941.
[59] *Daily News*, 12 January 1932, p. 7; *Sunday Times*, 17 January 1932, p. 13; *Dawn*, 20 January 1932.
[60] Rischbieth, MS2004/5/1330, 14 December 1931.
[61] MS2004/5/1325, 9 December 1931.

in favour of his trusty storm lantern.[62] Wilson, 28, had recently been appointed economist in the Statistician's Branch on the advice of Giblin who earlier had engineered his entry to the Commonwealth Public Service as the first graduate appointee. It was the beginning of a brilliant career: Wilson was appointed Commonwealth Statistician in 1936 at the age of 32; during the Second World War he was Secretary of the Department of Labour and National Service; and in 1951 he became head of Treasury. As a temporary guest in the Wilson home, Giblin typically threw himself into the physical work of helping the Wilsons begin a garden. One Saturday he worked for six hours digging and planting a strawberry bed in the previously unworked soil.

When it seemed likely that Lyndhurst Giblin would be one of the Australian party to the Ottawa Imperial Conference to be held in July/August 1932, Eilean delayed returning to Australia so that they could meet in London after the conference. Ultimately Giblin was not included in the delegation, at which British Commonwealth countries negotiated bilateral agreements providing limited Imperial preference, but with her arrangements for delay already in train, it was the middle of September before Eilean joined the *Moldavia* in Marseilles for the return journey to Melbourne. Her health had improved: 'You are certainly able to stand a great deal more than of recent years,' Lyndhurst wrote to her.[63] Nevertheless, in 1933 Giblin cited his wife's health as one of the reasons why he could not take the permanent position of Commonwealth Statistician. Eilean's reluctance to live in Canberra was also a factor. While she was in England she told her husband 'rather firmly of not returning to Canberra'[64] but eventually she agreed to go there temporarily. After her return from England the Giblins rented a house in National Circuit, Forrest, for about three months until just before Christmas 1932.[65]

The Giblins were to return to Canberra in the crisis of the Second World War, but in the meantime Melbourne presented Eilean with an unexpected opportunity to achieve an enduring feminist legacy.

---

[62] Wilson, p. 18.
[63] MS366/1, Canberra, 6 July 1932.
[64] MS366/1, Canberra, 27 July 1932.
[65] MS366/1, Canberra, 7 September 1932.

Chapter 5

A Room of One's Own

Melbourne 1930s

When Eilean Giblin returned to Melbourne at the beginning of 1933 to resume a life disrupted by two temporary residences in Canberra and about nine months overseas, she was about to enter the most publicly productive period of her life. Within a few months she was launched in the surprising role of acting chair of a committee that aimed to establish an independent non-denominational women's college at the University of Melbourne. Within four years she had steered the committee from a tenuous hold on a bare site to the opening of a residential college accepting its first students. This had been a long-wished-for dream for many university women, notably Dr Georgina Sweet, a zoologist, who was the first woman to reach acting- and associate professor level at Melbourne University and who had been chair of the women's college provisional committee since it was established in 1917. She was supported by an array of prominent women including the committee's Honorary Secretary, Elizabeth Lothian, a classics teacher who had graduated from the University of Melbourne and studied at Newnham College, Cambridge, and lecturer, Jessie Webb, who on several occasions was acting professor in charge of the University's history department. Eminent university men, among them the Chancellor, Sir John MacFarland, and Professor of Law, Sir Harrison Moore, were also active supporters.

During the 1920s the committee had been tantalisingly close to securing a site. In 1920 the chair of the college committee, Dr Sweet, reported that the Victorian Government had taken steps to reserve three acres of the old cattle and pig market site opposite the University for the proposed Women's College. Successive governments repeated the promise of a site, both in letters to Dr Sweet and to deputations in 1921, 1924 and 1928. In 1929, however, the site was reserved for a new Melbourne

General Hospital.[1] Meanwhile committee members were frustratingly aware that non-denominational women's colleges had been established in some other capitals long before, for example, at Sydney University in 1894 and at the University of Queensland in 1914. Women student numbers continued to grow at the University of Melbourne but only about 75 could be accommodated in two halls associated with denominational men's colleges, Janet Clark Hall at Trinity College and St Mary's Hall which was associated with Newman College but located in two houses in The Avenue, Parkville.

A breakthrough occurred in October 1932 when the Victorian Premier, Sir Stanley Argyle, supported a proposal that an area of unused Crown land in Parkville should be reserved as the site for a non-denominational women's college associated with Melbourne University. This triangular area bounded by Royal Parade (Sydney Road), College Crescent and Cemetery Road and on the north by Princes Park was well-situated opposite Ormond College and close to other University denominational colleges. In 1873 the site had been given to the Carlton Cricket Club but the club later obtained another site although the land grant had never been rescinded. By the time the bill to reserve the site for a women's college came before the Victorian Parliament in 1933, Eilean Giblin had become acting chair of the provisional committee, taking the place of Georgina Sweet who left on a lengthy overseas visit.

Why Eilean Giblin? She was a relatively obscure newcomer to the Melbourne world of women activists. Her only foray into feminist politics in Melbourne, in the Victorian Women's Citizenship Movement, had petered out and she had spent most of 1931 and 1932 either overseas or living in Canberra. Committee minute books are missing for the period from 1920 to 1934 so it is impossible to discover from College records the circumstances of her election. Why was she preferred, for instance, to such a prominent supporter as Eveline Syme who had attended a prestigious pinnacle of women's education, Newnham College, and had a Master of Arts degree and an established reputation as a painter and printmaker? Eilean was not a graduate of a university, a rare situation among the active members of the provisional committee several of whom had been at Newnham or Girton. She had an association with the university as a professor's wife but Lyndhurst Giblin, despite his public reputation, had had little time to acquire influence at Melbourne University before moving temporarily to Canberra. Perhaps she was chosen because of some rift among the active members of the committee

---

[1]   University Women's College, *First Annual Report*, 1937.

after the departure of such a prominent leader as Dr Georgina Sweet. She may have been a compromise between opposing factions but there appear to be no informal records or memoirs that could enlighten a searcher so long after the event. Committee members may have been aware of Eilean's reputation as an active member of the WNPPL in Tasmania, the high regard in which she was held by the president of the Australian Federation of Women Voters, Bessie Rischbieth, and her capacity for consistent hard work. They may also have admired her active membership of the Victorian Women's Citizenship Movement and her attempt to change its direction. Perhaps, after their hard and devoted work over so many years, committee members decided a new public face would be an advantage. Eveline Syme stated later that Eilean Giblin was chosen at the suggestion of committee member Jessie Webb, whose judgment members respected, although at the time most did not know Giblin – and Syme did not even know her by sight.[2] As Jessie Webb was a friend of Georgina Sweet's, committee members probably believed Giblin was Sweet's choice as her successor. However she came to the position, Eilean Giblin was described in an account of the early history of the college as 'a most suitable replacement for Georgina Sweet'. She was 'an intellect, a socialist ... a person of independent mind', a person whose views on social questions 'were ahead of her time' and who was known 'for what was then regarded as unconventional dress'.[3]

By 23 June 1933 Eilean Giblin was acting chair of the committee. The following month she prepared a document putting the case for the Carlton site for the proposed University Women's College including the argument that the laying of a foundation stone would be 'a notable and far-reaching function for Melbourne's Centenary in 1934' and 'would serve as a memorial to the work of Melbourne's pioneer women graduates in medicine, law, education and science'. Supporting material included a history of committee's efforts since 1917 to obtain a site and raise funds for a college. It concluded, following a reference to Virginia Woolf's great polemic feminist work, *A Room of One's Own*, with a plea for a college that would:

> ... give our women students in cramped boarding houses, and our ambitious country girls a setting of comfort and beauty and good

---

[2] UC Archives, Council minutes, 30 November 1955.

[3] Alan Gregory, 'Getting the College on the Ground: Background to the Establishment of a Non-Denominational Residential College for Women', in Margaret Campbell ed., *University Women's College: A Record of Events of 1937 – The First Year*, University College Association, 1988, p. 9.

fellowship ... [W]omen deserve as much as men to have granted them the freedom of the University and the chance to give back to the world in fine scholarship what they have been set free to acquire at leisure.[4]

Eilean Giblin's consistent energy marked her leadership of the college committee. Her first effort was to write to every member of the Victorian Parliament seeking support for the bill reserving the old cricket ground site for the proposed college.[5] The demands of the chair's position escalated when a sizeable opposition developed against what was regarded by many residents as alienation of parkland. The local member, William P. (Bill) Barry, the recently elected ALP member for the seat of Carlton, who had supported the idea of a women's college, became a strident opponent of the transfer of the cricket ground site, leading many protests. At the height of the controversy the *Argus* published a photograph of the old cricket ground site with a lively lacrosse game in progress,[6] contradicting some of the claims made by supporters of the college in letters to the editor that the site was a largely unused, weed-infested wasteland. Lyndhurst Giblin was one of the letter writers supporting the use of the land for a college. Although he acknowledged the need for preserving open spaces, he described the proposed site as 'an awkward triangular area' with an 'uninviting' surface and 'a covering of weeds, not grass'. He claimed this indicated 'the very small extent to which it is used'. He also argued the value of 'collegiate life' as part of university education.[7] Elizabeth Lothian, secretary of the provisional committee, promoted the advantages of the proposed college as a training ground for 'those important servants of the public, teachers, doctors and lawyers', and claimed that it would through scholarships 'give an equal chance of education to all ambitious girls, no matter what their private means may be'.[8] In its caption to the lacrosse game, the *Argus* had referred to the proposal 'to acquire the land for the erection of a hostel for women students at the University'. College proponents vehemently denied this 'boarding-house' claim, insisting their proposal was for a college that

---

[4] University College Archives, 01/01, Establishment of the Provisional Committee, 24 July 1933.
[5] UC Archives, 01/13, Correspondence between Mrs E.M. Giblin and Members of Parliament.
[6] Photograph of Old Carlton Cricket Ground, *Argus*, 31 July 1933, p. 10.
[7] L.F. Giblin, letter to the editor, *Argus*, 31 July 1933, p. 10.
[8] E.L. Lothian, letter to the editor, *Argus*, 31 July 1933, p. 10.

would offer all the advantages of university life including tutorials and the opportunity to mix with visiting lecturers and other experts.

The dispute about the land escalated when six hundred residents of Carlton and adjoining suburbs signed a petition opposing the transfer of the old cricket ground site for a women's residential college and the local member, Bill Barry, at a public meeting claimed the land was used by 'thousands' and should not be 'filched'. The petitioners' main argument was that the University had sufficient land to accommodate a college within its site.[9] Barry went far further when, on the night of 11 August 1933, with a small group of enthusiastic followers, he pegged out the site and declared it a mining claim. He claimed he had been told by an old resident that gold had been found in the area when sewerage pipes were being dug about 1898. This publicity stunt drew newspaper headlines but there appear to have been no further developments.[10]

In August 1933 Eilean led a deputation to the Premier, Sir Stanley Argyle, in support of the proposed college, gathering support from an impressive list of women's organisations including the National Council of Women, the Australian Women's National League, the Country Women's Association, the Housewives' Association and the Women's Organising Committee of the Labor Party. Prominent women who supported her included Dr Constance Ellis, a Melbourne obstetrician and gynaecologist, a pioneer in the field of women's health and a founder of the Lyceum Club, and Mrs Gladys A. Hain, a lawyer, then working as a journalist with the *Star* (the evening paper published by the Argus and Australasian Ltd), later president of the Housewives' Association. The Chancellor of the University, Sir John MacFarland, also joined the deputation[11] which was successful in maintaining the momentum for the grant of the site. On 5 September 1933, the Carlton Land Bill providing for the permanent reservation of the old Carlton Cricket ground as a site for a residential college for women students of the University of Melbourne was signed by the Governor after passing through the Victorian Parliament.[12] In the euphoria of this success, the women's college committee optimistically floated the idea, supported by the Premier, that sufficient money might

---

[9] 'Residents make emphatic protest', 'Residents petition Parliament', *Argus*, 2 August 1933, pp. 7, 8.
[10] *Argus*, 12 August 1933, p. 21.
[11] 'Two Deputations', *Argus*, 12 August 1933, p. 21.
[12] *Argus*, 6 September 1933, p. 8.

be raised to enable the foundation stone to be laid during the Melbourne Centenary celebrations in 1934–35,[13] but this proved impracticable and far beyond its fundraising capacity.

Early in 1934, after acting as chair of the provisional committee for the second half of 1933, Eilean Giblin took the position officially when Dr Georgina Sweet resigned because of ill health.[14] The files of correspondence and minutes of committee meetings and other records of the development of the plans for the proposed college indicate that she was an energetic and practical chairperson and an indefatigable letter writer. She sought people to join the committee, she appealed for donors, she sought advice on building plans, she explored costs of operating a college and she sought legal advice on affiliation with the University.[15] Before and during construction she had extremely detailed correspondence with the architects, A. and K. Henderson, on planning, estimating, equipping and constructing the first wing and associated problems, large and small. These ranged from major plans for the building, arrangements for the connection of water and telephone lines, choosing suitable electrical fittings and the design of the wrought iron balustrading, to such details as brackets in bedrooms and obtaining information about a suitable griller for the kitchen. (An illustration of one suggested model, now looking decidedly antique, remains in the archives.) She was often in contact with the Department of Lands and Survey and other departmental and municipal instrumentalities. She discussed affiliation of the proposed college with the University and other colleges; she sought Professor Kenneth Bailey's legal advice on a constitution and she corresponded with the Governor's wife, Lady [Eleanor] Huntingfield, seeking and arranging her involvement in the project.[16]

At the first meeting under her presidency, Eilean Giblin gained support for her proposal that a small executive consisting of the president and secretary be authorised to make immediate decisions between meetings.[17] The

---

[13] *Argus*, 8 October 1933, p. 22.

[14] E.I. Lothian and Eveline Syme, *University Women's College, University of Melbourne: A Brief History*, Melbourne, 1954, p. 5.

[15] UC Archives, 01/06 Correspondence of the President of the Executive Committee, 1933–37.

[16] UC Archives, 01.06, Correspondence of the President; 01/08, Architects' correspondence; 01/13, Correspondence re site.

[17] UC Archives, Minute Book Executive Committee Women's College, Book III, 9 July 1934.

provisional Executive Committee at this time consisted of about 16 members, including many whose names were associated with the early struggles for a college site; the provisional general committee included in its membership of approximately 75 many women prominent in the educational, organisational and social life of Melbourne and of the university. The Executive Committee held frequent meetings during the rest of 1934, discussing such items as liaison with government departments, the architect's plans, reaction to the plans and arrangements for an appeal and the appointment of a fund organiser. At one meeting Eilean reported that Professor Douglas Copland had agreed to contact the Rockefeller and Carnegie institutes regarding the possibility of financial support.[18]

When Eilean left on the *Ormonde* early in 1935 for her usual three-yearly visit to England, Eveline Syme took over as acting president (the position was sometimes called president, at other times chair). As the year unfolded, 1935 turned out to be a year when activity stalled. Just as a building appeal for the proposed Women's College was to get under way, organisers became aware that Melbourne University planned a major appeal for a students' union building. As it was impracticable for the two appeals to proceed together in a city that was only gradually emerging from the worst of the Depression, the Women's College appeal was postponed until the autumn of 1936. Eilean was back in Melbourne in October 1935 and chaired the college committee meetings held in the latter part of that year and in the build-up to the appeal the following year.

The women's college appeal for £25,000 was finally launched at the beginning of May 1936 at Melbourne Town Hall by Lady Huntingfield, wife of the Governor, in her role as president of the appeal committee. In the course of her speech she advocated the reading of Virginia Woolf's book *A Room of One's Own*. 'I believe such a college will be of lasting benefit to girls in the country and the community as a whole,' she said.[19] Members of the appeal committee were: Eilean Giblin, Chair of the Executive Committee, Eveline Syme, vice president, Mrs Muriel Cowling, Honorary Secretary, Sir Walter Leitch, honorary treasurer, and Mrs M.M. (Ray) Phillips who was appointed appeal organiser. A foundation member of the Lyceum Club and the Club's treasurer, a position she had held since 1920, apart from the 1923–24 year when she was Club president, Mrs Phillips set up the appeal

---

[18] UC Archives, Minute Book Executive Committee, Book III, 17 November 1934.
[19] R.J.W. Selleck, *The Shop: The University of Melbourne 1850–1939*, Melbourne University Press, Carlton, Vic., 2003, p. 653.

office in Capel Court in the city. Dr Georgina Sweet then in London was the first subscriber with the very substantial donation of £1000.[20] As part of the publicity effort, the *Argus* published a plan of the proposed building. In its final form it was to be a four-sided structure, enclosing a central quadrangle, to accommodate 120 students with a dining room to hold 130, but the initial plan was for the building of the south-eastern corner only, to accommodate 20 students in individual rooms.[21] The design had some similarities to Cambridge's Newnham College.

Many events were held to raise funds for the appeal. Eveline Syme donated proceeds from her exhibition of lino cuts and wood engravings at the Arts and Crafts Society's Gallery in Collins Street; Lady Huntingfield attended a fundraising lecture on 'Cave Men of Australia' by Mary Cecil Allen, the Australian modernist artist, writer and lecturer on art, then visiting Melbourne from the United States;[22] Mrs J.A. Lyons, wife of the Prime Minister, spoke at a Rotary Club function on the women's college; Professor Giblin gave a lecture on 'Icelandic Heroes' at the home of Sir Harrison Moore, former head of the Law School, and many bridge parties and dramatic performances were held. This struggle to raise funds, with its emphasis on numerous low-key events mainly aimed at a female audience, rather than major appeals to captains of commerce and industry, was an eerie reflection of the handicaps that women faced in raising funds for the first women's colleges at Cambridge in the nineteenth century. Virginia Woolf described the reasons for their struggle in *A Room of One's Own*:

> At the thought of all those women working year after year and finding it hard to get two thousand pounds together, and as much as they could do to get thirty thousand pounds, we burst out in scorn at the reprehensible poverty of our sex. What had our mothers been doing then that they had no wealth to leave us? Powdering their noses? Looking in at shop windows? ... If only Mrs Seton and her mother and her mother before her had learnt the great art of making money and had left their money, like their fathers and grandfathers before them, to found fellowships and prizes and scholarships appropriated to the use of their own sex ... we might have looked forward without undue confidence

---

[20] Gregory, p. 8; *Argus*, 2 May 1936, p. 22.
[21] *Argus*, 5 May 1936, p. 8.
[22] Eveline Syme, 'Women and Art', *Centenary Gift Book*, eds Frances Fraser and Nettie Palmer, Women's Centenary Council/ Robertson & Mullens, Melbourne, 1934, p. 85.

to a pleasant and honourable lifetime spent in the shelter of one of the liberally endowed professions ... there could be no doubt that for some reason or other our mothers had mismanaged their affairs very gravely ... Certainly our mothers had not provided us with any thing comparable to all this [men's well endowed colleges] – our mothers who found it difficult to scrape together thirty thousand pounds, our mothers who bore thirteen children to ministers of religion at St Andrews.[23]

Driving the momentum of the Women's College appeal was an underlying fear that if it were not a success and building could not begin, the site could be forfeited. During the appeal, the Member for Carlton, Bill Barry, renewed his attack on the use of the site for a women's college, claiming the college would be just a 'glorified boarding house'. Eilean Giblin and Muriel Cowling refuted this claim in a letter to the *Argus* in which they made an eloquent case for the college:

In a women's college there is ... a highly qualified principal who can advise and guide the students in the light of her own wider experience; there are tutors who work in small classes, discussing and amplifying the work done in university lectures, and smoothing out difficulties. This intimate contact with more mature minds is invaluable to the student, and in the dining hall and common room she finds ample opportunity of discussion with those of her own age. A library and facilities for games, and for meetings of students' societies are provided, and pleasant, airy bed-sitting rooms allow the student to have as much privacy as she pleases, and to arrange those intimate little gatherings which are sometimes purely "for fun", but when mind meets mind in the most valuable intercourse.

In such a college when the aim is the development of the individual and the pursuit of true learning, a corporate spirit grows up which is a splendid and lasting influence. Such a spirit is impossible in any boarding-house, however "glorified", for there is no common aim to bind its inmates together, nor can they forget the commercial nature of their dwelling-place.

---

[23] *A Room of One's Own*, Ch. 1.

It would be a crushing blow if the admirable site granted for the new women's college were to be taken away at the very moment when the first wing is in sight.[24]

Although the appeal fell far short of its target – it raised about £6000 – Eilean announced in July 1936 that plans had been prepared, tenders called and the building of the first wing would begin with the money in hand. This included about £8000 raised during earlier appeals.[25] On 13 August 1936 she signed the contract for the building of the first section of the new college and work began the next day. The following month, in a ceremony on the site, Lady Huntingfield declared the foundation stone 'well and truly laid' and the architect, Kingsley Henderson, presented her with a silver trowel. A press report states that in her speech Lady Huntingfield 'eulogised the work of Mrs Giblin', but there is no amplification of this in the news item. In her reply Eilean Giblin reviewed the history of the movement for the college from the setting up of the first committee in August 1917 to the present when, after what she described as 'worries, alarums and excursions', the preliminary task was over and the committee could give way to a college council. She read messages of congratulations from Dr Georgina Sweet in Geneva and Miss Freda Bage, head of Women's College at the University of Queensland.[26] A few days later the sandstone foundation stone disappeared in what was suspected to be a students' prank. When asked whether a new stone would be laid, Eilean said the ceremony already held was symbolic and 'as such, sufficient'.[27] The following month the Victorian Government announced the membership of a management committee for the college site. It included four of the women who had been most closely associated with the movement to obtain the site and build the college: Georgina Sweet, Eilean Giblin, Jessie Webb and Eveline Syme, plus the University Vice Chancellor, Raymond E. Priestley, the Dean of the School of Law, Professor Kenneth H. Bailey, and the Victorian Director of Education, John A. Sietz.[28]

---

[24] *Argus*, 7 July 1936, p. 8.
[25] *Argus*, 17 July 1936, p. 3; EG to Susie Williams, 16 September 1936; UC Archives 45/1, Folder 7.
[26] *Argus*, 18 September 1936, p. 3.
[27] *Argus*, 22 September 1936, p. 10.
[28] *Victoria Government Gazette*, No. 184, 15 September 1936, p. 2447.

Figure 5.1 The first section of University Women's College, the Georgina Sweet Wing, built in 1937. (University College Archives)

Once the College building began, a Council replaced the provisional committee and Eilean became Chair of the Council. The Committee of Management, set up under the new Council, made many decisions, some forced by financial problems. Although the original intention had been to advertise for a principal at a salary of £500 to run the College, funds were so short this was not practicable. Instead Eilean wrote to Miss Susannah J. (Susie) Williams, a former long-term principal of Women's College at the University of Sydney, an eminent classical scholar and a Newnham College graduate, setting out the financial position and asking her if she would take the job as principal for one year at a nominal salary. The Council could not start 'with a more experienced or wiser head to help us launch the College, & put it on right lines', she wrote. When Susie Williams who was visiting England and Europe cabled accepting, Eilean wrote:

> I cannot tell you how relieved & pleased we are ... Really it is very good of you to help us like this & I feel personally deeply grateful, & that my worries & difficulties will be nothing now we know that we are to have some one as experienced as you to take charge next year.[29]

---

[29] UC Archives, 1/15/07, EG to Susie Williams, 10 September 1936.

She held out the hope that the College would be able to pay a salary if an interview she had scheduled with the Premier was successful. At the meeting Eilean asked for a government grant of £1000 a year towards salaries for the teaching staff, quoting the example of the women's colleges at Sydney and Brisbane, both of which received considerable help from their state governments,[30] but this did not eventuate. Eilean Giblin, Eveline Syme and Elizabeth Lothian kept in touch with Susie Williams, sending her encouraging reports of the progress of the College until she landed in Melbourne on 11 February 1937.[31]

In another decision forced by financial constraints the size of the college building was reduced to accommodate 16 rather than 20 students and staff and built-in wardrobes and washbasins were eliminated from the plans for students' rooms. The accommodation was later restored to 20 when committee members lent money for the purpose. The famed garden designer, Edna Walling, after conferring with Eilean Giblin and Eveline Syme, agreed to plan the garden for a nominal fee and to supervise its maintenance free of charge.[32] In these straitened circumstances, although the first call for funds was 'for building and furnishing', Eilean Giblin in a letter to the *Argus* appealed for special earmarked donations for a scholarship fund. With the first students soon to arrive 'the question of scholarships cannot be postponed', she wrote, appealing to 'public-spirited women ... to sacrifice some small luxury in the cause of learning'.[33]

The College opened for the start of the 1937 university year initially with seven students, three more coming into residence later. On 17 March 1937 Eilean Giblin was the first after dinner speaker addressing the students on the events leading up to the establishment of the College. The official opening of the first stage of the college, named the Georgina Sweet Wing, took place on Saturday, 26 June 1937. Lady Gowrie, wife of the Governor General, travelled to Melbourne especially for the event and left that night to return to Canberra by train. Eilean Giblin as President of the College Council welcomed Lady Gowrie and the other official guests including the Principal, Miss Susie Williams, the Chancellor of the University, Sir James Barrett, and the vice president of the council, Miss Eveline Syme. The

---

[30] UC Archives, 1/15/07, EG to Susie Williams, 16 September 1936.
[31] UC Archives, 1/15/07, Susie Williams correspondence re appointment; *Argus*, 12 February 1937, p. 4.
[32] *Argus*, 26 November 1936, p. 3; Ian Forster, 'From the Archives: The Letters of Edna Walling', *Frappe Fort*, February 2010, pp. 8–9.
[33] *Argus*, 31 October 1936, p. 18.

ceremony took place in the presence of an impressive and colourful gathering of Melbourne community leaders and University academics, many of whom wore the brilliant colours of their academic dress, described by the *Argus* as 'rich tints of scarlet, green, and blue in hoods and gowns, some of which were braided in scrolls of gold or silver, or edged with fur'. Conspicuously, Eilean Giblin wore none of these marks of scholarship but it was she who during the past four years had steered the college from a tenuous possibility to the opening of the first wing where students were already halfway through their first university year. This result had not been achieved in the previous two decades despite the strenuous endeavours of very dedicated people. Eilean Giblin devoted herself to the College 'whole-heartedly', Eveline Syme wrote, 'it became the great interest of her life'. To the many problems that arose 'she brought wise judgement'.[34]

Lady Gowrie described the main benefit of collegiate life as 'a general sense of culture and scholarship' and the opportunity to exchange ideas freely with fellow students of different traditions, background, and outlook. 'These discussions must be the chief value of a university college,' she said.[35] At the end of the ceremony, Eilean Giblin presented Lady Gowrie with an inscribed copy of Woolf's feminist and modernist classic *A Room of One's Own*. It was a book that had a special resonance for Eilean through her friendship with the Garnetts and association with the Bloomsbury Group. First published in 1929, it was based on papers Virginia Woolf gave at two Cambridge women's colleges, Newnham and Girton, in October 1928. Since its publication *A Room of One's Own* had become a powerful text in the women's liberation canon. Its title had entered the language of feminism. Its theme was appropriate to the opening of a women's college: College life encouraged independence and provided opportunities for social interaction but also privacy to study and to think, something Girton's founder, Emily Davies, had described as 'this great boon – the power of being alone'.[36]

The formal opening was the final act in the successful establishment of University Women's College, an achievement that was accepted during Eilean Giblin's lifetime as worthy if not particularly extraordinary. It has since been acknowledged in a history of the university that the founding

---

[34] Eveline Syme, UC Archives, Council minutes, 30 November 1955.

[35] *Argus*, 28 June 1937, p. 3.

[36] Daphne Bennett, *Emily Davies and the Liberation of Women, 1830–1921*, Andre Deutsch, London, 1990, p. 198.

Figure 5.2 Students at University Women's College with the first Principal, Susie Williams. (University College Archives)

of a university college in the aftermath of the Great Depression, at a time when existing colleges were hard hit by rapidly falling numbers of students and financial deficits, was 'a remarkable achievement' that followed 'a most effective public campaign'.[37]

Eilean left for England in September 1937 with another important task to undertake for the college. Although her husband planned to leave late that year on his first trip to England since the First World War, in order to spend the first half of 1938 at his old college King's at Cambridge, Eilean travelled ahead so that she could be in London in time to take a decisive part in interviews for a new principal to succeed Susie Williams. On 18 January 1938, not long after she arrived in England, Eilean sat on a panel, set up with the help of the British-based Universities Bureau of the British Empire, to interview applicants. One of the candidates, Danish-born Dr Greta Hort, 34, an expert in medieval history, theology, philosophy and mysticism, who was a research fellow at Girton College, Cambridge, and had gained a doctorate while at Newnham, stood out. She had been strongly

---

[37] John Poynter and Carolyn Rasmussen, *A Place Apart. The University of Melbourne: Decades of Challenge*, Melbourne University Press, Carlton Vic., 1996, p. 42.

recommended by Dr Helen Wodehouse, the head of Girton, whose advice had been sought by the College councillors. Wodehouse had supported Hort's research on medieval mysticism that led to publication of her first book, *Sense and Thought: A Study in Mysticism*, published in 1936, and she and Hort continued their research on mystics in later correspondence. Panel members interviewed Hort at length and invited her to lunch. Eilean Giblin, as the only member with local knowledge, was influential on the interviewing panel. She was a strong supporter of Greta Hort and the panel recommended her with enthusiasm, stating in their report, 'unless there was a very strong local candidate, no one was more suitable for the appointment than Dr Hort'. The letter containing the panel's advice to the College Council included Eilean Giblin's endorsement that she could work with Dr Hort and that she would find her a loyal colleague.[38]

When the final decision was to be made in Melbourne the following month between Greta Hort and three Australian applicants, culled from a list of many more, Eilean sent an 'emphatic cable' recommending Hort's appointment. The Council's Selection Committee gave great weight to her opinion: 'As Chair of the Council, and as one of those in whose judgment the Council has had reason to rest an absolute confidence, she naturally carries great weight with the Committee when she commits herself so explicitly'.[39] Greta Hort, described as a most distinguished scholar, a teacher and writer in the fields of literature and philosophy, a creative and original thinker with a vivid and vital character, gained the position. One of the unsuccessful candidates was the Australian teacher and author, Flora Eldershaw,[40] who with Marjorie Barnard, had written several notable historical books, under the name of M. Barnard Eldershaw.

Dr Greta Hort arrived in Melbourne on 23 June 1938 to take over from Susie Williams. Eilean Giblin remained a strong supporter and friend through her eight years at University Women's College including periods when differences emerged between Hort and the Council. In 1940, when Eilean and her husband discussed her possible move to Canberra, Lyndhurst Giblin recognised that a factor against the move was Hort's need for Eilean's support, 'someone firm to calm her down', as he wrote, endorsing Edward

---

[38] UC Archives 1/15/07 Greta Hort – selection, appointment, resignation; John Stanley Martin, 'Greta Hort: Scholar and Educationalist', *Nordic Notes*, Centre for Scandinavian Studies, Vol. 8, 2004, http:diemperdidi.info/nordicnotes.

[39] UC Archives 1/15/07 Report of Final meeting Selection Committee for Post of Principal, 19 February 1938.

[40] UC Archives 1/15/07, 19 February 1938.

Dyason's opinion that following worry over events in Europe, 'Dr Hort was getting out of step with her students, & they were resenting a good many of her actions', and she was becoming 'agitated and upset'.[41] Greta Hort appreciated Eilean's support. She told Eveline Syme: 'I should be sorry for anyone who could not appreciate the simple goodness of Eilean Giblin. But I know that all of us who worked with her ... did appreciate it.'[42]

To art historian Dr Ursula Hoff, whom Hort was instrumental in bringing to Melbourne, she was 'brilliant but eccentric'. Hoff had arrived in Melbourne in 1939 to become secretary at University Women's College, a position Greta Hort offered as sanctuary to a Jewish female scholar, in the crisis of the spread of Nazism and the persecution of Jews in Europe. Already highly qualified in art, Hoff was overqualified for the position at University Women's College. She became a distinguished art historian and critic and gained appointment as Assistant Director of the National Gallery of Victoria.[43] Apart from her personality and accomplishments, Greta Hort had a characteristic that would have appealed to Eilean – they were alike in having no regard for dress. Although she appears strikingly attractive in a photograph as a young woman, Greta Hort was described by one of her College students, Diana Dyason, as 'almost a caricature of the Girton bluestocking, sparse fine hair drawn into a wispy bun from which it was always escaping, little dress sense and a penchant for thick grey, often holey, stockings'.[44] Another student, Rosemary Derham, described Hort in a similar way as 'mostly dressed in a variety of shapeless clothes' with her 'wispy brown hair parted in the middle and drawn back into a small bun that didn't stay together for long'.[45]

In December 1938, Eilean arrived back in Melbourne on the *Monterey* from Canada, where she had travelled with her husband, who gave evidence at a Canadian Royal Commission on Dominion/Provincial Relations in Ottawa.[46] She was back in time to be present at a ceremony at the College

---

[41] MS366/1, Canberra, 3 June 1940.

[42] Eveline Syme, 30 November 1955.

[43] Sheridan Palmer, *Centre of the Periphery: Three European Art Historians in Melbourne*, Australian Scholarly Publishing, North Melbourne, 2008, pp. 60–5, 74–7; Colin Holden, *The Outsider: A Portrait of Ursula Hoff*, Australian Scholarly Publishing, North Melbourne, 2009, pp. 15–18.

[44] Hume Dow, ed., *Memories of Melbourne University: Undergraduate Life in the Years since 1917*, Hutchinson, Richmond Vic., 1983, p. 92.

[45] *Nordic Notes*, Vol. 8, 2004.

[46] MS366/1, 16 September 1938.

to accept a painting of the first Principal, Susie Williams, presented by Professor R.M. (Max) Crawford, professor of history at Melbourne University, on behalf of donors. The portrait was painted by W.B. McInnes, seven times winner of the Archibald Prize. Many distinguished people including the Chancellor, Sir James Barrett, and those associated with the founding of the College, including Dr Georgina Sweet, Eveline Syme and Jessie Webb, were present at the ceremony.[47]

During 1938 the College gathered momentum with many more applicants for residence. A third storey was added to the original Georgina Sweet Wing and the building of the second wing, named after Constance Ellis, began. This wing was opened the following year but the outbreak of war in September 1939 'inevitably cancelled all thought of building plans'. This was described in the *Annual Report* as 'a serious set-back to a young college' and 'of grave educational concern as the education of women becomes more and more important'.[48] Eilean remained President of the College Council until she resigned the position in December 1940, some months after she had moved from Melbourne, and Eveline Syme, formerly deputy president, succeeded her.

There was no mention of the role Eilean Giblin had played in getting the College built, opened and functioning, in the College's *Annual Report* for 1940, the year she resigned as Chair of the College Council. She remained a member of the Council through the war years and until her death but there is no tribute to her role although the College's annual reports made a practice of mentioning the achievements of people associated with the College. The *Annual Report 1941*, for example, records tributes to Miss S.J. Williams, the first Principal, Enid Derham, a University lecturer in English, and Kingsley A. Henderson, the College architect.[49] An appreciation of Eilean's work in establishing the College, written by Eveline Syme, was included in the College minutes following her death in 1955.[50] The College remained close to Eilean – she made efforts to attend Council meetings during the Second World War, despite restrictions on interstate travel, but she also developed other interests that allowed her to expand her artistic and literary life. From this time her life followed a more private path.

---

[47] *Age*, 13 December 1938, p. 3.
[48] University Women's College, *Annual Report 1939*, May 1940, p. 7.
[49] University Women's College, *Annual Reports* 1941–57.
[50] Eveline Syme, 30 November 1955.

Professor R. M. Crawford, on behalf of the donors, yesterday presented the portrait of Miss S. J. Williams, the first principal of the University Women's College, to the chairman of the college council, Mrs. F. Giblin. On the left is Dr. Greta Hort, principal of the college.

Figure 5.3   Eilean Giblin (right) at the handing over of the portrait of Susie Williams, first principal of University Women's College by Professor Max Crawford on behalf of donors. Dr Greta Hort, principal 1938–1946 is at left. (*Age,* 13 December 1938 p. 3)

* * *

In 1938, the hard work of establishing University Women's College over, Eilean Giblin prepared for a more rounded life. As President of the College Council she still had an important role requiring energy, diplomacy and tact, but the intense pressure of the years of negotiating, building and opening the college was past, leaving her free to return to or take up other interests. Throughout her life she had had an ambition to write and to be published. The travel manuscript she took back to England covering her Australian adventures from 1913 to 1916 had promised much. Initially it appeared to have an excellent chance of being published but as the war news escalated with huge casualty lists from the Western Front, pre-war travel adventures had less and less appeal and eventually the manuscript was relegated to the background as their marriage, and Giblin's narrow escapes from death on the Western Front, made it seem unimportant. Nevertheless, it carried so many of Eilean's early hopes for a career as a writer that, almost certainly, she brought the manuscript to Australia with her in 1919. During the next decades she kept writing by keeping a journal on the regular trips she made to Europe. In 1935 when she sent her journal of her tour of Greece back to her husband, he replied:

> I came back [from Sydney and Canberra] to find your noble journal – 3 parts – about 8000 words. It would make a good little book with what is to come. The point of view is very individual & it makes a very readable & attractive narrative, that would be appreciated even by people with no personal interest in the writer.[51]

Twenty years after her abortive attempt to have her pre-war manuscript published, Eilean Giblin had another travel manuscript. When she was on her way to England on the *Almakerk* in September 1937, her husband wrote: 'Have you got it with you, – & are you thinking of revising on the voyage? And have you any idea about a publisher?'[52] Eilean's reply indicated that fellow passengers were so interested in her manuscript she was holding readings for them.[53] It is possible this was the Australian manuscript Eilean

---

[51] MS366/1, 8 May 1935.
[52] MS366/1, 17 September 1937.
[53] MS366/1, 2 October 1937.

had tried to get published 20 years before but it was probably a new one based on the six trips she had made to Europe during the 1920s and 1930s. Although Homefield was always her main destination on these trips, she travelled widely on each journey, sometimes to the Middle East or the Mediterranean, to countries in Europe, or to Scotland, Ireland and many parts of England, sometimes attending conferences and always observing the social and political atmosphere. It may be that the manuscript describing these later travels incorporated some of her original Australian material.

In England in 1938 while he was supernumerary fellow at King's College, Cambridge, Lyndhurst Giblin made a concerted effort to help in marketing Eilean's manuscript through his contact with David Garnett, the author son of his old friends, Edward and Constance Garrett. Early that summer David Garnett collected him from Cambridge and took him to stay at his home at Hilton where he was living with his wife, Ray, a book illustrator who was connected to the Bloomsbury Group through her sister diarist and writer, Frances Partridge, and the Garnetts' two young sons, Richard and William. It was the first time Giblin had seen David Garnett since the First World War when Garnett, a pacifist and conscientious objector, was living with Duncan Grant, Vanessa Bell and other members of the Bloomsbury Group at Charleston. Since then Garnett had established a career as a novelist and in the 1930s had published a major collection of the letters of John Galsworthy and had a similar work in progress on T.E. Lawrence. Giblin found him a 'complete surprise'. 'Nothing of the David of 1919 & little of what I had built up round that on his writing,' he told Eilean. 'Something of the boy, Bunny, of 1904–5, a good deal of Edward – Edward in serious run, without his impish side. – All somehow familiar, so that I felt on terms, pleasantly, at once.'[54] As he had on previous meetings, Giblin made an unforgettable impression and the Garnetts marked his visit by renaming their recently acquired two-seater folding German Faltbot canoe, 'The Giblin'. To Garnett, Giblin was 'the most splendidly all-round man' he had ever known. 'It was the month before Munich,' he wrote, 'and Lyndhurst Giblin's presence gave me hope that when it came to the test we should be strong enough'.[55] By the summer of that year Garnett's marriage was in trouble and he was a lover of Angelica Bell, the daughter of Vanessa Bell and his former lover Duncan Grant. After the death of his first wife in1940, Garnett married Angelica Bell.[56]

---

[54] MS366/1, King's College Cambridge, 15 February 1938.
[55] David Garnett, *The Familiar Faces*, Chatto & Windus, London, 1962, pp. 185–6.
[56] Frances Spalding, *Duncan Grant*, Chatto & Windus, London, 1997, p. 363.

Garnett and Giblin agreed that Eilean should cut her manuscript, by about '1 page in seven', to 'make a more continuous story' and to avoid the 'danger of the whole thing being rather discursory'. Giblin also advised her to sharpen the beginning before sending it to her preferred publisher, Gollancz: 'In these days, you must catch the reader with the first few pages', he wrote.[57] Whether revised or not, the manuscript does not appear to have interested a publisher. Some of the problems are obvious from Giblin's comments but Eilean's timing was bad, as it had been with her previous manuscript during the First World War. The escalating crisis in Europe following the rise of fascist dictatorships in Germany and Italy and growing evidence that another world war was becoming inevitable – in spite of the false hope of Chamberlain's 'peace in our time' – made publication of a travel manuscript less likely. This was not the end of Eilean's ambition to become a published writer but, inevitably, it was a setback and she turned in a new direction.

Back in Melbourne in 1939 with University Women's College running successfully, she decided to pursue in a serious way an interest in pottery at a time of growing nationalistic interest in Australian endeavours in literature, painting and arts and crafts. Eilean saw around her the artistic accomplishments of some of the friends she had made through University Women's College Council, particularly Eveline Syme, a painter and printmaker. Syme had trained at the Grosvenor School of Modern Art in London in the later 1920s with fellow Australian artists, Dorrit Black and Ethel Spowers. There they came under the influence of British artist, Claude Flight, who pioneered and popularised linocuts as a democratic art form and, largely through his influence, they evolved into 'a distinct form of 20th century art'. His teaching inspired Syme: 'I had seen nothing more vital and "essentially" modern in the best sense of the word', she wrote.[58] Syme, together with Black and Spowers have been credited with introducing to Australia this particular form of modernism which aimed to bring art to the wider public through affordable linocuts.[59] All three were represented in an exhibition of prints organised by Dora de Beer in Melbourne in December 1930 and Syme and Spowers were founding members of the Melbourne

---

[57] MS366/1, Cambridge, 22 April 1938.

[58] Roger Butler, *Woodcuts and Linocuts of the 1920s and 1930s*, National Library of Australia, Canberra, ACT, 1981, quoting Eveline Syme's article on Claude Flight and his teaching published in *The Recorder*.

[59] Betty Churcher, *Hidden Treasures*, 'Linocuts of Black, Syme & Spowers, video clip, 2008.

Contemporary Artists group which from 1932 held regular exhibitions promoting modernism.[60]

It is unclear why Eilean was drawn to study pottery rather than some other form of art – she had some training in painting and she pursued this at times during her life. But it is evident that she was influenced by the ideas of modernism which were permeating arts circles and some levels of the Arts and Crafts Society. When she developed her studio pottery, she was influenced by the work of a founding member of the Arts and Crafts Society, Frances Derham, in turning to Aboriginal designs for decorative motifs. Derham's design for the cover of the Arts and Crafts Society's journal, *The Recorder* – a roughly hewn geometric design featuring a simplified figure surrounded by spirals and dots – was influenced by designs on woven baskets from Arnhem Land, and her spiral designs resembled concentric circle patterns in Aboriginal work from Central Australia.[61] In May 1939 Eilean enrolled in pottery classes at Melbourne Technical College (later RMIT University) under Jack Knight and she pursued this new career with enthusiasm and talent for a decade or more.

Early in September 1939, just before she began her second term in pottery at the College, Germany invaded Poland and the Second World War, so long threatened, began. From then on Lyndhurst Giblin, in addition to his role as Ritchie Professor of Economics at the University of Melbourne, increasingly was called to Canberra to advise the government. In addition, he retained his positions as a member of the Grants Commission, to which he had been appointed a founding member in 1933, and as a member of the Commonwealth Bank Board to which he was appointed in 1935. Late in 1938 the Federal Government had appointed him chair of a newly established Financial and Economic Committee with Commonwealth Statistician, Roland Wilson, and Leslie Melville from the Commonwealth Bank, as members. Its task was to advise the government on the economic consequences for Australia of an outbreak of war. Once war was declared, and other economists including Douglas Copland and James Brigden (and later Dr H.C. Coombs) joined the committee, it became the government's chief source of advice on managing the war economy. Within a few days of war being declared, Giblin was on a train to Sydney with Cabinet ministers

---

[60] Chris Deutsher and Roger Butler, *A Survey of Australian Relief Prints 1900–1950*, Deutsher Galleries, Armadale, Vic., 1978, p. 43.

[61] Jonathan Parsons, 'Aboriginal Motifs in Design: Frances Derham and the Arts and Crafts Society of Victoria', *La Trobe Library Journal*, Vol. 11, No. 43, Autumn 1989, pp. 41–2.

(on the train he complained to a sympathetic Prime Minister Menzies about the ABC banning German music[62]), then to Canberra for the Federal Budget and a premiers' conference. From then on his life became almost a routine of travelling to Canberra for visits that were initially scheduled for a few days but which usually lasted much longer. In addition he often had to visit Sydney for a Commonwealth Bank Board meeting. After snatching a few hastily arranged days at home in Melbourne, he would have to leave again. Most of his travel was by train – the journey between Melbourne and Canberra was an overnight trip of about 12 hours. Sometimes he got a lift by car but this took at least as long. As he wrote to Eilean, Canberra, where the weather in spring was 'superb', would be a great place for her to holiday, 'if it was not so far away, & difficult to get a car to'.[63]

As his visits to Canberra became more frequent and lasted longer, and his letters began to contain more news about the city, Eilean must have become accustomed to the idea that she might have to move to the capital. This was underlined by concerns about her husband's health. In May 1940 he was in Canberra Community Hospital briefly with bronchitis and later that month he caught a cold on a car trip back to Canberra and was in hospital again with no voice, this time at the small private hospital in Forrest. His health problems combined with the escalation of the war began to make the move to Canberra inevitable. The 'blacker than ever'[64] war news from Europe included the rumour that the Germans had got to the French coast, and suggestions that the English would evacuate Essex. Eilean momentarily proposed offering to evacuate her nephew and niece, Peter and Gillian Burton, to Australia. Giblin agreed 'it is too far to propose taking them, but I'm sorry it is so'.[65] Probably conscious of the successive upheavals in their life already, Lyndhurst Giblin appeared reluctant to raise the subject of moving even after he had concluded that he must stay in Canberra indefinitely. When he did raise the prospect, he recognised two problems: Eilean's commitments at University Women's College and the difficulty of getting accommodation in Canberra: 'There's partly Women's College & potting. I suppose Dr Hort rather wants your support. ... Accommodation here is fitful. There's nothing available at

---

[62] MS366/1, 5 September 1939.
[63] MS366/1, 11 September 1939.
[64] MS366/1, 22 May 1940.
[65] MS366/1, 17 August 1940.

present, but occasionally something furnished offers & there are private possibilities.'⁶⁶

Once it was known Giblin was looking for a house possibilities arose, including J.B. Brigden's in Mugga Way – Brigden was moving to Melbourne as head of the new Department of Supply and Development – but he considered Brigden's house too large. Another on the outskirts of suburban development had more disadvantages – no sleep-out and about 40 minutes' walk with no bus near and 'buses are the devil anyway'.⁶⁷ Towards the end of July 1940, Giblin had the offer of a house at 29 Empire Circuit, Manuka, where the distance was right and where sleeping-out was possible although not ideal. After taking the house for six months, he told Eilean to decide what to bring to Canberra, what to store and what to send to Hobart. He specified the gramophone, some records and books and a coffee pot, adding that 'a case or two of beer' would be worth bringing as there were no liquor outlets apart from the Hotel Canberra bar. Then she could sell off most of the furniture. He enclosed a rough plan of the Empire Circuit house,⁶⁸ adding that he wanted to move as soon as possible as the current occupier, J.T. Browne, had some seedlings ready for planting.

For the third time – Hobart in the 1920s, Melbourne in the 1930s, Canberra in the 1940s – Eilean began a new decade in a new Australian city. It was a momentous time. The second world war in her lifetime, with all its potential for many millions of casualties and world upheaval, was nearing the end of its first year when she moved to Canberra.

---

[66] MS366/1, 3 June 1940.
[67] MS366/1, 24 July 1940.
[68] MS366/1, 10 August 1940.

Chapter 6

War and the *Dunera* 'enemy aliens'

Canberra, Hay, Hobart 1940

Australia had been at war for nearly a year when Eilean Giblin arrived in Canberra at the end of August 1940 to live in a furnished, rented house at 29 Empire Circuit, Forrest. Canberra had a population of about 12,000 living in a few scattered suburbs on either side of the Molonglo River. Forrest was south of the river, close to Parliament House and to the few government departments then located in Canberra, principally the Prime Minister's Department, Treasury and Taxation. The house the Giblins rented was well located between Arthur Circle and Franklin Street, only a few blocks north of the Manuka shopping centre in a suburb that was the home of many senior public servants. They drove up from Melbourne – Eilean as usual did all the driving – spending two nights on the way, at Benalla and Yass. It was the longest drive she had ever done and it was an unusual achievement for a woman in an era when women who had driving licences, still a small minority, usually drove only short distances. In Melbourne the Giblins left behind 142 Domain Street, South Yarra, their home for the previous ten years, dividing all their possessions, some to go to Canberra, some to Hobart and some to be sold.

Although chosen as the site for the capital more than a quarter of a century earlier, Canberra's development had been severely disrupted and delayed by the successive calamities of the First World War and the Great Depression. By the beginning of the Second World War, although the city was the seat of government and the place where parliament met, it was home to only a small number of the departments and agencies of government. Most notably, the defence departments were still in Melbourne. It had a few scattered monumental buildings: the provisional parliament house opened in 1927 on the southern side of the meandering Molonglo River and facing it on the northern side at the other point of a central axis, the gradually rising War Memorial with its striking cupola, resonant of the Middle East where Australians had fought many battles in the First World War. Two main office buildings, East Block and West Block, were on either side of the provisional parliament house. Plantings of exotic and native trees defined the main avenues and the streets of the widely separated, sparsely settled suburbs. Apart from the sound of birds, the place seemed unusually silent and deserted to people who came from cities where crowds walked in the streets and trams rattled along the roads. M. Barnard Eldershaw in a novel set in Canberra in the late1930s, *Plaque with Laurel*, described the embryonic city as 'silent, dignified, and embowered'.[1]

Eilean Giblin arrived only a few weeks after a dramatic aeroplane crash near Canberra on 13 August 1940 in which three cabinet ministers were killed – the Minister for the Army, Brigadier G.A. Street, the Minister for Information, Sir Henry Gullett, and the Minister for Air, Mr James Fairbairn – as well as the Chief of the Army General Staff, Sir Brudenall White. The destabilising loss of three such senior members of the government and the head of the Australian Army came at a time when the Menzies Coalition Government was struggling to establish and maintain a war effort. The war news, with one disaster in Europe following quickly on another, was catastrophic but the war itself seemed remote to most Australians apart from those with husbands or sons in the AIF in the Middle East. Ambivalence towards the war effort was compounded and inextricably bound up with an uncertain political situation. Robert Menzies, who had been Prime Minister leading a United Australia Party and Country Party coalition government since the death of Joseph Lyons in April 1939, had a comfortable majority in parliament but he had many critics who found his leadership weak and uninspiring. Faced with the prospect of by-elections for the three seats of the cabinet ministers who had been killed, he announced that a general election would be held on 21 September 1940, although it was not due until towards the end of the year. Many commentators expected the Australian Labor Party, which earlier that year had won an important by-election with a substantial swing, would come close to defeating the government.

Although Eilean Giblin approached her move to Canberra with the equanimity she had approached other moves, it was almost certainly

---

[1] M. Barnard Eldershaw, *Plaque with Laurel*, George G. Harrap & Co., London, 1937, p. 23; Patricia Clarke, 'Canberra in the 1930s: A Fictional Look at the National Capital', *Canberra Historical Journal*, May 2012, pp. 15–22.

unwelcome. She had made a satisfying life in Melbourne with a prestigious position as chair of University Women's College Council and she was developing her expertise at pottery. The women she had worked with over nearly a decade establishing University Women's College remained her friends and the College was her spiritual home, to which she was to return whenever possible. The move to Canberra was a necessity rather than a pleasure. She was in a different position from her husband who had the satisfaction of being needed in an important position with great responsibility for which he had given up his University chair. While some women were able to make useful and happy lives in Canberra building social networks through voluntary organisations, others found the atmosphere barren and sterile. Dr H.C. ('Nugget') Coombs in his autobiographical book, *Trial Balance*, recorded the deep unhappiness of his wife Mary Alice (Lallie) Coombs in Canberra during wartime. Women found Canberra 'burdensome and without intellectual or cultural stimulus', he wrote; so much so that the Coombs family moved back to Sydney at the first opportunity. An early entry in the diary Eilean kept in Canberra reinforces this view. She recorded a comment by Mrs Hood, the English-born wife of John D.L. Hood, a senior officer in the then tiny Department of External Affairs, that many women were discontented in Canberra: 'They have come here having made up their minds that they are not going to like it – and they won't like it,' she said.[2]

Canberra was a young, artificial society still finding its way. It lacked the long-established progressive women's networks Eilean had found in Hobart and Melbourne. There was no equivalent to the WNPPL in Tasmania or the Victorian Women's Citizenship Movement in Melbourne and no organisation affiliated with the Australian Federation of Women Voters. Its only tertiary institution was Canberra University College, a small adjunct of the University of Melbourne providing limited undergraduate courses. From the arrival of the first influx of public servants in 1927, the energies of Canberra women, mainly women with children, had been channelled to establishing basic community groups centred on the churches and sporting, service and social groups. The major women's initiative, not surprisingly given the make-up of the community, was the Canberra Mothercraft Society. This began in 1927 under the officially inspired, guided democracy model which was a feature of the early establishment of the planned city under the Federal

---

[2] MS366/6/1, 10 September 1940.

Capital Commission, the body charged with administering the capital.³ In the 1930s the Society's main initiative was the establishment of health clinics for mothers and babies.

In 1939 a meeting of Canberra women formed the National Council of Women (ACT), joining women from the six states of Australia, each of which had already formed a Council, and which had federated in 1931 as the National Council of Women of Australia (NCW). The NCW was a coordinating body for state and territory councils which themselves comprised affiliated organisations. Eight Canberra organisations joined the new National Council of Women ACT: Canberra Mothercraft Society, Canberra Relief Society, St John's Ladies' Guild, Presbyterian Church Ladies' Guild, Canberra Community Hospital Auxiliary, Canberra Croquet Club, Women's Hockey Association and the YWCA.⁴ This list of organisations underlined the absence in the National Capital of any women's group in which Eilean Giblin could pursue the interests she had been associated with in the past: the pursuit of equal citizenship in all its manifestations and the provision of equal educational opportunities for young women. She seemed to be aware of this lack before she moved to Canberra and had prepared for a different life.

Eilean Giblin arrived in Canberra with two ambitions that gave meaning and purpose to her move. She intended to establish a pottery studio, the first in the capital, and she intended to keep a diary that she believed would be an important record of the country at war. She was conscious that she was moving to the National Capital at an important time in its history. Ostensibly, it was the centre of government for the conduct of the nation's part in a world war. That was why her husband had been called to Canberra and had decided that, although he was in his late 60s, he should give up his chair at the University of Melbourne for this wartime role. It was why she began recording life in the capital from the day she arrived. As her diary enfolds, however, it reflects the historic fact that Canberra fulfilled its expected role as the seat of wartime management to only a very limited extent. Its development had been undermined by the financial stringency of the 1930s leaving it without the infrastructure, offices and housing to handle an influx of departments and public servants and this was compounded by a lack of government will

---

³   Freeman Wyllie, 'The Community Spirit – Social Service Idealism in Canberra 1925–1929', *Canberra Historical Journal*, September 1997, pp. 7–17.

⁴   Freda Stephenson, *Capital Women: A History of the National Council of Women (ACT) 1939–1979*, NCW (ACT), Canberra, 1982, pp. 1–6.

in the later part of the 1930s to move important government departments to the capital.[5] In Eilean's diary there are innumerable occasions in which she records her husband being called to Melbourne or Sydney where cabinet and important departmental meetings were often held. She also records the reported reply of the Chiefs of Staff of the three services when told to travel from Melbourne to Canberra to consult with Cabinet, 'We are pretty busy, why not come here?' Her comment: 'Who rules this country, Parliament or Chiefs of Staffs?'[6]

When Eilean began her diary the Second World War was still distant to most Australians and, as the early part of her diary demonstrates, the war had barely touched the routine of daily life, an attitude she records with surprise and sometimes with shock. Many of her entries highlight the leisurely pace of life in Canberra where the omnipresent Commonwealth Department of the Interior was the city's administrator and landlord, responsible not just for normal municipal services but minor maintenance problems, even the replacement of electric light bulbs and the repair of dripping taps in houses that were mostly government-owned. To Eilean, more familiar than many Australians with European events and receiving constant news from her family in London, the war was all too close and immediate. She was unable to understand the complacency of Australians while she agonised over the bombing of London, losses in Europe and the Middle East and the enormous waste of human life and resources that war caused. From Hitler's invasion of Poland and the declaration of war in September 1939, one Allied calamity had followed another. In the first half of 1940 Denmark, Holland, Belgium and Luxembourg fell to the German Blitzkreig. When the British Expeditionary Force in France had to be evacuated from Dunkirk and Paris fell to the Germans, invasion of Britain appeared imminent.

The beginning of Eilean Giblin's diary coincided almost exactly with the first all-night bombing alert in London on the night of 26–27 August 1940. A week or so later the London Blitz began and a German invasion appeared even more likely ('perhaps it may be proceeding now', she wrote in her diary in mid-September), a prospect that made Australia suddenly more vulnerable unable to rely on Britain for its security. The contrast with the complacent atmosphere in Canberra just as the blossoms of early spring were

---

[5] Jim Gibbney, *Canberra 1913–1953*, AGPS, Canberra, 1988, p. 207.
[6] MS366/6/1, 15 February 1941.

flowering was stark. 'Prunus is in flower, weeping willows are vivid green, and the gardens are gay with japonica,' she wrote.[7]

Her first adjustment was similar to that of other new arrivals from populous cities. 'I am no longer expecting to hear the Melbourne trams,' she wrote. Soon she was juxtaposing placid Canberra, its quietness and lack of activity and seeming unawareness of world events – the peace that 'reigns in the Capital' – with the bombing of London and the human cost of war. On 9 September she wrote of the German air raids over the East End and the Thames Estuary in which 400 people were reported killed and 1500 wounded:

> It all seems incredibly stupid – here are two countries piling up munitions and planes and sending their young men to Berlin and London and to other places, to drop bombs on innocent people, and people who are very much alike – who don't want war – who want work and security, and to dig in their back gardens and grow cabbages! ... Here in Canberra it is difficult to realise such horrors are going on in Europe. It is so peaceful and lovely. There are so few sounds and I listen for them – the voice of a child crying in the distance, a hen clucking, a car passing, a kookaburra beginning his first note, the drone of a plane circling over Canberra and making its way to the aerodrome on the flat beyond Duntroon.[8]

In the midst of the devastation occurring elsewhere she found the ordered peace of Canberra 'with these curving roads, broad belts of flowering trees, houses nestling among wattles and prunus and cypress ... slightly nauseating'. It left her feeling as though she 'had eaten too many chocolates, as though I was looking at a picture on a chocolate box as though a little disorder would have added to the attraction'.[9] When she walked with her husband to Mugga Way, Canberra's premier street, with its 'fairy-land of well established gardens, houses enclosed by pink and white double prunus, gums and cypresses', past the house that had recently become the United States Chancellery, the first American diplomatic presence in the city, the unreality of Canberra struck her again and she contrasted it with the plight of Londoners. 'At one particular spot I felt as though I was back in my

---

[7] MS366/6/1, 31 August 1940.
[8] MS366/6/1, 9 September 1940.
[9] MS366/6/1, 10 September 1940.

childhood at a Drury Lane pantomime with the transformation scene before me,' she wrote. 'And London has had its seventh night of bombing with thousands of innocent people killed and wounded.'[10]

An habitual walker, Eilean was unfailing in noticing the beauty of the trees and plants, the sounds of the birds and the cycle of the seasons. She noted the white poplars on the way to the Manuka shops with underneath them in springtime their carpets of green catkins, the bronze purple of prunus, apple trees in glorious blossom, the unfolding green leaves on the branches of fig trees and the brilliance of bottle brushes in flower. As summer approached she watched Capital Hill turn brown, then in autumn she wrote of the magnificence of the elms and pin-oaks as these and other exotic trees changed to yellow or gold or red. Through her diary entries she records the environmental landscape of Canberra in the 1940s.

Every now and then she was surprised, as were other newcomers and visitors, by the curious intermingling of development with continuing rural activities. One day she recorded the scene as she crossed the Molonglo:

> I noticed many sheep crossing the river, a scene I have several times wished to photograph. This time I had my camera with me, so I got out and scrambled down the side of the embankment to the parched flat, which at times is flooded, and took a photo of a stream of newly shorn sheep slowly crossing the river.[11]

She noted the architecture of the gradually rising War Memorial on the northern side of the Molonglo opposite Parliament House. It was 'a big stone pile, simple and impressive' but she disagreed with its purpose. 'What a farce', she wrote, 'what a waste of money with nations now at each other's throats.'[12]

While English cities suffered sustained German bombing attacks and the nation prepared for a possible invasion, Australia was absorbed with a federal election. The Giblins were able to listen to Prime Minister Menzies' policy speech, owing to the fortunate fact that their rented house had a radio. When her husband, usually named 'L.' less frequently 'Lynd', in her diary, said he wanted to listen to Menzies she wrote, 'an ordinary remark for most people, but we had stood out against a wireless set, preferring our own music

---

[10] MS366/6/1, 15 September 1940.
[11] MS366/6/1, 11 November 1940.
[12] MS366/6/3, 20 September 1940.

Figure 6.1   The 'bush' capital in the 1940s with a flock of sheep in front of the then Parliament House. Eilean Giblin describes a similar scene in her diary. (Old Parliament House, Canberra, with sheep in foreground. R.C. Strangman, 194-?. BibID: 3773047. National Library of Australia)

and getting our information from the papers'. Eilean thought Menzies' speech good on the whole, except when he brought in God. 'Are not the Germans and Italians appealing to God and saying He is on their side?' she wrote. 'And what can He do?'[13] When the election resulted in an evenly balanced parliament with the Menzies Government dependent on two Independents to continue in office she observed unsuccessful government overtures to the Labor Party to form a national government, as she dined at the Hotel Canberra, a centre of political intrigue. Citizens of the National Capital did not have a vote in federal elections but with its preponderance of public servants it was an intensely political city and the fate of governments, ministers and their departmental heads dominated local gossip. Through her husband's central position as a government adviser Eilean heard a great deal of high-level gossip, including approaches to her husband for advice from journalists and Labor politicians which she interpreted as widespread concern at the political situation but reluctance to bring down the government.

---

[13]   MS366/6/1, 15 September 1940.

'And who would want the responsibility of governing in such times as these,' she wondered.[14]

The Giblins kept in touch with left-wing thought through their subscription to the *New Statesman and Nation*[15] which arrived by sea mail well over a month after publication sometimes in batches of two or three editions. They also subscribed to the London *Times* and the *Manchester Guardian*. These sources of news and opinion augmented the more parochial news they read in the Australian dailies, including the *Canberra Times*, which Eilean judged 'a small and rather feeble publication'. It arrived by breakfast time, however, well ahead of the Melbourne *Herald* (the evening paper from the night before) and the *Sydney Morning Herald* which arrived about 10 am. Eilean's description of the arrival of these papers, 'thrown on to the front lawn by a skilful driver of a car who throws as he drives without slowing down',[16] appears to be one of the earliest descriptions of this method of newspaper delivery, which did not take over from hand delivery by newspaper boys in most cities and towns until decades later.[17] It was probably adopted earlier in Canberra, a news hungry city, because of the arrival of interstate newspapers after newsboys had gone to school.

In a city without the music and theatre they were used to, the Giblins attended lectures or gatherings on serious subjects but these were relatively rare events. They were in the audience when Professor Kenneth Bailey, their friend from Melbourne University, lectured on 'Federation, League or Anarchy' for the University Association at the Hotel Canberra. Eilean recorded that she saw the British High Commissioner, Sir Geoffrey Whiskard, 'wince' when the speaker pointed out that federation would mean Britain giving up its Navy. She found herself sharing an 'innate feeling of pride and absolute confidence' in the British Navy, reinforced by memories of being taken by her father on childhood visits to the Portsmouth dockyards and Nelson's *Victory*.[18]

The Giblins were always glad to entertain or meet friends when they visited Canberra. Anne Dyason made a particular impression – she was about to leave on an adventurous journey through Burma and over the

---

[14] MS366/6/1, 28 November 1940.
[15] The two periodicals amalgamated in 1931.
[16] MS366/6/1, 29 September 1940.
[17] Victor Isaacs, *How We Got the News: Newspaper Distribution in Australia and New Zealand*, Australian Newspaper History Group, Brisbane, 2008.
[18] MS366/6/1, 14 September 1940.

Himalayas to return to Chungking, the headquarters of the National leader General Chiang Kai-shek during the Sino-Japanese war. Eilean recorded that in Chungking, a city that was more heavily bombed than London, Anne Dyason expected to spend a great deal of time in 'very deep and safe air raid shelters excavated into the sides of a sand stone hill'.[19] Her accounts of her dramatic experiences at the Nationalist headquarters were published in the *Austral-Asiatic Bulletin*, the journal of the Victorian Division of the Australian Institute of International Affairs, founded in 1937 by her estranged husband, economist and stockbroker, Edward Dyason.[20]

When she first arrived in Canberra, Eilean's next-door neighbour Mrs Hammersley remarked: 'I don't go out much; I'm not one of the society people; some of them are never at home (with a glance at me). If you are one of those social people you hardly are at home.' Eilean replied, 'Oh, I am not one of those sort of people.' It is apparent from Eilean's diary – and very much in keeping with her character – that purely social events did not interest her. Inevitably, however, she was invited to important functions and she was expected to join women of similar standing in social and community groups, particularly those working for the war effort providing amenities for members of the services. Her arrival was noteworthy in the small world of Canberra: 'Mrs Giblin has joined her husband, Professor Giblin, at their new home at Empire Circuit', the *Canberra Times* recorded in its social notes.[21] She was invited to official events, receptions and dinners and Mrs Pattie Tillyard, the matriarch of social Canberra, invited her to afternoon tea. A graduate of Newnham College, Cambridge, Mrs Tillyard was highly regarded for her efforts in welcoming newcomers to Canberra and her visitors' book became a valued and evocative record of the city's social life in the 1930s and 1940s.[22]

Eilean's diary portrays aspects of the social life of the upper echelons of Canberra society and her reluctant forays into this world. She made token appearances at a few diplomatic gatherings, attended dinners at the homes of top public servants, went to several afternoon teas and invited guests to

---

[19] MS366/6/1, 18 October 1940.

[20] Anne Dyason, 'The Private Persistence of Man', *Austral-Asiatic Bulletin*, April–May 1941; 'Wanted – A Minister', 'It Might Happen to Anyone', June–July 1941; 'The Private Persistence of Man', August–September 1941.

[21] *Canberra Times*, 25 September 1940.

[22] Patricia Clarke, 'Tillyard, Pattie (1880–1971)', *Australian Dictionary of Biography*, 12, p. 232.

her home. At this social level, Canberra was a small hierarchical society of public servants and their wives in which gender division was pervasive. At a dinner at the home of James F. Murphy, head of the Department of Commerce and Agriculture, and his wife Beatrice, at which Sir William Clemens, former head of the Public Service Board and Chair of the ACT Division of the Red Cross, and Lady Clemens, were fellow guests, Eilean caught tantalising snippets of her husband's talk with the other men about 'politics, the standard of various government departments, how the war is to be paid for', but she was expected to join the women in discussing a recent fete at Government House to raise funds for the Lady Gowrie Services Club. The evening ended with Mrs Murphy giving Lady Clemens a cake recipe while, from the other side of the room, Eilean heard a man's voice say, 'Well, I think Beasley would do quite well.'[23] This comment on the prospects of John Albert (Jack) Beasley, a member of the breakaway ALP (Non-Communist) Party, should Labor form government, was another teasing snatch of a conversation about politics in which she would have liked to be included. Beasley was later Minister for Supply and Shipping in Curtin Labor governments.

Her diary records several other instances of her alienation from the social round. At a diplomatic cocktail party to welcome the newly arrived wife of the first United States Minister to be appointed to Australia, Clarence E. Gauss, Eilean had a few words with the Gausses, 'drank a glass of sherry, ate 2 or 3 little biscuits with fancy savouries on them, spoke to a few people, and came away early – the first to leave I think'. It was 'a dull party,' she wrote.[24] She described an official gathering at Parliament House for a goodwill mission from Thailand in a similar way. She spoke to the host, the Minister for External Affairs, Sir Frederick Stewart, and Lady Stewart, John Hood and his wife, Lady Knowles, wife of the Solicitor-General, Sir George Knowles, and Una Mitchell, headmistress of Canberra Girls' Grammar School, but she commented: 'The heat was oppressive and I felt I had had enough – so I slipped out, having spent a quarter of an hour at the party.'[25] Lyndhurst Giblin was as averse to social events as his wife and seldom accompanied her – he often had the excuse of pressing work and he was often away from Canberra either for a Commonwealth Bank Board meeting in Sydney or to advise at Cabinet meetings, frequently held in Melbourne.

---

[23] MS366/6/1, 14 October 1940.
[24] MS366/6/1, 28 October 1940.
[25] MS366/6/1, 21 November 1940.

***

'What are we fighting for, if England can do such things?'

20 September 1940

In such a restricted social milieu and at a time when she was more deeply moved by the war news from Europe than many of those around her, Eilean Giblin received a welcome challenge when an unexpected plea arrived from a friend in England seeking her help for three refugees deported to Australia as enemy aliens on *HMT Dunera*. It was a plea that aroused all her instincts of fairness and freedom and she made it a personal mission. It came from Nellie Heath, an artist, whom she knew through the Garnetts. Nellie Heath had grown up in a house owned by Constance Garnett's sister just down a woodland track from the Cearne[26] and she had been Edward Garnett's lover for many years. In 1935 Edward Garnett wrote an introduction for a book of Heath's paintings of rural scenes and portraits[27] but when he died two years later she abandoned painting and devoted the rest of her life to humanitarian causes, her concern for the *Dunera* deportees being just one of these.

Many of those deported to Australia on the *Dunera* later won fame for their achievements as scientists, economists, musicians, art historians and in many other fields. Yet when they arrived in Australia from Britain in September 1940 they were classified as enemy aliens and regarded with hostility and suspicion, although most were refugees who were bitter enemies of Nazism and fascism. Initially only a small minority of Australians showed sympathy for the internees, as headlines such as 'Enemy Aliens Arrive' announced their arrival. The stories that followed emphasised Britain's fear of a fifth column should Germany invade the country. According to one report hundreds of the deportees 'had been carrying out subversive work in England'[28] and the British officer in charge of the guard on the *Dunera*, addressing a Legacy audience, gave a vivid account of fifth column activities

---

[26] David Garnett, *The Golden Echo*, pp. 48–51.
[27] E.M. Heath, *Thirty Paintings, with a Foreword by Edward Garnett*, Jonathon Cape, London, 1935.
[28] *Daily Telegraph*, 7 September 1940.

in Britain.[29] In the same newspapers Australians read of British cities being bombed relentlessly and of the imminent threat of invasion by German forces, heightening the impression among the Australian public that a shipload of dangerous subversives had been deported to Australia.

The arrival of about 2500 prisoners on the *Dunera* was part of a move by Britain at the height of the invasion threat to deport those classified as enemy aliens to Commonwealth countries. Although deported as enemy aliens, most had fled from the Nazis to escape persecution or death and many were Jewish. This was little appreciated at the time, as Eilean Giblin's diary reveals. She was among a small minority among Canberra residents stirred by the plight of the *Dunera* enemy aliens and she met a generally hostile reaction when she tried to win sympathy for them. The three refugees she was asked to help were Viennese-born Peter Stadlen, who had established an international reputation as a concert pianist and conductor before fleeing to Britain,[30] his brother Erich, an interpreter and translator,[31] and Stefan Petoe, a tutor and musician, originally a Hungarian Jew and later of Austrian nationality.[32] Peter and Erich Stadlen described themselves on their internment files as Protestant although they appear to have been partly Jewish. The files of all three state that they were 'refugees from Nazi oppression'. Peter and Erich Stadlen fled from Austria in March 1938 at the time of the Anschluss when Austria was annexed by Nazi Germany and a campaign of violence against Jewish people began. Peter Stadlen arrived in England soon after he had achieved some notable musical successes. In 1937 he had given a world premiere performance of Anton Webern's Variations for piano Op. 27 in Vienna and in the same year at the Venice Biennale he conducted a performance of Schoenberg's 12-note suite for septet Op. 29. In England he re-established his musical career. In May 1940 at London's Wigmore Hall he gave a widely advertised solo performance playing sonatas by Mozart and Schubert and works by Bartok.[33]

Just over a month later, on 26 June 1940, he was interned in London as an enemy alien and his brother, Erich Stadlen, and Stefan Petoe were interned at the same time. They were caught in the round-up in Britain of all 'Class C'

---

[29] *Argus*, 13 September 1940.
[30] Bayan Northcott, 'Obituary: Peter Stadlen', *Independent*, 23 January 1996; NAA Peter Stadlen, MP1103/1, E40708, 8618388.
[31] NAA Erich Stadlen, MP1103/1, E40707, 8618387.
[32] NAA Stefan Petoe, MP1103/1, E40358, 8618043.
[33] London *Times*, 8 May 1940.

enemy aliens who had previously been regarded as no threat to security, unlike those in higher risk categories. Enemy aliens in Class A had been interned at the start of the war and those in Class B had had their movements restricted. The internment of all Class C enemy aliens was ordered the day France capitulated, at a time when a German invasion of Britain appeared imminent. Very influential people including the German novelist and Nobel laureate Thomas Mann, who had left Germany when the Nazis came to power, the Jewish violinist Yehudi Menuhin, and Eleanor Roosevelt, wife of the president of the United States, signed an application for Peter Stadlen's release, and the renowned English composer, Dr Ralph Vaughan Williams, used his influence with the British Home Office. Although the Home Office ordered Stadlen's release, enemy aliens were deported very swiftly before any individual claims could be investigated. By the time that Peter Stadlen's release order came through, he was already on the *Dunera* on the way to Australia.[34]

To Eilean, more aware than most Australians of the campaign being mounted in England for the release of the Class C deportees, through her reading of the English press, particularly the *New Statesman and Nation*, their situation was distressing. They were '*sans peur* and *sans reproche*', she wrote, yet they had been deported to Australia 'with suspects and prisoners of war'. She wrote: 'Such people it seems to me can only hate the Nazis as they would the devil. What are we fighting for, if England can do such things – how can we lead a crusade for democracy and freedom if we put such people in a concentration camp?'[35]

The *Dunera* called first at Melbourne, where some prisoners were sent to Tatura prisoner-of-war camp. The remaining prisoners disembarked at Sydney on 6 September 1940 and were taken in several trains to the Riverina town of Hay, 750 kilometres south-west of Sydney, a centre for the sheep stations spread over the vast and virtually treeless saltbush plains of south-western New South Wales, that appeared as a desert to the internees.

As Eilean discovered, when she raised their plight among women in Canberra, there was not a great deal of sympathy in Australia for the deportees. Only a small minority seemed aware that many were Jewish or anti-Nazi refugees who had fled from Germany or Nazi-occupied countries to escape persecution or death. She attempted to win support for the deportees among Canberra women, beginning with Mrs Pattie Tillyard, but initially found her unsympathetic. 'You must guard against the fifth

---

[34] Ronald Stent, 'Obituary: Peter Stadlen', *Independent*, 27 January 1996.
[35] MS366/6/1, 20 September 1940.

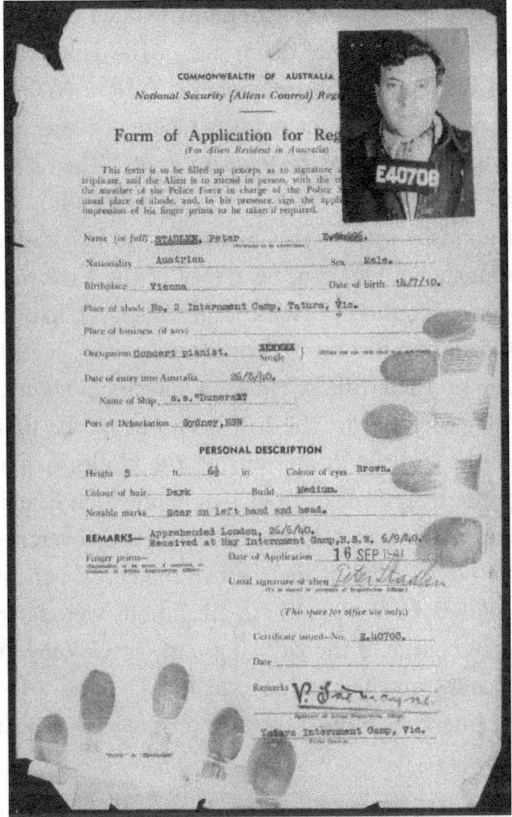

Figure 6.2 Peter Stadlen's application for registration as an alien resident of Australia (National Archives of Australia MP1103/1 E40708 8618388)

column,' Mrs Tillyard said. When Eilean protested that many were anti-Nazis, Mrs Tillyard replied, 'Oh, it is one of the unfortunate things that happen in wartime.'[36] These responses reflected Australian public opinion at the time. Later when confronted with further evidence of injustice, Mrs Tillyard became more receptive and asked for the address of the camp as 'we might be able to send some garments'. During her visits to Mrs Tillyard on this mission Eilean met another visitor, Sir Llewellyn Dalton, former chief justice in Tanganyika, whom she appears to have interested in the cause of the internees as he was later appointed by the Commonwealth Government as an Official Visitor to wartime internment camps.

---

[36] MS366/6/1, 23 October 1940.

She found a few allies among Canberra women although all reported instances of resistance to the deportees. Mrs Edwards, wife of the headmaster of Canberra Grammar School, Canon W.P. Edwards, told Eilean of her meeting with eight women where she was accused of being 'pro-German' when she raised the *Dunera* issue. 'They were at me like a pack of wolves – one said she simply did not believe it – … I came away feeling "all het up",' she said.[37] Mrs Edwards and her husband put Eilean in touch with Constance Duncan, Secretary of the Victorian International Refugee Emergency Council (VIREC), and Bishop Charles Venn Pilcher, the Anglican Coadjutor Bishop of Sydney, who had visited the camps at Hay and Tatura in their official roles. Constance Duncan was an old acquaintance from Melbourne; she had been one of the first speakers at a University Women's College dinner during the College's first year and she was Secretary of the League of Nations Union of which Eilean was an active member. Constance Duncan told her of the serious overcrowding and ill-treatment on the *Dunera* and of the theft of internees' personal possessions by the British soldiers in charge. These allegations were later substantiated when the officer in charge of the British guard, Lt Colonel W.P. Scott, was court martialled and convicted on his return to England.[38] Deeply moved at the plight of the internees robbed of their possessions, Eilean wrote in her diary:

> It is a ghastly story – that afternoon I went to Manuka and bought 3 each of shorts, shirts, jerseys, hats, fly veils, razors and soap, which Miss Duncan said were urgently needed. If my fellow countrymen can behave in such a way on the ship, I felt, as a gesture, I must do something. But I think it possible the people on the ship thought the prisoners of war were Nazis and that they were fair game – that they would get one back on them although that does not excuse brutality and thefts.[39]

She also tried to enlist the British High Commissioner, Sir Geoffrey Whiskard, in the cause of the internees, but his response was guarded. When she talked with Bishop Pilcher, however, he told her 'it was encouraging to find someone sympathetic and interested in the internees'. He described the

---

[37] MS366/6/1, 6 November 1940.
[38] London *Times*, 27, 28 May, 30 June 1941; Cyril Pearl, *The Dunera Scandal: Deported by Mistake*, Angus & Robertson, Sydney, 1983, pp. 138–40.
[39] MS366/6/1, 6 November 1940.

attitude of many churchwomen to whom he had spoken as 'deplorable'.[40] An example of public reaction appeared in the *Canberra Times* in a letter to the editor from 'Indignant' who wrote that Britain had got 'rid of the Hun who was ready with fifth column techniques'. This is 'total war', 'Indignant' continued. All energies should be directed to 'finishing the Hun for all time', not providing 'friendly aid to the enemy'.[41]

From the time she was asked to help the Stadlens and Petoe, Eilean made efforts to contact them by letter and by sending newspapers only to have the letters delayed and the papers returned by the Censor. As she became more disturbed at the lack of news from the internees, particularly after she heard some Class C enemy aliens had been released from detention in England, she began to wonder about the possibility of visiting Hay herself. 'If there were not petrol rationing, I almost think I would go there and try to find what the conditions are like,' she speculated.[42] When she was frustrated further in attempts to send newspapers, she decided to seek a permit to visit Hay, although it would involve a difficult journey of some 500 kilometres. She applied first for a permit to the Officer in Charge of Internment Camps in Melbourne but when after some weeks she had received no reply she applied as well to the Camp Commandant at Hay, Lt Colonel Charles S. Thane. Her permit arrived late in November. Soon after, she became one of the first visitors to the internees, even pre-dating a visit by Rabbi L.A. Falk on behalf of the Australian Jewish Welfare Society in December 1940, and by representatives of the Quakers in January 1941.

She set out on her long journey on 2 December 1940, driving alone in her small Morris car to the rail junction at Junee, a good deal of her trip, apart from the Hume Highway section, being on gravel roads. Although she missed the turn to Murrumburrah at Bowning she regained the correct route after some distance and arrived at Junee that evening. The next morning, leaving her car at a hotel, she caught the 8.18 train to Narrandera. 'What a country I have come to,' she wrote, 'dry and flat and bare'.[43] After a journey of about two hours she had three-quarters of an hour wait at Narrandera before boarding a rail motor, a single carriage train, which left at 11.15 for the slow trip of nearly four hours on the single line track to Hay. The carriage was driven by a motor located under the chassis and the driver sat in a small

---

[40] MS366/6/1, 21 November 1940.
[41] *Canberra Times*, 19 November 1940.
[42] MS366/6/1, 21 October 1940.
[43] MS366/6/1, 3 December 1940.

central box-like structure at the centre front of the vehicle. On either side of the driver's enclosure were two seats one facing sideways and one facing the front. Eilean had one of these favoured first class seats so she was able to look ahead through the small window.[44] In the heat of December the windows at the front and the side of the train provided the only ventilation for the few dozen passengers in first and second class. There was no scheduled stop for tea but, as she describes, the driver stopped at one of the small stations on the route and she went to a tiny refreshment room 'where two hot looking women were pouring out tea and handing cups with scones or cakes or sandwiches to the passengers'.[45]

Finally after her two-day journey Eilean arrived in Hay about 3 pm only to face an anti-climax. After booking into a hotel, she took a taxi to the internment camp on the outskirts of the town. But, after she showed her permit to the sentry, she was told as it was nearly 4 o'clock it was too late to see anyone that afternoon and she would have to return the next morning. She walked back to the hotel in the December heat carrying the large heavy fruit cake and the bundle of papers she had brought for the Stadlens. At the hotel she was surprised to find a friend from Canberra, astronomer Dr Richard Woolley, Director of the Mount Stromlo Observatory. Woolley had flown to Hay to investigate recruiting highly skilled internees for the optical productions workshop he was establishing at Mount Stromlo as part of the war effort. He told Eilean he had discovered 'at least 40 highly skilled mechanics and tool-makers' among the internees. 'Just what we want,' he said. 'But the unions might make trouble if they were released and given jobs, and there are all sorts of difficulties about getting them out. Not the least is Laby.'[46] Despite Professor Thomas H. Laby, who was chair of the wartime Optical Munitions Panel, Woolley succeeded in recruiting several *Dunera* internees for optical munitions work, including Hans Meyer and Ernst Frohlich although they were not released until the following year.[47]

Next morning Eilean walked to the camp on the outskirts of town carrying her cake which, she wrote, 'seemed to get heavier and heavier'. At

---

[44] Information on rail motors and railway timetables from transport historian Victor Isaacs.
[45] MS366/6/1, 3 December 1940.
[46] MS366/6/1, 3 December 1940.
[47] NAA Hans Meyer, MP1103/1, E40244, 8617929, transferred to Canberra, 2 July 1941; Ernst Frohlich, MP1103/1, E39534, 8617219, transferred to Canberra 11 August 1941.

the entrance the sentry asked again for her permit and she sat in his shelter while he telephoned for an escort:

> Presently, an officer came up and said, 'Come with me', and he took me to another long hut divided down its length with fine wire netting with benches on either side, and 3 young men arrived from the other end. ... We sat down, and they began to talk, telling me of the voyage out, which must have been a nightmare, Erich the youngest doing the most talking. 'When we got to Sydney', he said, 'the Australian soldiers brought us tea. We were surprised, we could not believe it after the treatment from the English soldiers on the ship.'
>
> A Sergeant stood by the open door, and a soldier with a rifle at the far door, both out of hearing. I poked cigarettes through the wire saying I felt I was feeding the monkeys at the zoo. The Sergeant passed behind me, but we went on talking. Presently I realised he was looking at me, and he came up saying, 'Time's up', and 'You have had longer than usual.' Half an hour is the time allowed, and we had ¾ of an hour, and I had not said half the things I intended to. 'Shall I write to your mother?' I asked the Stadlens, and they gave me her address.[48]

Eilean was taken to the orderly room where she was asked to sign a form stating that she had not given the internees any parcels and that they had talked only of personal and spiritual matters. When she remarked, 'I wonder what spiritual means', the elderly lieutenant replied, 'that refers to a bottle of whisky'. She handed over her gifts for the internees and their names were written on them. The newspapers were a different story.

> 'About these papers', I said, 'can they be given to the Stadlens?' 'No', the clerk said, 'they must all go through the Censor's office in Sydney.' 'But', I said, 'I sent a bundle addressed to the Stadlens at the Censor's office, and I got a slip of paper in a letter saying all papers must be ordered through the Commandant.' 'A new order has just come out', I was told.

Eilean returned to the camp that afternoon and succeeded in seeing the Stadlens for another half hour as well as some other prisoners whom friends

---

[48] MS366/6/1, 4 December 1940.

had asked her to contact. They included Erich Frankl, an Austrian Jew, Dr Edward Weisz, an Austrian Jewish physician, and 'Doc' Kurt Sternberg, a Prussian Jew who had been a film producer in Germany and who stayed in Australia after the war and produced films for the Commonwealth Film Unit.[49] Erich Frankl told her about the camp: 'Good food plenty of it, the troops kind to them – but little to do, but sit about and worry! The men are taken to the river in batches for swimming but that does not come very often.'[50] When time was up, Eilean wrote: 'I felt it was most inadequate to smile through the wire netting and say goodbye. I wished to shake hands, one can express something in a hand grip which one cannot express in words, and there was so much that one could not say. Regret at this cruel injustice, desire to help, shame for the behaviour of one's fellow-countrymen.' Next morning she left Hay to retrace her journey to Junee 'not sorry that I had done what I had intended to do, but glad that it was over'.[51]

While interned at Hay, Peter Stadlen formed a choir of 75 male voices and arranged a concert performance of Handel's oratorio *Israel in Egypt*. He had brought a piano transcript with him and managed to keep it on the *Dunera* and to transcribe scores for violins and voices on precious lavatory paper. At Hay he also arranged performances of Mozart's C Major Mass, a Palestrina Mass and the Prisoner's Chorus from *Fidelio*. He was described as 'a constant source of cheer to his fellow prisoners'.[52] Stefan Petoe taught mathematics classes and Erich Stadlen, using his skills as an interpreter, prepared a memorandum of their claims on behalf of the internees.

In the months following her visit Eilean Giblin recorded in her diary several snippets of information about the possible fate of the internees gleaned either from information in letters she received from the Stadlens or from some Canberra gossip – at one stage Roland Wilson told her that 150 of those interned in Hay were to be released in Australia.[53] In Britain, public pressure forced the British Government to send Major Julius Layton, a distinguished London Jewish banker and stockbroker, to Australia to investigate the claims of the internees that they had been wrongly

---

[49] NAA Erich Frankl, MP1103/1, E39488, 9905992; Edward Weisz, MP1103/1, E40900, 8618580; Kurt Sternberg, MP1103/1, E40756, 8618436.
[50] MS366/6/1, 4 December 1940.
[51] MS366/6/1, 5 December 1940.
[52] Ronald Stent, *Independent*, 27 January 1996.
[53] MS366/6/1, 4 May 1941.

deported. He made his first visit to Hay in April 1941. As a result, many of the internees returned to England, others volunteered for service in the Australian Military Forces employment companies and some were released to work in Australia in specialist fields.

Peter and Erich Stadlen and Stefan Petoe chose to return to Britain although ship travel was dangerous, being frequently the target of enemy attack. Despite all the efforts that had been made to have Peter Stadlen released, it was Erich Stadlen who was the first to leave Australia. He sailed in mid-1941 on the *Themistocles*, one of the first ships to take deportees back to Britain. Peter Stadlen, after being moved to Tatura Internment Camp, left Australia in November and Stefan Petoe left in December 1941. As soon as Peter Stadlen landed in Liverpool, towards the end of 1941, the Home Office official who had signed his release papers advised him to contact Dr Vaughan Williams. 'He tried very hard to get you back to England,' the official told Stadlen.[54] Within weeks of returning to Britain Stadlen was performing in public. On 13 February 1942 he played a program of Schubert's music before a large audience at the National Gallery in London, a newspaper report describing him as 'safely returned from travels which he did not seek'.[55] Stadlen became a British citizen in 1946 and resumed his international concert career, introducing Schoenberg's Piano Concerto and Hindemith's Four Temperaments to European audiences. From 1947 to 1951 he ran a master class in modern piano music at Darmstadt Summer School and in 1952 he was awarded the Austrian Government's Schoenberg Medal. In Britain he held a lectureship at Reading University and was a visiting Fellow at All Souls, Oxford, in 1967–8. Later he pursued a career in broadcasting and journalism, joining the London *Daily Telegraph* where he was chief music critic from 1977.[56] His wife, Hedi Simon, a member of a prominent Austrian Jewish family, whom he married in 1946, was a grand niece of Johann Strauss. Peter Stadlen died in 1996. Erich (Eric) Stadlen joined the BBC's News Department where he worked for more than 25 years, mainly as an editor on Radio Newsreel. He was later in charge of training new employees at BBC News and he taught at the City University Graduate Centre for Journalism. He died in London in 1995.[57] Petoe's subsequent career has not been traced.

---

[54] Peter Stadlen, 'Obituary, Dr R. Vaughan Williams', London *Times*, 5 September 1958.
[55] London *Times*, 14 February 1942.
[56] Bayan Northcott, *Independent*, 23 January 1996.
[57] Gerard Marshall, 'Obituary: Eric Stadlen', *Independent*, 23 January 1995.

Eilean Giblin's support for the Stadlens and her publicising of the plight of the *Dunera* internees was her immediate response to injustice ahead of, and largely in defiance of public opinion, and in the face of general wariness and hostility. It became part of an international momentum of concern for the plight of the internees.

* * *

After retracing her journey by train to Junee Eilean began driving to Melbourne where she intended to ship her car to Tasmania for the Giblins' usual Christmas holiday. Just beyond the small township of The Rock she picked up a hitch-hiker who was surprised that a woman driving alone would stop for him. 'You don't seem to have any fear,' he said. 'Why should I have fear,' Eilean asked, '... when I saw you I said to myself, supposing I was walking in this heat, I should be glad of a lift.'[58] She dropped the hitch-hiker at Albury and continued down the Highway until 'disaster' struck. As thunder rumbled, lightning flashed and rain started to fall, her car made a strange noise and stopped. Eventually some RAAF officers stopped to help and towed her car to Wangaratta. She left for Melbourne by train that night but had to wait a fortnight in Melbourne for her car to be repaired and to arrange to have it shipped across Bass Strait.

As she drove from Launceston to Hobart she found preparations for war spreading 'even in this little island at the other side of the world'. At Brighton she saw 'row after row of huts, where young men are trained to fight for freedom, or for democracy, or whatever it is we are fighting for. There is no escape from the horror of the machine that is grinding at the life of the people of Europe.' She feared democracy and freedom might disappear in the struggle, adding, 'some people would no doubt say they have already disappeared'.[59] Even the peace of Cobblers End at Seven Mile Beach had been disturbed by a zig-zag fortified trench built along the crest of the sand dunes where troops from Brighton trained 'to repel an invader'. She heard that shipping was suspended while minesweepers cleared a route through enemy mines laid at the mouth of the Derwent and paravanes – a form of towed underwater glider designed to destroy enemy mines – were fitted to ships. In Hobart HMAT *Zealandia* filled with

---

[58] MS366/6/1, 8 December 1940.
[59] MS366/6/1, 20 December 1940.

troops and, as Eilean watched the troop carrier moving slowly up the river in the grey mist, she wrote in her diary 'to many parents in Tasmania life must seem grey – indeed to many parents all over the world'.[60] Returning to the mainland, she found in Melbourne 'noise and strain and worry', but when she reached Canberra it was 'full of silence' and 'the impression of emptiness'.

In Canberra she continued writing her diary and establishing her pottery as the war raged in Europe and the Middle East.

---

[60] MS366/6/1, 7 January 1941.

Chapter 7

A studio pottery in a time of war

Canberra 1940s

Establishing a pottery workshop gave an extra interest and focus to Eilean Giblin's move to Canberra, where she was a pioneer in a field that was not only personally satisfying but added a new cultural dimension to a city lacking most of the intellectual and cultural diversity of larger centres. As a world war raged, making pots also provided a temporary refuge from news of disastrous battles and, after Japan entered the war, the fear of invasion. Working on her pots was a 'solace', Eilean Giblin wrote several times in her diary. The development of her pottery appears as a sub-story in her diary, occasionally to the forefront but usually incidental to the major story of a world at war. It is extracted and pieced together here as an account of a pioneering achievement.

As soon as she arrived in Canberra, Eilean Giblin began setting up a pottery workshop at first at the rented house the Giblins leased for six months in Empire Circuit, Forrest, then in the government-owned house they were allocated in National Circuit. When an official from the Department of the Interior came to connect her potter's wheel to the electricity supply she rather expansively told him she intended 'to start a new industry'.[1] In Melbourne she had taken lessons from Jack (John Arthur Barnard) Knight, who taught pottery in the art and architecture department at Melbourne Technical College and was later head of the ceramics department. During the years he was at the College from 1936 to 1970, Knight was credited with training most of the potters working in Victoria. He had learnt pottery at the Hoffman Brick, Tile and Pottery Company, one of about half a dozen commercial potteries then operating in the Melbourne suburb of Brunswick. Many artist potters were associated with Hoffman's including Merric Boyd

---

[1] MS366/6/1, 5 September 1940.

who in the 1930s had his pots fired in Hoffman kilns.² Knight regarded himself as 'a very strict teacher' and Eilean records having 'a chastening lesson' from him after he discovered she was centring incorrectly when she returned to the College for a refresher lesson.³ Knight's pottery was in an 'elegant Art Deco' style with simple glazed decoration. He was a friend of artist Napier Waller who taught at the College until 1938 when Murray Griffin, who was to become famous for his paintings of prisoner-of-war life under the Japanese, succeeded him. Napier Waller, later noted for his design of the mosaics and stained glass windows in the Hall of Memory at the Australian War Memorial, decorated some of Knight's pots.⁴

Eilean enrolled in Knight's class for the second and third terms of 1939 and the first term in 1940.⁵ She began establishing her pottery within a few days of her arrival in Canberra. In her diary she describes getting her wheel operating, setting up her kiln, her endless search for suitable clay and the development of her skill as a potter, and she also records the interest Canberra women took in her pottery. Each step was difficult, even connecting her wheel to electricity. When she first arrived she suggested to an official that she could just run a flex from the house to the potter's wheel in the garage but this was too simple, and possibly dangerous, a solution in bureaucratic Canberra. The official explained that there were 'regulations about that sort of thing'; he would have to put in a report and the report might not be dealt with for two or three weeks. He was unmoved by her plea for urgency because she wanted to start a new industry.⁶ Eventually the power was connected but she had to call a mechanic several times when the chain came off disconnecting the motor. Exasperated, she decided that she would discard the electric motor and alter the wheel to a foot-operated one, but Roland Wilson, the Commonwealth Statistician, a friend of the Giblins since he had been a young Tasmanian Rhodes scholar, advised her to keep the motor, as peddling was tedious, and he would try to fix it for her. Wilson continued to help in making adjustments and repairs to get her wheel restarted after its frequent break-downs. 'He is a practical man,'

---

2   Melbourne Technical College, *Art prospectus*, 1939, 1940; Royal Melbourne Institute of Technology, Oral history interview, J. Knight with Tony Dare, May 1979; Kenneth Hood, *The Arts in Australia: Pottery*, Longmans, Melbourne, 1961, p. 24.
3   MS366/6/2, 30 May 1942.
4   Grace Cochrane, *The Crafts Movement in Australia: A History*, NSW University Press, Kensington NSW, 1992, p. 147.
5   RMIT Archives, No. 90, Box 7 – Student Revenue Cards.
6   MS366/6/1, 5 September 1940.

Eilean wrote, 'with a workshop and various gadgets worked by electricity.'[7] Wilson was so successful a handyman that during the Second World War, when petrol was rationed, he constructed an electric car on a baby Austin chassis which he drove to his office, avoiding the bike riding forced on many other Canberra public servants.[8] After the creation of the Department of Labour and National Service in 1940 he moved from the position of Commonwealth Statistician to head of that department.

Getting her potter's wheel operational was one problem, just as essential was locating a source of clay. As Bernard Leach described in his highly regarded potters' guide, 'a potter's prime need is good clay'.[9] It was possible then, although probably very expensive, to buy clay from Sydney or Melbourne suppliers and have it sent by rail to Canberra. Today commercial potters' clay is used almost universally. Eilean, however, searched far and wide for clay, sometimes in the Australian Capital Territory, often over the border in New South Wales, sometimes guided by a report on the location of clay by Dr Walter Woolnough, geological adviser to the Commonwealth Government. She found and experimented with clay from such widespread places as Mulligan's Flat to the north, Naas to the south and many other places around Canberra, including Captain's Flat, Bungendore, Queanbeyan and the Cotter River. She also searched widely in Canberra and hardly any building site in the capital was safe from her digging, even the foundations for the statue of George V being erected in front of Parliament House. A friend remarked that she was 'clay-minded'. Like most of the best studio potters at that time, Eilean believed that a true potter must dig her own clay. She agreed with Leach that there was 'no comparison between the satisfaction of finding one's own local clay and that of buying a ready-made article'.[10]

When she searched for clay during weekends her husband often accompanied her and they would boil a billy and have a picnic lunch with a bottle of wine on the way. During the week a woman friend often accompanied her, sometimes Mrs Alma Mehaffey, wife of the Director General of Works, at other times Mrs Coombs, wife of 'Nugget' Coombs, then a senior economist in Treasury. Rural landowners expressed astonishment when Eilean asked

---

[7] MS366/6/1, 6 October 1940.
[8] Selwyn Cornish, *Sir Roland Wilson: A Biographical Essay*, Australian National University, Canberra, 2002, pp. 26–27.
[9] Bernard Leach, *A Potter's Book*, Faber, London, 1948, p. 43.
[10] Leach, p. 46.

permission to dig for clay. 'Well, I have been asked for many things, but I have never been asked for clay before,' one remarked.[11] Nearer home she found clay at several sites and when petrol rationing drastically curtailed private driving she favoured a site she found behind the Presbyterian church at Forrest. On a rare excursion out of Canberra at the height of the war she found all road signs had disappeared as a precaution in case of invasion. When she collected clay from sites near her home, the economist Dick Downing, or Joan Rogerson, a classics teacher at the Girls' Grammar School and a former student at University Women's College, sometimes helped.

On some of her trips out of town Eilean followed vague hints of the existence of clay deposits. After she was told of an abandoned sawmill site near the old mining town of Captain's Flat, she and her husband set out one Sunday, Eilean driving in icy rain over a corrugated, pot-holed road until they finally located a saw pit beyond the town. She described their dig:

> Half rotten timbers lay on the ground and others were still standing. The pit was about 6 ft. deep, but in places the walls were broken down, and here we slipped down into it. They were partly stone and partly earth with patches of grey with white clay. I dug my hands into the clay, and squeezed handfuls into lumps, while L. dug with a spade. A man and a boy appeared above us, and the boy came down and helped me fill a tin, while the man told us of other places where clay could be found. 'There is clay at Bungendore', he said.[12]

They returned to the car wet and cold but with their tins full of clay and sat in the car in the rain eating food they had packed and drinking their wine.

The next day Eilean searched in the central suburb of Acton, much nearer home, where foundations were being dug for the new Canberra Hospital. The foreman helped her fill a bucket with clay and assured her, 'There is plenty of clay here and if you want any more just come along and you can have all you want. This here is the well for the hospital lift.'[13] Construction of the new hospital had begun just a month before, in August 1940. With wartime delays it was not completed until February 1943 when it was requisitioned by the United States Army. It remained a military hospital until the end of that year.

---

[11] MS366/6/1, 29 September 1940.
[12] MS366/6/1, 29 September 1940.
[13] MS366/6/1, 30 September 1940.

Eilean wrote to Melbourne for a sieve to clean the clay she had collected, recording that gradually she was getting 'the necessary gear together' and had made 'a rough, but solid stool to sit on at the wheel'. When the sieve arrived she worked the Captain's Flat clay through it, a 'slow process' until she learnt the technique and the amount of pressure to put on the hard brush without slopping it over. The result was 'a silky cream-like substance' that she poured on to a sack on the ground to dry. A couple of weeks later after working the different clays she had collected, manipulating them through the sieve, she laid the clay in the sun and had a supply that she expected would last a few months. Then she found she had another problem in keeping the clay damp in Canberra's dry air. She kept experimenting with clay from different places and attempting to perfect her technique, recording her efforts in her diary:

> In the morning I did some essential chores (my essential would not be the same as most women's) and soon after 11, I went to the garage. After some preparation I started the wheel, but found the clay very difficult, as I have for some weeks. It is a tough clay that needs considerable pressure and this slows down the wheel and I cannot get slow steady revolutions. I felt in despair, and that I must write to Sydney for some new clay. And then the idea leapt to my mind – try the red clay from Acton. So I went to the reserve with a tin and cut off a lump and started to make it up. It was sticky and difficult to wedge as it would not come away clean, but after a time I decided to use it as it was, and I threw a lump on to the wheel and began. To my joy I found it quite different from the Captain's Flat clay. Very little pressure centred it, and the wheel revolved gently and evenly, and soon I had made a fair sized bowl. By this time it was nearly 2 o'clock, and I was hungry and tired ...[14]

She searched for books on pottery at the National Library of Australia, then housed in a building on Kings Avenue and functioning as a lending library for Canberra citizens, but was disappointed when she could not find a practical book 'with drawings' describing a kiln.[15] Nevertheless she had a kiln assembled quickly, as by the time the Giblins had to move from the Empire Circuit house, it took three men to move her kiln from the garage to a lorry for the journey of a few blocks to the house in National Circuit.

---

[14] MS366/6/1, 30 October 1940.
[15] MS366/6/1, 11 September 1940.

The move itself was preceded by uncertainty. As their six months' lease on the Empire Circuit house neared an end, the search for a new place to live became urgent. Although Eilean contemplated the possibility of camping, the Giblins' plight did not remotely approach the predicament of many other people who had recently arrived in Canberra as a result of the expansion of departments and the functions of government. In the wartime accommodation crisis that developed, as public service staff and military personnel swamped a city that already had a severe backlog in the provision of housing, an incredible 74 people were reported crowded into and around a 4-bedroom boarding house and two young men were reported to be camping out on Mount Ainslie.[16] Eilean's initial inquiries at the Department of the Interior for a government house to rent were unsuccessful and she came away from one visit thinking 'if we can't get a house, we had better camp in the motorists' camping ground' where she had heard there were some 'quite good huts' which they could supplement with a tent.[17] But when Lyndhurst Giblin used his contacts, his essential role in the war effort ensured that they were given the keys to two vacant houses in Forrest, so they could make a choice. They chose 50 National Circuit, a 7-roomed house, its chief attraction to Eilean being that it was 'well closed in with trees and shrubs', although the garden had been neglected. The Giblins had very little furniture but their move was complicated. Apart from the three men needed to move Eilean's kiln and other pottery equipment, hens had to be transported in several trips in the back of her car. Some new furniture arrived by van from a store in Queanbeyan while another van brought furniture from storage in Melbourne. When they came to unpacking their books, Lyndhurst Giblin exclaimed, 'Why ever did we bring all these from Melbourne?'[18]

The Giblins' house faced vacant lots on the other side of the road so that from their front windows they looked across the slope of Capital Hill to the top of the National Library and the Patent Office on Kings Avenue and beyond to the War Memorial at the base of Mount Ainslie. Eilean recorded the scene:

> In the morning before the mists have evaporated, the Memorial is shrouded and indistinct, except where the sunshine touches the curve of the dome and parts of the walls on the same side. Then it is an enchanted palace full of mystery, a setting for a story from

---

[16] Gibbney, p. 224.
[17] MS366/6/1, 24 February 1941.
[18] MS366/6/1, 17 March 1941.

the *Arabian Nights*. When the sun is high and the light is hard and clear the appearance is imposing, but it has not the fairy-like quality of the morning.[19]

After the Department of the Interior had cleared up the garden, they planted shrubs and trees: in the front, tamarisk, laburnum, holm-oak, kurrajongs and casuarinas and at the back apples, pears, peaches, nectarines and a fig. Eilean hoped future tenants would appreciate the fruit as she thought it unlikely they would still be living there when the trees began to bear fruit.

Once settled in the house, Eilean had her wheel operating and was turning out pieces within a few days but getting the kiln connected proved difficult. Eventually after she complained to the head of the Department of the Interior, Mr Carrodus, several men worked for some days to connect the kiln to the electricity supply, but problems remained as she described in her account of her first firing:

> Directly after breakfast yesterday I took the pots to [the kiln] in the sleep-out, and slowly, and with pauses to think and plan, I filled it and arranged supports to hold plates with a second storey for more pots. At 10.20 I closed it and switched on the current, leaving the ventilating plugs out, and at 12 closed them as well. In the next two hours, I went to the kiln several times and applied my eye to the spy hole, but no glow was to be seen, and I began to wonder if anything was wrong. I went to the meters, there are three of them, and found two were working but the third was not, and it seems that the third wire cannot be connected. So my troubles with the kiln are not yet over.[20]

She described her next bake as 'Another experiment and the result may be failure as I know nothing about glazing.'[21] A few days later she wrote 'Pottery-making gives one startling surprises' when she saw the colours of her pots as she took them from the kiln and noticed her fingermarks where she had held the pots to glaze them. 'And so one learns,' she concluded.[22]

Soon after their move to National Circuit Eilean described calling her husband from the backyard where he was building a pen for their hens to take

---

[19] MS366/6/1, 5 April 1941.
[20] MS366/6/1, 20 April 1941.
[21] MS366/6/1, 24 April 1941.
[22] MS366/6/1. 27 April 1941.

a call as a member of the Commonwealth Bank Board on their telephone in her pottery workshop. 'If only the people in Sydney could see him,' she wrote, in the midst of 'wheel and clay and pots and colours, at a table made by me of slabs of pine (half bark, half wood, of which the hen house is being built) on a stool made by me of the same material, and at the other end [in Sydney], there are grand and opulent offices with staff running here and there.'[23]

After she had been experimenting for some months Eilean wrote for the first time of the designs she was using to decorate her pottery. She described two pieces, a bowl made from a mixture of red and white clay and a vase from red clay, as 'bigger and more ambitious' than anything she had done before. 'The red vase,' she wrote, 'must be decorated with a black design, and in that I am following the early Greeks.'[24] She continued searching for ideas for designs for her pottery pieces, making sketches of designs she found in a book on prehistoric Chinese pottery and experimenting with Aboriginal designs. The immediate inspiration for the Aboriginal designs came from her visits to the new Victorian Government Tourist Bureau, which opened in Collins Street, Melbourne, early in 1940. The Bureau's main booking hall featured a distinctive rubber floor inlaid with what were described as 'cream and black facsimiles of aboriginal carvings found in caves in Central Australia'.[25] Eilean did many designs based on the Aboriginal motifs she saw at the Tourist Bureau but described her results as 'primitive'. 'My style is developing, by that I mean my decorations are changing,' she wrote. 'Nearly all these pieces have Aboriginal designs on them, done roughly ...'[26] When she decided she wanted a green and black grasshopper design for a plate she temporarily trapped one under a glass in the garden while she made drawings from which she could develop a stylised design.[27]

She found inspiration in buildings in Canberra, particularly the Institute of Anatomy (now the National Film and Sound Archive), one of the best examples of Art Deco architecture in Australia, with its Corinthian-style columns and marble floored foyer. She described it as 'the finest building in Canberra, modern in style, but simple and not aggressively modern'.

---

[23] MS366/6/1, 29 March 1941.
[24] MS366/6/1, 17 February 1941.
[25] 'Victorian Government's new Tourist Bureau: Distinctive Australian Motifs the Keynote of the Architectural Treatment', *Decoration and Glass*, February 1940, pp. 16–19; MS366/6/2, 6 February 1942.
[26] MS366/6/2, 22, 26 February 1942.
[27] MS366/6/2, 28 February 1942.

She noticed the carvings on the capitals, the pillars and direct on to the stones above, and the carved design of two conventionalised lizards which was repeated along the front of the building. In the foyer she noted the large Perspex skylight, typical of the stripped classical style of architecture, with its stylised platypus. She made a rough drawing, describing it as 'a stiff platypus design in blown glass with yellow feet'.[28]

Pottery became so much a part of her life that trips away from Canberra without her wheel were a trial. During one visit to Tasmania her husband suggested that she try to make figures in clay, 'never mind how Epsteinish they may be'. She was at first reluctant but when he persisted she sat outside in the shade of the house for an hour manipulating a lump of clay 'into the shape of a squatting man'. After another half hour's work, she 'called to Lynd to come and look, for something had appeared – with apologies to Epstein'.[29] After she had made several figurines, however, she decided her heads were 'crude and grim' and she had 'a lot to learn'.

There were very few potters in Canberra when Eilean Giblin began in 1940 and none operating a studio pottery. The YWCA had introduced a course in 1934 under Mavis Thorpe who had studied with Nell McCredie, an established potter in the Sydney suburb of Epping. The YWCA students used clay brought from Sydney and learnt the built-up method which Mavis Thorpe described as 'strip, coil & slab work'. Canberra Brickworks offered to fire the first pots the students produced but the usual practice later was to send the unglazed pots to the McCredies' studio in Sydney for firing and glazing. A recorder of the early history of pottery in Canberra, Loma Rudduck, described the students preying on people travelling by train to Sydney, asking them to take the frail pots with them. The class averaged 10 to 12 students but appears to have ceased after some years.[30] When Eilean Giblin arrived in Canberra she found Mary McFarlane, wife of the head of Treasury, had done some pottery, but she had learnt the built-up method not the use of a potter's wheel. Another early potter, Dr Herbert Angell, Principal Plant Pathologist with CSIR, and his wife Kate, advised Eilean of sources of clay, particularly in the Wells station area near Hall, and introduced her to palaeontologist, Nelly Ludbrook, with whom she discussed sources for pottery clays and the qualities of clay in the Canberra

---

[28] MS366/6/1, 24 February 1941.
[29] MS366/6/2, 18 January 1942.
[30] NLA MS907 Loma Rudduck Papers.

region.³¹ Dr Angell became a well-known Canberra studio potter after the Second World War but during the time Eilean was developing her pottery, he was absent from Canberra on war work developing the flax industry in Victoria.

Eilean's early pottery experiments aroused much interest among women in Canberra, particularly those looking for interesting activities, intellectual stimulus and respite from the worries of war. Almost as soon as she moved to National Circuit a neighbour, Mrs Florence Green, wife of Lyndhurst Giblin's old Army mate, Frank Green, became her first pupil and Mrs Coombs joined briefly. Later, when Mrs Green decided to give up, Una Cunningham took her place and Valeska Wilson, wife of Roland Wilson, also became a pupil. Una Cunningham was a prize pupil with an eye for form. When she remarked on the shape of a dipper, Eilean wrote – 'how many people think of a plain homely dipper and its shape? That is the one thing pottery does – it gives people a new vision, it makes them think about the things they handle every day, about the shapes and colours.'³² She was sorry when Una Cunningham gave up pottery after she began attending Technical College classes to train as a munitions worker. Eilean wrote: '... she would be a potter quite soon. Mrs Wilson has also stopped, temporarily, but I do not think she will ever be a potter.'³³

Eilean's search for suitable clay was never-ending, particularly when she had failures with the clay she had collected. When she opened the kiln containing her third batch of pots made from clay she had collected at Pipe Clay Lagoon during a visit to Tasmania, she found four pieces broken. Clay dug from a drain at a bowling green near the Giblins' home was also a disappointment. 'Clay is queer stuff in my short experience of it,' she wrote. 'There is a lot to learn about it and I am buying my experience.'³⁴ Her best find came when she noticed some patches of white clay among stones and earth near the Presbyterian church on State Circle, only half a mile from her home. After enlisting her husband to help with digging, she discovered patches of mauve and yellow near the white clay and decided it was 'a most interesting spot'.³⁵ When petrol rationing drastically curtailed private driving, she relied on this accessible clay. She labelled clays from each different location

---

[31] MS366/6/1, 22 April 1941.
[32] MS366/6/1, 6 August 1941.
[33] MS366/6/2, 28 March 1943.
[34] MS366/6/1, 27 May 1941.
[35] MS366/6/2, 16 March 1943.

and kept them in the backyard. Testing them took a long time, she wrote: 'they must be soaked with water in buckets, they probably need mixing with other clays, they need drying, they need maturing. I bake about once a month so that from the time one has dug up the clay weeks must pass before one can know what it will eventually be like; that is if it is good for pottery.'[36] Soon she remarked that her collection of clay was becoming 'unmanageable' and her handwritten labels attached to each container became weathered and sometimes unreadable. She continued to experiment with mixtures of clay. After she had made two pots and lids from a mixture of Bungendore and Presbyterian church clay she noted, 'easy to work, but on the soft side'.[37]

About 18 months after she first set up her potter's wheel and kiln she recorded some success. After one bake 'the pots came out well glazed' and she had good results with some of her experiments with clay mixtures. One in particular was a delight. When glazed it came out an orange colour, 'a lovely clay', and she planned to make it one of her standard mixtures.[38] Later, when she turned out some bad work, she arranged a refresher lesson in Melbourne. 'I am doing better work on the wheel, and Mr Knight's lesson was of value,' she wrote. 'Yesterday afternoon I made 4 pots, fairly good, but I want firmer clay and I shall run out of supplies if I cannot get the new lot to dry. It is now on the kitchen floor where it can stay until tomorrow morning.'[39]

The major outlet for Eilean Giblin's work was the Arts and Crafts Society's shop in Melbourne. At first she sent consignments by train but many pots arrived broken. Later she usually managed to get Dick Downing, Jim Nimmo, a Treasury official who had been one of Giblin's University research assistants in the early 1930s, or her husband to take them in suitcases when they were called to Melbourne on government business. She also donated many pots for patriotic fundraising in Canberra. She records Mrs Murphy collected 14 for the Red Cross Fair held at the Prime Minister's Lodge in April 1942. Another consignment went to the YWCA for fundraising and she turned out 30 or so small pots, mostly ashtrays for another fund-raiser. As news of her talent spread friends commissioned jugs, teapots and coffee pots and the YWCA asked her to take a class in pottery. When it became

---

[36] MS366/6/1, 6 August 1941.
[37] MS366/6/2, 10 March 1942.
[38] MS366/6/2, 28 March 1942.
[39] MS366/6/2, 10 June 1942.

Figure 7.1   Eilean Giblin's pottery in the National Gallery.
(Eilean Giblin 1884 Great Britain – 1955. Tea set comprising teapot with lid, water jug with lid, milk jug, sugar bowl, cup and saucer 1943–44. Earthenware. Gift of Dr and Mrs H.R. Angell 1990. Acc. No. 90.563.1-5. National Gallery of Australia)

apparent they wanted a class using the hand-built method, not one using a potter's wheel, Eilean declined. It would be 'a case of the blind leading the blind' she replied, adding that she did not think the person who approached her knew the difference between the two methods.[40]

The arrival in Canberra of Yseult Bailey, wife of Professor Kenneth Bailey, added a new dimension to Eilean Giblin's pottery making. Since the outbreak of war, Professor Bailey had been called on frequently to advise the Commonwealth Government and when he was appointed to the position of consultant on constitutional matters and foreign affairs in the Attorney-General's Department, which he was later to head, the Bailey family moved to Canberra. Kenneth and Yseult Bailey and their three sons had known the Giblins in Melbourne and in Canberra they lived only a few houses apart in National Circuit. Eilean Giblin and Yseult Bailey had a similar background as Englishwomen who had been to the same school and they both had

[40]   MS366/6/2, 13 October 1943

Figure 7.2 Yseult Bailey, a student and later a colleague at Eilean Giblin's pottery studio.
(Portrait of Yseult Bailey, c. 1924, Falk Studios, Sir Kenneth Bailey Photographic Collection, BibID: 1461736. National Library of Australia)

artistic interests. Yseult had studied sculpture at the Slade School at the University of London before her marriage to Australian Kenneth Bailey in Melbourne in 1925. Soon after she arrived in Canberra she became one of Eilean's pottery students, taking two lessons a week. Less than two months later Eilean wrote that Yseult was 'getting on' in her lessons, adding: 'She is a nice person and I like having her here, and our origins are alike, Wycombe Abbey, and London – I must be 20 years older than she is, but that does not seem to make much difference, and we can talk freely.'[41] Yseult Bailey became Eilean's closest friend, always unobtrusively at hand when needed. Eilean recorded that after one of her trips to Melbourne she found that Yseult had been around and left her house 'swept and tidy', a contrast with

[41] MS366/6/2, 26 April 1943.

the 'depressing clutter' she usually found on her return.[42] Later Yseult took Eilean into her home to convalesce after an illness.

By the time Yseult Bailey began taking lessons Eilean had become an accomplished potter. After three years of persistent searching for clays, of perfecting her technique on the wheel, the timing of her bakes, and experimenting with designs, she described her satisfaction with her work:

> Today, and all this week, I have been working hard at pots in various stages. L. went to Melbourne last Friday and took a suitcase full with him. I want 50 pieces for an exhibition in Canberra in aid of the Kindergarten Society, which will probably be early in October. I want more for the Arts and Crafts Exhibition in Melbourne in the same month, and some I should take with me to Melbourne when I go there towards the end of this month. At least I hope I am going, I have written asking for a permit, but no doubt it will be some days before a reply comes. On Tuesday I worked on the wheel and made 5 good sized jugs which came easily, and were fairly correct – perhaps the best things I have done. The clay was good, and it seems as though at last I have got a good mixture, after the many experiments I have made since I have been here – just three years.[43]

A few months before, Lyndhurst Giblin had told his sister, Edith Hall, that Eilean was potting more assiduously than ever. 'She has at last got the better of teapots – spouts are tricky,' he wrote, 'and we drink out of an ample and freely pouring prehistoric Chinese.'[44]

Eilean and Yseult Bailey became not only close friends but fellow potters and Yseult's student son, Peter, often volunteered to dig for clay at sites in and around Canberra, carting his finds back in the boot of Eilean's Morris car.[45] When Yseult became founding president of the Canberra Nursery Kindergarten Society Eilean directed some of her output towards raising funds for the organisation. A sale of 'Giblin Pots' was held to raise funds for a nursery school at Acton, a project organised by Yseult Bailey, who worked to establish pre-schools in Canberra and later became president of

---

[42] MS366/6/2, 30 June 1943.
[43] MS366/6/2, 23 July 1943
[44] MS366/3, 29 April 1943.
[45] Interview Peter Bailey, 18 June 2007.

the Australian Pre-School Association.[46] When the nursery school opened in the former Isolation Block of the old Canberra Hospital, a site now in the Australian National University, Eilean and Yseult made individual earthenware pipkins (small pots with handles and legs) as drinking mugs for the children. The pots were described as 'made from local clay, thrown on the Giblin wheel and fired in the Giblin kiln by potters Giblin and Bailey'.[47]

Eilean's satisfaction with her hard-won technical skill and the success of her output was one aspect of her pottery. In a deeper sense potting was an important distraction from her anguish at the enormous loss of lives and the destruction of war that she recorded so often in her diary. She felt she was creating objects of beauty and utility while the rest of the world was destroying so much, even civilisation itself. When destruction was too much to bear she turned to the 'solace' of her pots. Long after her death, Dr Angell and his wife presented examples of Eilean Giblin's pottery to the National Gallery of Australia.

* * *

'These things are happening to one's own kith and kin'

2 March 1941

Eilean Giblin's recording of her efforts at establishing a pottery studio remained a subsidiary story to her record of the war. The tragedy of war gnawed at her consciousness as she wrote of one devastating disaster after another in Europe or the Middle East, while around her the slow pace of suburban life went on and the trees changed with the seasons. In January 1941 she noted the dispatch of the AIF 8th Division to Malaya as Japan moved warships to the Gulf of Siam and reasserted its policy of expanding through its Greater Asia Co-Prosperity Scheme. She also noted the United States fortifying Guam and Samoa in the Pacific and sending warships

---

[46] Loma Rudduck, 'A short story about a long time ago 1943–1988,' *Canberra Historical Journal*, March 1989, pp. 8–15.

[47] NLA MS 907, Loma Rudduck Papers.

to visit Australia in a reassuring show of power. Parliamentarians rushed from Canberra by special train, she wrote, 'to be at the various functions of welcome' to the Americans in Sydney. Although she recorded these developments in Asia and the Pacific, disasters in Europe and the Middle East remained more immediate to her. As the Blitz on English cities continued, she recorded the toll in lives lost and buildings destroyed.

> Every fresh development gives one a shock, although one has read of such possibilities. And one feels this is more than can be borne. A few days go by and one has adjusted oneself to the new horror, and a sort of indifference comes to one's help. Then some new happening takes place, such as the bombing of Coventry, or the sinking of a ship, the *[HMS] Jervis Bay* for example, and one goes through the same cycle. There are days when one picks up the paper and one's eyes fall on some news and one says to oneself, 'These things don't happen, they are incredible', and then comes realisation that they are happening, and not to people of a different nation, but to one's own kith and kin.[48]

She recorded the loss of Greece when most of the British forces (including Australian and New Zealand battalions), after retreating before the German advance, escaped from Greece through Piraeus, the Port of Athens, to Crete. While Greece was still being defended, she wrote:

> Tomorrow is Anzac Day and a holiday. And the sons of the men who fought on Gallipoli are now fighting in Greece (perhaps on Parnassus), withdrawing slowly and inflicting great losses, with 'extraordinarily light' casualties, we are told, which seems difficult to understand. Sometime there will be a tale unfolded of these last few weeks and of the retreat of the British forces from line to line and from mountain to mountain as they moved south fighting the Germans, to be, I suppose, evacuated, perhaps under similar conditions to those at Dunkirk.[49]

Her day-to-day recording of the progress of the war does not have the impact now that it would have had for contemporary readers. Now, when the outcome of the German advance through Greece and Crete and the number of lives lost and prisoners taken and the outcome of battles in the Middle

---

[48] MS366/6/1, 2 March 1941.
[49] MS366/6/1, 24 April 1941.

East – the capture and then the fall of Benghazi, the siege of Tobruk – are recorded in histories of the Second World War, the surprise, dismay and horror she felt have lost their effect. However, her general comments on war, particularly its futility, retain their timeless force. After recording the fighting on Crete in June 1941, the 'concentrated terror of modern science' that had 'fallen on our men', she continued:

> And I can garden and work at my wheel, and I can forget everything. What is the use of remembering, for what can I do? And mothers of sons in the fighting forces rush about and fill their days with committee meetings, and bridge parties and service at canteens, in the attempt to stifle the anxiety gnawing at the core of their existence.[50]

In Canberra politics dominated the news and conversation. The House of Representatives remained evenly balanced with two Independents keeping the Menzies Coalition Government in office. Public perception grew that the government was incapable of undertaking a sustained war effort or of adopting unpopular policies. Strikes in essential industries were frequent. 'Why is there so much unrest and dissatisfaction among the workers?' Eilean wrote.[51] The absence of the Prime Minister, Mr R.G. Menzies, for nearly four months from February to May 1941 on a visit to London where, in contrast to his reputation in Australia, he won acclaim as a war leader, did not help the government's fortunes. During his absence the leader of the Country Party, Arthur Fadden, was Acting Prime Minister, but he also failed to gain public support for decisive action.

As Eilean records the war news and life in Canberra, there are glimpses of the high-level talks among senior government officials, some of them held in the Giblins' lounge room. Soon after Menzies returned from London, Eilean was an almost invisible observer, as she sat in her lounge room knitting by the fire, while officials gathered against a background of political instability to discuss the government's plans for a total war effort. The urgency and importance of their discussions is evident from the fact that they met on three successive days outside working hours – on Friday night, Saturday night and Sunday afternoon. Their discussions were suddenly overtaken by the momentous German attack on Russia, sometimes described as the turning point of the Second World War. Eilean Giblin recorded this

---

[50] MS366/6/1, 1 June 1941.
[51] MS366/6/1, 17 July 1941.

moment: 'For the last two evenings I have sat by the fire knitting, listening to plans being thrashed out, ideas ventilated, personalities discussed, and this afternoon [Sunday] there has been a continuation ... L. came back after dark and told me that Germany had declared war on Russia. This is an extraordinary state of affairs.'[52]

In August she left on a visit to Melbourne travelling by service car to Albury then on by train, remarking before she left that in Melbourne she would wear different clothes and different shoes and she would wear a hat which she rarely did in Canberra, 'in short, I shall ascend a rung of the ladder of civilisation'. Most of all she would stay with friends and talk with them.[53] In Melbourne she attended a meeting of University Women's College Council but there was also another purpose to her visit to the city. During her visit she arranged for the diary she had kept since her arrival in Canberra to be typed and, after giving it the title 'Canberra Calling', she sent it to Angus & Robertson, the only major Australian publisher. While she waited to hear whether it would be published she stopped writing entries. She did not resume her diary until the beginning of 1942, leaving no record of the months from August to December 1941, a time that was momentous for Australia and the Allies. In Europe the Germans advanced through Russia, reaching to within 30 kilometres of Moscow before the Soviet Army launched a major counter attack. In Australia, towards the end of August 1941, criticism of Prime Minister Robert Menzies culminated in his resignation. Arthur Fadden, the Leader of the Coalition Country Party, formed a UAP/CP government but this lasted not much more than a month. On 7 October 1941, the two Independent members of parliament, Arthur Coles and Alex Wilson, both from Victoria, voted with the Labor Opposition to bring down the government and a Labor Government under John Curtin took office.

Within a short time the new Government faced the greatest crisis in Australia's history. There had been an ominous foreshadowing of how close the war was approaching with the loss off the Western Australian coast on 19 November 1941 of *HMAS Sydney* and her crew of 645, the greatest Australian disaster so far in a war that had seemed remote. The Japanese attack on Pearl Harbor in December 1941, Australia's declaration of war against Japan and the rapid advance of Japanese forces through Asia and the Pacific were such momentous events that Eilean Giblin decided to start a

---

[52] MS366/6/1, 22 June 1941.
[53] MS366/6/1, 13 August 1941.

new diary, even though she had not heard from Angus & Robertson of the fate of 'Canberra Calling'.

Amid the rush of startling war news Eilean recorded in the first entries in her new diary, she also noted that when the United States Congress passed America's Declaration of War on Japan there was a sole dissenter, Jeanette Rankin,[54] whom she remembered from the days of the International Woman Suffrage Alliance. A pacifist and leader in the women's suffrage movement, Jeanette Rankin had been elected to the United States Congress from Montana in 1940 on an anti-war platform. She had also voted against United States entry in the First World War, 'following the principles of the International Woman Suffrage Alliance and her own womanly heart'.[55]

---

[54] MS366/6/2, 1 January 1942.
[55] Regine Deutsch, *International Woman Suffrage Alliance: Its History from 1904 to 1929*, Alliance Board, London, 1929, p. 23.

Chapter 8

The country under threat

Australia 1942

The Japanese attack on Pearl Harbor on 7 December 1941 and the rapid Japanese advance through Asia in the next few months brought the war close to Australian shores with the stark possibility of invasion. During the early months of 1942, Malaya and Singapore, then the Dutch East Indies, fell to the Japanese. In Papua New Guinea Rabaul was captured and Australian soldiers fought on the Kokoda Track to stop the Japanese advance on Port Moresby. An Allied fleet of 12 cruisers was lost in the Battle of the Java Sea. In Australia Darwin and other towns including Townsville, Katherine, Wyndham, Derby, Broome and Port Hedland were bombed and Sydney Harbour raided by midget submarines as the country moved to a total war footing with the mobilisation of industry and labour and the introduction of rationing. Eilean Giblin records in her diary the fear women felt at the prospect of invasion by Japanese forces. It was not until August 1942 that Australian battalions inflicted the first defeat on the Japanese at Milne Bay and it was November before Kokoda was retaken. By then masses of American troops, who had begun arriving in Australia soon after Pearl Harbor, were fighting with Australians in the Pacific.

Eilean Giblin recorded in her diary these and many other events as news of them reached her. She had no benefit of hindsight, no way of seeing losses and gains in a long-term context. She was also a victim of pervasive wartime censorship. When Darwin was bombed on 19 February 1942 she recorded that 17 people were killed, the official figure released at the time. It emerged later that at least 243 people were killed and between 300 and 400 injured but, with the fall of Singapore only four days earlier, the Government was so concerned about the effect on national morale if it revealed the true casualties that it concealed the disastrous extent of the air raids from the public. Some time later, as people who had been in Darwin began to appear in Canberra, Eilean reported the chaos and lack of preparation they talked about. It seemed to her 'almost as bad as Pearl Harbor and almost impossible when one knows that for weeks a Jap raid has been possible, and probable'. She concluded that 'there must be incompetent men in control', which she expected would be revealed in the report being prepared by the Commission of Inquiry set up under Mr Justice Lowe to report on the panic, desertion, looting and disorder that followed the bombing.[1] In individual instances like the Darwin raid the Government could conceal the true extent of losses but there was no way of disguising the overwhelming advance of the Japanese through Asia and the islands to the north of Australia or the fall of Tobruk in the Middle East or German advances on the Eastern Front.

The first entry in Eilean's resumed diary is dated 1 January 1942. Although written at Cobblers End, Seven Mile Beach, Tasmania, which she reached between Christmas and New Year, it begins with a retrospective account of her experiences in Canberra during December from the time Japan attacked Pearl Harbor and the country moved to a crisis war situation. A few days before she planned to leave Canberra for the break the Giblins usually took in Tasmania, Eilean met the wife of Nelson Johnson, who had succeeded Charles Gauss as the United States Minister to Australia. Mrs Johnson remarked, 'Haven't you heard? The bombing of Honolulu was over the air at 11 o'clock and hundreds of people have been killed.' This was the first Eilean had heard of the Japanese attack on Pearl Harbor and Australia's declaration of war and she was stunned by the news.

In the few weeks before the end of 1941, the Japanese advanced down the Malayan peninsula, captured Hong Kong and invaded Sumatra and Borneo with their rich oil fields. Guam, Wake and other American islands were taken and the Philippines was soon to fall. Despite these events, bringing the war close to Australia's north, Eilean was still able to travel by rail service car to Albury, by train to Melbourne and to cross Bass Strait by ship to Tasmania where she resumed her diary at the beginning of 1942. On Seven Mile Beach she found a zig-zag trench had been dug along the crest of the sand dunes and she heard that a RAAF squadron was about to arrive. 'Even Tasmania, a drop on the map of Australia, is involved in these fantastic incredible happenings,' she wrote. As she listened to an air raid siren giving a short blast to demonstrate that it was in working order, she commented on the possibility of invasion:

---

[1] MS366/6/2, 4 April 1942.

One can hardly imagine that Japanese planes would raid Tasmania, but the authorities must take precautions, and with the possibility of more islands being occupied and further Japanese successes the invasion of Australia becomes more likely. And if they made an attempt I do not see that we could do much to stop them, with the enormous coast line stretching for thousands of miles and the small population scattered in a country as big as the USA.[2]

The situation in Malaya quickly became disastrous. Nearly all front line British aircraft were destroyed when the Japanese attacked RAF airfields in Singapore and the British naval squadron was crippled by the loss of the battleship *Prince of Wales* and the battle cruiser *Repulse* off the coast of Malaya. As the Japanese with their superiority in the air and sea advanced down the Malay Peninsula, Eilean saw the story of the defeats in Greece and Crete being repeated, despite reading 'over and over again about the impregnable defences of Singapore'. When the Japanese landed in Rabaul in New Guinea Eilean, by then back in Canberra, believed some place on the mainland of Australia was likely to be bombed before long, perhaps Newcastle or Sydney, and she agonised about the world catastrophe that had been brought about by 'highly civilised peoples'. She hoped 'a different pattern of civilisation' could be worked out so that the world would not periodically suffer from 'an incredible waste of lives, of resources, of money'.[3] As the war news became 'even more depressing' with the bombing of Singapore and cities in the Dutch East Indies, Japan's advance in Burma and British forces being pushed back by the German army under Field Marshal Rommel in Libya, Eilean wrote, 'Our British pride has had many hard blows in the last two years, and it looks as though we are to have many more, perhaps even harder.'[4] She turned from war news to her pottery and the garden but the 'hard blows' continued as she recorded the Japanese landing in Singapore on 8 February. She regarded this Japanese success as 'the same old story on our side of insufficient supplies, although we have been told again and again that Singapore is impregnable and has ample munitions'. She speculated that if Singapore fell, it would be 'Australia's turn' next, unless 'great armadas of battleships, planes and men and munitions' arrived in time from the United States.[5]

---

[2] MS366/6/2, 13 January 1942.
[3] MS366/6/2, 15 January 1942.
[4] MS366/6/2, 6 February 1942.
[5] MS366/6/2, 11 February 1942.

In Australia the Prime Minister announced the government would take complete control of the economy and manpower 'to promote the greatest effort in the crisis now on us'. A couple of days later what seemed to Eilean 'all the economists in Canberra', as well as 'several young men recruited from Melbourne' gathered at the Barton flat of Professor Douglas Copland, the Prices Commissioner and a member of Giblin's Financial and Economic Committee. Eilean stayed for only a short time but the economists' discussions continued past midnight on new regulations to implement the Prime Minister's total war statement. The party had gathered originally to meet economist Jean Polglaze who had been recruited on Copland's advice from her job as an economics lecturer at the University of Melbourne to run a statistical section in the Department of Defence. She had been called to Canberra to present to War Cabinet graphs showing the state of the Australian war effort. Eilean reported with great satisfaction the success of a woman in this important role, 'I am told she made quite a hit,' she wrote.[6]

Another notable woman, the writer Flora Eldershaw, who was also employed in Canberra at this time, crossed paths with Eilean Giblin. After a career as a teacher, Eldershaw joined the Division of Reconstruction in the Department of Labour and National Service in June 1941 and worked for nine months in the capital she had portrayed in a novel, *Plaque with Laurel*, written with Marjorie Barnard under the name of M. Barnard Eldershaw, and published in 1937.[7] In August 1941 she gave a talk to the National Council of Women (ACT) on 'Women's part in Post-War Reconstruction'.[8] In February the following year she was a guest at dinner of Eilean Giblin and her husband,[9] who was an early advocate of the need to plan for a post-war world even as the war drew nearer to Australia. As well as the interest in reconstruction she shared with Lyndhurst Giblin, Flora Eldershaw had in common with Eilean an interest in the education of young women. A former long-serving senior mistress at Presbyterian Ladies' College, Burwood, she had been an unsuccessful candidate for the position of head of University Women's College in 1938. She was by that time well-known as an author and a writing activist. As president of the

---

[6] MS366/6/2, 13 February 1942.
[7] Clarke, 'Canberra in the 1930s'.
[8] Freda Stephenson, *Capital Women: A History of the Work of the National Council of Women (ACT) in Canberra 1939–1979*, NCW (ACT), Canberra, 1992, p. 9.
[9] MS366/6/2, 10 February 1942.

Sydney branch of the Fellowship of Australian Writers she had transformed the previously staid and conservative organisation into a radical political lobby group. In 1938, representing the Fellowship, she had been successful in persuading the conservative Lyons Government to triple the budget of the Commonwealth Literary Fund, enabling it to initiate grants for writers and to support engaging writers to undertake lecture tours. In 1939 she was appointed to the Advisory Board of the Commonwealth Literary Fund as its only female member and she remained on the Board until 1953. This brought her into contact with the highest level of government as from 1939 the Board was chaired by the prime minister of the day.[10] Soon after her dinner with the Giblins, Eldershaw moved to the Department of Labour and National Service's Division of Industrial Welfare in Melbourne where she was responsible for the development of policies on industrial relations and for research on personnel practice in munitions factories.[11]

As the disaster in Singapore unfolded, crisis meetings continued in Canberra, as Eilean Giblin recorded in her diary:

> L. came in this evening and said, "The Government has had bad news. I do not know what it is but Ministers have not been able to see people, they have been shut up together." "I suppose that means that Singapore has fallen," I said. "Probably worse than that," he said, "they are very upset. I can only think that some place in Australia has been bombed and that people have been killed, or that the AIF in Singapore has been wiped out."[12]

Singapore fell to Japanese forces on 15 February 1942 and 15,000 members of the Australian Army's 8th Division were taken prisoner. With about 7000 Australians captured in other parts of Asia they were to remain in Japanese captivity until the end of the Second World War. Four days later Darwin was bombed and British, Dutch and Australian forces withdrew from Sumatra to defend Java. Eilean, who also noted the escape of German warships from a months-long British blockade at Brest, wrote, 'The happenings all round are as black as they can be.' As usual when she was unable to do more than read about catastrophes, she turned to activities within her control: to bottling tomatoes and 'the solace' of her pots, although she doubted whether these occupations could suppress 'this nightmare, which is not a nightmare, but

---

[10] Maryanne Dever, 'The Case for Flora Eldershaw', *Hecate*, Vol. XV, No. 2, 1989, p. 40.
[11] Dever, *Hecate*, p. 40.
[12] MS366/6/2, 13 February 1942.

facts happening at the present moment'. She continued: 'I suppose one will adjust oneself to these latest horrors as one has done in the past, and that this heartache will pass – leaving one more callous, less responsive to individual suffering than one was – at any rate for the present.'[13]

As Australians absorbed the shock of the fall of Singapore, the Japanese advance in Papua New Guinea, the bombing of Darwin and a warning by General Gordon Bennett, commander of the 8th Division AIF, who had escaped from Singapore after the surrender, that Japanese attacks on Australia would come 'very soon', invasion appeared almost inevitable. Mrs Edwards, wife of the head of Canberra Boys' Grammar, told Eilean that as a mother with daughters she 'felt sick at heart when she thought of what might happen if there was a Japanese invasion'. Another friend, Mrs Kate Angell, told Eilean that 'she felt she could stand up to bombing, but at the idea of an invasion and Japs coming, she felt sick for her children'. Eilean added, 'and evidently she was terrified'.[14] Soon Eilean began hearing of the toll of the war on Australian soldiers and airmen overseas – Lady Knowles who had lost a son, fighter pilot Ft Lt Lindsay E.S. Knowles, in the Middle East, and Lady Clemens, whose son Lt P.C. Clemens was killed at Gemas in Malaya while leading a platoon of the 2/30 Battalion AIF. Suddenly the war that had been so remote was part of the lives of Canberra people. The war that had been 'so far away' and 'quite apart' had now been suddenly 'brought right into their lives'.[15]

War regulations came in quickly. At an afternoon gathering at the home of Frances Elizabeth (Betty) Calvert and her husband Dr Pat Calvert, both scientists, Eilean Giblin heard from other guests that a total blackout was in force. When she returned home she had to hastily improvise by closing shutters, hanging blankets over glass doors and a ground sheet over a window under instructions from the local ARP (Air Raids Precautions) warden. A week or so later when the air raid siren sounded while the Giblins were visiting the Coombs, the party moved quickly to the dining room which, Eilean wrote, 'Dr Coombs had prepared' for the blackout.[16] Eilean bought some blackout paper at Cusacks and tacked it on part of the big window in the Giblins' gramophone room, leaving another part to be covered by a blanket, and she continued using removable blankets for the rest of the

---

[13] MS366/6/2, 16 February 1942.
[14] MS366/6/2, 21 February 1942.
[15] MS366/6/2, 28 February 1942.
[16] MS366/6/2, 12 February 1942.

windows. She did not follow many other Canberra residents in having an air raid trench dug in her garden. When her neighbour, Mrs Castieau, told her of four people nearby who had dug air raid trenches, Eilean commented that if there were an air raid she would stay in bed. She told a young woman canvassing the neighbourhood for the ARP to record how residents could assist in an emergency, that she could put up one bombed-out person and could make tea or coffee for relief workers; she had no camp stretchers but she could spare two dark grey blankets.[17] Later, rumours swept Canberra that 900 RAAF ground crew trainees would be billeted in private homes,[18] but nothing came of this.

When Eilean walked to the Manuka shops she saw an air raid trench being dug behind St Christopher's Church and heard that trenches were being dug at all the shopping centres. She wondered if they would be needed:

> … it is difficult to imagine that bombs may actually fall here in Canberra … One thinks sometimes that death may come soon – at least in the last few weeks with the war coming nearer and nearer, I have thought about it … much more definitely these last few days since the collapse of Java. … Under normal circumstances I should, I suppose, live another 10, 15, or 20 years, and there is much in life of great interest, there is much which gives great pleasure, beauty first of all, what we see around us. … This afternoon I worked at the wheel, wondering sometimes what could become of my pots …[19]

She had trouble sleeping at night thinking of the destruction as Japanese bombs crushed the Allied Forces in Java and destroyed towns and cities 'as the Germans have done, the Italians, the British and the Russians'.[20] The loss of human lives tormented her, as well as 'the incredible waste all over the world', the ships lying at the bottom of the sea, wrecked planes rotting and rusting in Europe, Africa and Asia, and men and women 'sweating and toiling to make more planes, and more ships, and more guns in order to feed the insatiable maw which consumes and destroys …'.[21]

---

[17] MS366/6/2, 8 March 1942.
[18] MS366/6/2, 8 May 1942.
[19] MS366/6/2, 12 March 1942.
[20] MS366/6/2, 28 February 1942.
[21] MS366/6/2, 9 March 1942.

Suddenly married women, previously barred from even temporary work in government departments, were in demand and young women began arriving in the capital to take the place of men who had enlisted in the services and to work in the rapidly expanding departments and agencies of government. Mrs Nelly Ludbrook, a palaeontologist, told Eilean she had secured her first ever full-time job in the Department of External Affairs. 'It seems that married women can get taken on by any Department,' she said, 'I have never been able to get a job in my own line, and here I am de-coding cables.'[22] Later Mrs Ludbrook was employed as a geologist, a job more suited to her training. Two recently arrived young women, Joan Rogerson and Norma McArthur, whom Eilean knew as graduates of University Women's College, called on her soon after they arrived in Canberra. Rogerson had been recruited to teach classics at Canberra Girls' Grammar School and McArthur, a mathematics graduate, was employed at Mount Stromlo Observatory. She told Eilean she had little to do at the Observatory and was pleased when she was given the job of writing a history of wartime munitions making at Mount Stromlo.[23] Norma McArthur later became a distinguished demographer and specialist in Pacific studies at the Australian National University.

Incongruously, in the midst of the acute shortage of labour, three men turned up from the Department of the Interior to lay a gravel path after Eilean complained that so much water had accumulated in their back yard she had to lay a plank to get out the back door. She records several other instances of the extraordinary overhang of ordinary life during the crisis of threatened invasion. Soon after writing of the fear several women friends held for their children if the Japanese landed, she records the arrival at her door of a travelling saleswoman for Lucas's corsets. In other entries she notes a Chinese market gardener appearing at her door selling vegetables, a man who arrives ready to sharpen knives and a messenger who still calls for her weekly grocery order. Their continued appearance is a minor indication of the difficulties the Government faced in turning the economy to a total war footing. Strikes, which Eilean often records with dismay, were another manifestation of this difficulty, in this case changing workers' views from their long-standing antagonism to employers to a realisation of the country's grave danger. Eilean found it hard to believe that miners would still go on strike even at the height of the invasion scare. A Melbourne friend she talked

---

[22] MS366/6/2, 7 February 1942.
[23] MS366/6/2, 13 September 1942.

to, physician Dr Marion Wanliss, commented, 'Don't they realise that the Japs may come and cut their throats.'[24]

With the arrival of United States General Douglas MacArthur in Australia on 19 March 1942 the war entered a new phase. 'It is true,' Eilean wrote in her diary, 'one feels there is a different atmosphere, there is more confidence, more assurance. ... One feels ... that we are not alone, seven million people, in this great country.'[25] About a week before she had noted the 'different drone' of nine Kittyhawk fighter aircraft which flew so low before landing at Fairbairn aerodrome that she could see the United States markings on the planes, which were painted 'brown and green in patches'.[26] Although the Americans moved quickly from Fairbairn to northern bases, they made an impact in Canberra during their short stay. Eilean heard from Elsie Harry, a departmental librarian, who called to see her pottery, that Gorman House, a government-controlled hostel for women, had introduced restrictive regulations after Americans had been found in girls' bedrooms late at night.[27] Although she reported this puritanical reaction without comment, Eilean Giblin's attitude was usually more libertarian. On one occasion when she read of several young men and women being prosecuted for 'scandalous behavior' (nudism) in Sydney, she commented: 'What a fuss to make about an innocent amusement.'[28]

It was May 1942 before some good war news came, with the Battle of the Coral Sea off the north-east coast of Queensland. The success of the United States and Australian navies in this battle stopped a Japanese seaborne landing at Port Moresby and was regarded at the time as saving Australia from invasion. Eilean, however, continued to hear and record much bad war news and she felt overwhelmed by 'the many scenes of fighting, and the sufferings of the common man and woman in various parts of the world'. The 'madness' sweeping over the world, she wrote, was 'putting the wheels of progress back, stopping constructive developments, social reforms, the slow but sure improvements of evolution'. She was particularly moved by the fate of the starving refugees and the sick and wounded retreating from Burma to India before the Japanese advance and lamented that British imperialism had failed to win the trust of Indians and

---

[24] MS366/6/2, 26 February 1942.
[25] MS366/6/2, 21 March 1942.
[26] MS366/6/2, 8 March 1942.
[27] MS366/6/2, 12 April 1942.
[28] MS366/6/1, 2 March 1941.

Burmese people. She speculated that the Burmese people would prefer to be overtaken by an Asian rather than a European race. She also interpreted some of the extreme fear of invasion among Australians to a racist attitude to the Japanese. '... the Japanese threat to Australia has shaken people here as I think a possible German invasion would not have done,' she wrote, 'although that is hard to judge because a German invasion has been beyond the probabilities.'[29]

Rationing of essential commodities was soon a part of life. Petrol rationing, introduced early in the war, was tightened significantly and the use of gas producers encouraged. Tea, at that time drunk in great quantities at and between meals, was rationed when supplies ceased from major sources in the countries taken by the Japanese. At first it was rationed to one ounce a week per person through a system of registration with a retailer but this proved ineffective and in June 1942 ration books were issued. As labour was directed to essential industries and much non-essential production ceased, many items disappeared from shops, sometimes in one part of the country, sometimes in another. Eilean records some of the commodities that were unavailable in Canberra: '... no treacle or golden syrup, ... no lime for the garden, no ground ginger, no marmite, tea rationed, and coffee very short. No dried fruits such as prunes and apricots, although we hear that the troops get so many that they are sick of them.' She attributed the coffee shortage to the amount drunk by the American troops.[30] Matches – essential to light fires for cooking and heating, as well as for lighting cigarettes and pipes – were also in short supply, but Eilean's particular grievance was against the continued, although curtailed, operation of the cosmetics industry. With no thought for morale, she believed the industry should be shut down for the duration of the war:

> I cannot believe it is necessary for women to put colour on their faces and on their nails in these times. ... I have been in chemists' shops and have watched little girls, lots of them, discussing with the chemist and buying powder or rouge or face cream, or it may be nail colours. And it is not 10 years I suppose that the use of these things has become so usual. Probably I should be considered old fashioned.[31]

---

[29] MS366/6/2, 13 May 1942.
[30] MS366/6/2, 6 May 1942.
[31] MS366/6/2, 17 January 1943.

The announcement that clothes rationing would be introduced and that in the meantime stores could make only three-quarters of their normal sales per week brought chaotic scenes. Before the announcement, female public servants had been surveyed in an effort to find the average yearly amount women spent on clothes. Eilean thought the rumoured result of £35 a year too high – 'Last year I spent £5 odd on my clothes,' she wrote.[32] She described the 'wild rush of buyers all over Australia ... hordes of men and women struggling and fighting, pushing and grabbing to obtain new clothes' as 'an unedifying spectacle'. It meant that 'those with money have been able to buy'.[33] When 'Fashions for Victory' regulations restricting clothing styles were published, Eilean thought forcing people to dress 'simply' was 'a good move' but she sympathised with the men and women appointed to the 'National Council of Clothes Styling', whose job it was to decide on the restricted designs that could be manufactured. 'What a job,' she wrote, 'and won't they quarrel at their meetings'.[34] Sugar was rationed in August 1942, then meat and butter. Eilean heard rumours that beer, tobacco and cosmetics would follow but although production was reduced these commodities were never rationed by coupons. When she first heard from her husband of possible tobacco rationing at a different level for men and women she wrote, 'I went off the deep end and said, "Why the discrimination?" and L. looked rather sheepish.'[35]

Eilean recorded the Japanese midget submarine attack on Sydney Harbour on 31 May 1942 with the loss of 19 Australian and two British sailors and the sinking of a converted ferry, *HMAS Kuttabul*. Although a significant event in Australia's engagement in the war and a spark for further invasion fears, it was overshadowed in her diary by her recording of the devastating British raid on the German city of Cologne, the first 1000-bomber raid undertaken by the RAF under the command of Sir Arthur 'Bomber' Harris. Saturation bombing of German cities was the first step in opening a Second Front in Europe, agitation for which had begun soon after Germany attacked the Soviet Union. To Eilean saturation bombing was 'the first step towards the destruction of the great towns all over the world', bringing to an 'actual state' the world predicted in H.G. Wells's novel, *The War of the Worlds*, written

---

[32] MS366/6/2, 28 March 1942.
[33] MS366/6/2, 13 May 1942.
[34] MS366/6/2, 26 July 1942.
[35] MS366/6/1, 6 March 1941.

more than 40 years before.[36] As she recorded 'bad news on all fronts', she added: 'But a sort of philosophy comes to one, an acceptance of these things ... One accepts, as one accepts a violent storm, or great heat, or any other condition over which one has no control. But such things will pass, and one does not know when this breakdown of civilisation will pass.'[37] There was better news in the Pacific. After the naval success in the Battle of the Coral Sea and the even more decisive victory at the Battle of Midway in June, Australian forces in late August and early September 1942 inflicted the first land defeat of the war on invading Japanese forces, at Milne Bay, dispelling the myth of Japanese invincibility. It was the 'most cheering news we have had since war came to the Pacific', Eilean wrote.[38]

Despite the gravity of the war and wartime restrictions requiring permits for interstate travel Eilean managed several trips to Melbourne, usually obtaining permits that allowed her to travel to attend council meetings at University Women's College. During one of these visits she attended the funeral at Fawkner Crematorium of Miss Susannah Jane (Susie) Williams, whom she had recruited as first head of University Women's College. The simple service was 'impressive and peaceful, the building simple and the words stirring', she wrote. She attended the service with Eveline Syme and Dr Georgina Sweet after having lunch with them at the Alexandra Club.[39] The trips were important in re-establishing social and intellectual links, as Eilean wrote in her diary:

> I came in from gardening the other day, and I looked at my hands. The nails were full of earth, fingers were plastered with mud, the backs of the hands with clay. One side of my cardigan was smeared with clay, the other had a tear in it. My shirt was spluttered with clay, as were my shoes, which had not been cleaned for weeks – and I felt disgruntled with myself, and I thought it is time I went to Melbourne.[40]

She travelled on crowded trains and made her way through platforms congested with young men and women in uniform. In Melbourne she recorded some remarkable changes:

---

[36] MS366/6/2, 3 June 1942.
[37] MS366/6/2, 5 July 1942.
[38] MS366/6/2, 7 September 1942.
[39] MS366/6/2, 30 May 1942.
[40] MS366/6/2, 25 August 1942.

Melbourne is full of soldiers ... most of them American, it is full of men in uniforms – military cars and lorries painted khaki, or painted in several colours, are all over the place. Shop windows are covered up, or have fine wire netting over them or have a trellis work of cotton strips. Crowds of people swarm in the main streets, trams are full to overflowing ...[41]

When Douglas Copland, whom she met while changing trains at Albury, described Melbourne as 'a mad house', Eilean rejoined, 'The whole world is a mad house.'[42]

At a dinner at Douglas Copland's Canberra flat she met the Treasurer, Ben Chifley. The only other guest she mentions by name is Dick Downing, the young economist from Melbourne, who had been Giblin's research assistant and protégée and who had been recruited by Copland to work in Canberra. In her diary entry she relays several stories Chifley told of his electioneering experiences, then she records her impression of the man later to be Prime Minister: 'A shrewd and honest man Mr Chifley seemed to me – not used to talking to women. When he was sitting opposite me at table and telling these experiences he turned to D.B.C[opland], and then to Dick, back and forth, back and forth.' Dick Downing walked home with Eilean and Norma McArthur joined them for an evening of music, '*Cosi fan tutti*, brought by Dick – or rather selections chosen by him ... followed by the London Symphony Vaughan Williams – another world we were plunged into, and the party broke up at 12.'[43]

After her initial efforts at conforming to the social mores of Canberra society, Eilean moved towards friendships with people she and her husband found compatible and who shared their outlook on social and political issues and their musical interests. They found friends principally among scientists, economists and educationists, usually people with progressive, left-wing views on national and international issues. Close friends could be depended on to visit Eilean during her husband's frequent trips away to Melbourne and Sydney. She recorded one of these occasions when Richard Woolley and his wife, Dick Downing and Mick Shann, then a young public servant in Treasury later the diplomat Sir Keith Shann, visited:

---

[41] MS366/6/2, 30 May 1942.
[42] MS366/6/2, 3 June 1942.
[43] MS366/6/2, 19 July 1942.

Last Saturday evening L. went to Sydney, and Dick, Mick Shann, and the Woolleys came here. Dick came in the afternoon to do some gardening and I got him to come with me to the Drain as I wanted more clay. We went by car as kerosene tins filled with damp clay are very heavy to carry. Beethoven, and Bach, and the *New Statesman* were the entertainments of the evening. When I came in with coffee and cake about 11 o'clock I found them reading some of the several copies of the paper lying about, with one attending to the music, which was at that moment Bach Walton's *Wise Virgins*. The party broke up at 12 and it was 1 o'clock before I got to bed.[44]

Social events such as this at the Giblins' home were probably as close to a bohemian gathering as Canberra society came during the war years.

Towards the end of 1942, when Eilean read of the Allied landings at Algeria and other places in the start of the North African offensive, which led to the defeat of the Vichy French and the start of Allied attacks on German forces under Rommel, she felt for the first time since war broke out 'the weight of horror pressing on the top of one's head shifted slightly'. She hoped that some time in the future there would be an end to 'this monstrous machine' which was sapping the life of mankind and 'the resources and fruits of the earth'.[45] In November 1942 Australian troops recaptured Kokoda and the following month the Japanese were defeated at Gona and Buna on the north coast of New Guinea.

＊＊＊

An unusual Christmas Day at University Women's College

With the threat of invasion lifted Eilean planned, despite travel restrictions, to get to Hobart for Christmas. She reached Melbourne on 8 December 1942, hoping to get to Tasmania almost immediately, but weeks went by and Christmas came and went before she managed to get a berth on a ship. Stranded in Melbourne for much longer than she expected, she stayed at

---

[44] MS366/6/2, 19 October 1942.
[45] MS366/6/2, 10 November 1942.

University Women's College, apart from a brief visit to friends, Phillip and Margot Bowden, at Ivanhoe. She was at the College for Christmas Day, which she spent with Greta Hort and an exotic group of women separated from families and friends through the exigencies of war, a situation for them far more serious than her own temporary inconvenience.

The day was 'very unusual', she wrote. She described the group of five women who spent Christmas day together as 'a Dane, a Czech, a German (but of British birth), an Austrian and a Britisher'. They were an extraordinary group to find in the 1940s in Australia, which was still an insular, overwhelmingly Anglo-Celtic society. The women's stories typify the extraordinary upheaval of wartime, resulting in the disintegration of families, the forced abandonment of careers and the loss of fortune. Three of the group, Julie Moscheles, Ursula Hoff and Lacerta Finton, were refugees from the Nazis. Dr Julie Moscheles, a former professor of geography at Charles University in Prague, had fled to Australia from Czechoslovakia fearing for her life because of her Jewish background after German troops took over the country. She had been discovered by Greta Hort dressed as a bedraggled peasant – the disguise in which she had escaped from Czechoslovakia – wandering along Royal Parade near Melbourne University. Hort befriended her and their friendship developed into a lesbian relationship.[46]

Dr Ursula Hoff, then secretary of University Women's College, the woman Eilean described as 'German but of British birth', had been born in London in 1909, but soon afterwards her father, a German Jewish merchant, moved his family back to Germany. Ursula was educated in Hamburg where she studied art history. After Hitler became German Chancellor in 1933 following the overthrow of the Weimar Republic, the Hoffs left Germany for England where 23-year-old Ursula, due to her British birth, was able to take up British citizenship. After completing a doctorate at Hamburg University she returned to England. From 1935 she had temporary positions at the Courtauld Institute of Art and the Ashmolean Museum, Oxford, until such opportunities dried up in the later 1930s as the threat of war increased. Simultaneously the influx of refugees, mainly Jewish, from Nazi-occupied countries, strained English resources. In response to a British Government request, Australia agreed to take 15,000 of these refugees over three years. In this roundabout way Ursula Hoff came to University Women's College in Melbourne. Early in 1939 Greta Hort asked her friend Dr Helen Wodehouse, Principal of Girton College, Cambridge, whether it

---

[46] Martin, *Nordic Notes*.

would be possible to find a Jewish or part-Jewish refugee with a university degree who would like the job of College secretary in Melbourne. Ursula Hoff was offered the job and her voyage to Melbourne was sponsored by University Women's College.[47] On 31 October 1939, nearly two months after the start of the Second World War, she sailed on the *Orcades* for a position for which she was very overqualified. In the college milieu, however, she developed cultural contacts among intellectual women including Greta Hort, who as an émigré herself understood Hoff's background, and eminent and influential members of the Council such as Dr Georgina Sweet and Eveline Syme. She became a member of the Lyceum Club for professional women and was invited to be a member of the Catalysts, an elected group of women intellectuals that formed the core of the Lyceum Club and whose members met monthly.[48] She also began discussion groups on art at the College and when her expertise became better known she was asked by the recently appointed Director of the National Gallery of Victoria, Daryl Lindsay, to give lunchtime lectures on art at the Gallery.

The Austrian, Mrs Finton, an anglicised form of her Viennese name, was described by Eileen as the 'daughter of a Professor (of 'salamander' fame, I am told) married to an interior house decorator who died early this year, and she is now teaching at St Michael's', a description that gives only vague hints of Lacerta Finton's background. Mrs Finton's father was Dr Paul Kammerer, an Austrian experimental biologist, who was the subject of one of the great evolution controversies of the early twentieth century. His experiments with various amphibians, including salamanders and the midwife toad, at the University of Vienna, supported the Lamarkian argument that acquired characteristics could be inherited. This provoked an international battle with neo-Darwinians, led by British scientist William Bateson, who upheld the theory of chance mutations preserved by natural selection, and Dr G.K. Noble of the American Museum of Natural History. Kammerer's experiments were never replicated, leading to claims that they had been faked. In 1926, at the age of 46, Kammerer committed suicide. Twenty years before, he had married Baroness Felicitas Maria Theodora von Wiederspenger and their only child, Maria Lacerta, was born in 1907. Her father chose the name Lacerta after the *Lacertidae* genus of lizards: a previously unknown variety he had discovered and which had been

---

[47] Sheridan Palmer, *Centre of the Periphery: Three European Art Historians in Melbourne*, Australian Scholarly Publishing, North Melbourne, Vic., 2008, p. 61.

[48] Palmer, p. 98.

named *Lacerta fumana Kammerer*, after him.⁴⁹ The former Maria Lacerta Kammerer arrived in Australia late in September 1939 on the *Oronsay* as a refugee from Austria with her husband, Paul J. Finton, an Austrian architect and photographer, who had anglicised his name from Fischel. Their immigration sponsors included Professor Wilfred Agar, professor of zoology at the University of Melbourne, who had done research on the Lamarkian theory.⁵⁰ The Fintons were living in Toorak Road, South Yarra, and Maria Lacerta Finton was employed as a teacher at St Michael's Girls Grammar School in St Kilda when Paul Jacques Finton died on 14 October 1942, aged 56, at Royal Melbourne Hospital.⁵¹

Eilean named Dr Moscheles and the recently widowed Mrs Finton as the 'tragic' members of the group that gathered for Christmas dinner, but even the host, Greta Hort, although she had arrived in Melbourne in an uncomplicated way after being appointed principal of Women's College, had heard recently of the death of her sister and of her mother, whom she believed had been killed during the British bombing of Copenhagen. Ursula Hoff, too, worried about the aged parents she had left behind in England as refugees. She had identified with the plight of European refugees in Victoria by visiting the camp at Tatura, where some of the 2500 'enemy aliens' brought to Australia on the *Dunera*, were interned. During her visit, arranged through VIREC, she met internees who became well known in their post-war careers in Australia, including the art historian Franz Philipp and Peter Herbst, later professor of philosophy at the Australian National University.⁵²

Eilean described the dinner at University Women's College with this group of women from five different countries thrown together by the upheavals of war:

> Christmas day was very unusual. Dr Moscheles came to lunch and stayed on, and at 5 Dr Hoff arrived, and then a Mrs Finton ... We sat in the Common Room with the afternoon sun shining in, and there was good talk, give and take, remarks from one or the other, no one out of it – chiefly round and about 'men like war'. Sherry before dinner at 6.30, and I went along and there was

---

⁴⁹ Arthur Koestler, *The Case of the Midwife Toad*, Hutchinson, London, 1971; Mark A. Gillman, *Envy as a Retarding Force in Science*, Avebury, Aldershot, Hants, 1996.
⁵⁰ NAA, B13, 1939/50662.
⁵¹ Victorian Deaths, 11165/1942.
⁵² Palmer, p. 99.

a thread connecting all of us (or so it seemed to me) of sympathy, and understanding. Frontiers do not matter, there were 5 women from 5 different European cities celebrating a festival as far away as they could be from their birthplaces, just glad to sit and talk and be friendly.[53]

While she was in Melbourne Eilean attended a College Council meeting which she described as lasting three hours and which ranged widely, towards the end deteriorating into haggling over 'what is policy'. Philosophy professor, Boyce Gibson, ended the discussion with the answer, 'What is not administration.'[54] The most important decision of the meeting was to reappoint Dr Greta Hort for a further five years as College principal. During her time as head, Hort fostered high academic standards and in accordance with the ideals of the College Council she encouraged a higher degree of freedom and independence in students than was usual at the time. She tutored in philosophy, published several books and became president of the Victorian Branch of the Australasian Society of Psychology and Philosophy.[55] She provoked considerable antagonism, however, among some students who found her arbitrary and manipulative. 'There were rumblings of student revolt,' student Diana Dyason wrote, 'mostly the result of arbitrariness, use of pressure tactics, and what are best termed personality problems'.[56] Greta Hort did not complete her second five-year term. After the Second World War she visited Julie Moscheles in Prague and decided to stay there. As the Communist grip on power in Czechoslovakia tightened, she could find no employment apart from some translation work and after the death of Julie Moscheles from cancer in 1956 she escaped from the country and returned to Denmark. She was appointed professor of English at the University of Aarhus and became an authority on Commonwealth and post-colonial literature.[57]

Ursula Hoff became a legendary figure in the Australian and international art world. She began her career as an art historian in Melbourne with her lunchtime lectures at the National Gallery of Victoria. In 1943 she was

---

[53] MS366/6/2, 26 December 1942.
[54] MS366/6/2, 17 December 1942.
[55] Ursula Hoff, 'Hort, Greta (1905–1967)', *Australian Dictionary of Biography*, Vol. 14, Melbourne University Press, 1996.
[56] Hume Dow, ed., *Memories of Melbourne University: Undergraduate Life in the Years since 1917*, Hutchinson, Richmond Vic., 1983, p. 93.
[57] Martin, *Nordic Notes*.

Figure 8.1 Dr Greta Hort, principal of University Women's College, 1938–46. (University College Archives)

employed Assistant Keeper of Prints and Drawings and she was later assistant director of the Gallery and a visiting lecturer in the Fine Arts Department at Melbourne University.[58]

Lacerta Finton left her position as a teacher of German and French at St Michael's Grammar School in St Kilda at the end of 1944. When she applied for naturalisation in 1948, her application stated that she had been a nursing sister at the Women's Hospital in Grattan Street, Carlton, for three years.[59] Her sponsors who stated that she was 'a person of good repute' included Professor Wilfred Agar.[60] When Arthur Koestler, author of the famous *Darkness at Noon*, was researching his book on her father, Paul Kammerer, he contacted Lacerta Finton and acknowledged the letters she

---

[58] Jaynie Anderson, 'Obituary – Ursula Hoff (1909–2005)', *Symposium*, No. 30, July 2005.
[59] NAA, B78/4110780
[60] NAA, A435, 1948/4/3085.

wrote to him in his book, *The Case of the Midwife Toad*. Her letters conveyed, he wrote, 'an intimate portrait of her father but also of the life of intellectual élite of Vienna before the First World War'. Koestler's book suggested that Kammerer, who was a pacifist and socialist, may have been the victim of sabotage by a Nazi sympathiser at the University of Vienna. Its thesis vindicated a man he believed was 'in all probability himself betrayed'.[61] Maria Lacerta Finton lived in Melbourne until her death in the suburb of Canterbury on 14 November 1981, aged 74.[62]

The changing society Eilean noted at this Christmas dinner was not a passing phenomenon. On another visit to Melbourne for a College Council meeting, she had dinner with Greta Hort and Eveline Syme at a Jewish restaurant in Carlton which, she wrote rather in surprise, 'supplies good and unusual food, and one is surprised to hear English spoken by the foreign-looking people at the other tables'.[63]

While staying at University Women's College through December 1942, Eilean tried every few days to get a berth to Tasmania but with the movement of troops to and from the island, either on leave or to new postings, nothing was available. After many failures she contemplated abandoning her trip and returning to Canberra but eventually she heard that she could sail to Launceston on 29 December. When she reached the Giblins' cottage at Cobblers End, which had been vacant for a year, it presented a strange time warp. Items such as boxes of matches and tins of rice that not been in shops for months were on the shelves. A copy of the Hobart *Mercury* from a year before (2 January 1942), that was twice the number of pages allowed a year later, following the rationing of newsprint, lay on the table. Eilean read in the year-old paper of Churchill still proclaiming that Singapore and Malta would not fall to the enemy and of the Americans still fighting against the Japanese around Manila. She reflected on the enormous changes in the past year when the Japanese had come so close to Australia that an invasion seemed likely:

> The cottage has stood still, and life has not touched it – and so much has happened in the past year. War in the Pacific had only just begun last January and at that time, and for some months, a Japanese invasion of Australia was likely. Now it is possible, but it does not seem probable, with American troops and munitions

---

[61] Koestler, p. 15.
[62] Victorian Deaths, 27860/81.
[63] MS366/6/2, 30 June 1943.

here in large numbers, on Guadalcanal, and with the A.I.F. in New Guinea. There are not as many troops in this neighbourhood as there were a year ago, and I am told they are now stationed in small parts further away from the coast, and that they come for a week at a time from Brighton.[64]

Eilean's comment on the changing fortunes in the war foreshadowed a changed atmosphere in Canberra when she returned from Tasmania.

---

[64] MS366/6/2, 4 January 1943.

Chapter 9

War and peace

Canberra, Hobart 1943–1951

By the beginning of 1943 the fortunes of the Allied Nations had begun to turn, although the Second Front, with its promise of the recapture of European countries, was still 18 months away. In Australia there was an easing of tension, although Japanese submarines continued to attack coastal shipping, Darwin continued to be bombed and air raid trenches, brownouts and sandbagged buildings remained features of life in cities and towns. After she returned from Tasmania to Canberra Eilean Giblin had to be reminded by a warden that there was a brownout when she neglected to pull heavy blankets over some windows. She found out later that an enemy plane had been detected over Port Kembla. More than 20 Allied ships were sunk off the Australian coast and about double that number attacked by Japanese submarines. The worst disaster occurred on 14 May 1943 when the Australian hospital ship *Centaur* was torpedoed by a Japanese submarine off the coast near Brisbane. Eilean described the torpedoing of the ship with the loss of 268 of the 332 people aboard, including 11 of the 12 nursing sisters, as 'another horror'.[1]

In New Guinea, the successes against the Japanese at Milne Bay and Kokoda were reinforced in March 1943 with an Allied victory in the Battle of Bismarck Sea, north of New Guinea, when United States and Australian planes destroyed a Japanese convoy carrying troops to New Guinea. In the final phase of the battle Allied aircraft strafed escaping Japanese soldiers on life rafts to prevent them joining the Japanese offensive at Wau. In her reaction to this battle Eilean decried the cost of war not only in the loss of lives but in the lessening of moral judgment in its prosecution and she queried the double standard applied to Allied and enemy actions. She was

---

[1] MS366/6/2, 28 May 1943.

particularly scathing about General Douglas MacArthur's claim that 'A merciful providence has guarded us in this great victory', commenting:

> [It] sounds like a remark made by a covenanter, or even Cromwell himself. Thousands of Japanese troops were drowned or killed, and great quantities of supplies were lost. One American officer states that "we strafed the burning ships with our heavy machine-guns – then we turned our attention to the boats in which the Japanese tried to escape and strafed hell out of them". When escaping British sailors on rafts or in boats have been fired at by U boats, or by planes, there have been remarks about the outrageous brutality of the Germans or the Italians. But now we are doing it, and it seems as though it is considered the right thing to do. There is a deterioration of standards in war, and brutality becomes progressive. I suppose an American who was at Pearl Harbour in December 1941 would say that the Japs deserved everything that modern weapons could give them, but I cannot help feeling grieved that we can behave in such a way. If we do this now what may we not do before the war is over.[2]

She was momentarily heartened when she heard church bells ringing at Easter for a celebration that had continued 'in spite of wars and revolution, massacres and famines, and all the disasters that have befallen the human race' for two thousand years. Perhaps 'mankind will survive the present insane disaster', she wrote, and men and women would construct a better life in the future.[3] The following month, however, as Allied planes continued the saturation bombing of German towns and began bombing Italian towns in preparation for invasion, she recorded with dismay 'towns lying in ruin, young men burning to death in crashing planes, ships filled with food settling down to the bottom of the sea, or children playing in fields being blown to bits'. After concluding that 'we are in the grip of some terrible machine', she turned again to the consolation she gained from potting: 'At least I can make pots, and people must have mugs and jugs, vases and plates,' she wrote. 'Most people are working directly or indirectly to destroy, and I am trying to create.'[4]

---

[2] MS366/6/2, 5 March 1943.
[3] MS366/6/2, 26 April 1943.
[4] MS366/6/2, 28 May 1943.

As the threat of invasion receded and the Allies recorded victories against the enemy, the atmosphere of crisis relaxed. The recently created Department of Post War Reconstruction began planning for the future and Lyndhurst Giblin had time to talk to a Methodist Church men's group on the recently released British report in which Sir William Beveridge, in plans for a more equitable post-war society, proposed all people of working age should pay a weekly contribution in return for benefits to the sick, unemployed, retired or widowed. Giblin also began writing on post-war problems and that year he had several articles on the subject published in Britain and Australia, including 'The problem of maintaining full employment' in a series, *Realities of Reconstruction*, published by Melbourne University Press for Army Education.[5]

In Canberra there were more social occasions. One of these events, a farewell to the United States Minister to Australia, Nelson Johnson, held late in January 1943, was so important to Australia's alliance with the United States that the Prime Minister, Mr Curtin, attended. When her husband introduced Eilean, the Prime Minister recalled that they had met in Perth. Eilean wrote: 'I had forgotten this meeting, which must have been in 1923, 20 years ago' when she was on her way to Rome for the International Woman Suffrage Alliance conference. 'L.' commented: 'There is a Prime Minister for you.'[6] There was another farewell for the Johnsons a few days later, a picnic supper on the lawns of Canberra Grammar School, held before news arrived that Nelson Johnson would be staying on in Canberra, following the withdrawal of his proposed successor. Eilean's description of this occasion expresses the sentimentality that was an aspect of the American and Australian wartime relationship as well as the evocative sense of the enveloping bush in the sparsely settled National Capital. As the stars came out and the sky darkened, she wrote, above 'the murmur of conversation, men's voices, women's voices, came the low singing of "Waltzing Matilda" and the notes of a guitar'. Guests moved their chairs closer to Nelson Johnson, who had begun the singing, and joined him in negro minstrels and traditional songs. 'It was a wonderful evening,' Eilean wrote. In the near distance 'a bright light moving along a deserted road made the scene even more dramatic' as the tall Italian cypresses at the edge of the lawn disappeared in the blackness of night.[7]

---

[5] Others included 'Reconstruction in Australia', *Agenda*, 1943; 'Reconstruction: A Pisagh View', *Australian Quarterly*, September 1943.
[6] MS366/6/2, 31 January 1943.
[7] MS366/6/2, 31 January 1943.

By 1943, several major non-English speaking countries had established diplomatic presences in Canberra, a new phenomenon in a city where, in the 1930s, only the United Kingdom and New Zealand had been represented and the United States only since 1940. Their advent interested the well-known writer and critic, Nettie Palmer, when she visited Canberra to give two lectures on Australian literature for the Commonwealth Literary Fund. When she heard that the children at the Russian Legation did not attend schools but were taught privately and did not speak English, Eilean recorded her comment as 'really rather sinister'.[8] In her diary Eilean contrasted the Russian children with the children of Chinese diplomats who attended public schools and learnt English quickly. Nettie Palmer went with Eilean to visit Nien Cheng, a graduate of the London School of Economics, who was the wife of the Chinese Nationalist Minister in Canberra, Kang-chi Cheng.[9] After the war the Chengs returned to China but their fortunes changed following the victory of the Chinese Communist Party against the Kuomintang in 1949 and the retreat of the Nationalist Government to Taiwan. In 1968, some years after her husband's death, Nien Cheng was arrested as a spy and even after her release in 1973 was kept under surveillance. In her best-selling book *Life and Death in Shanghai* she described her incarceration in solitary confinement for more than six years during the Chinese Cultural Revolution and the murder by the Red Guards of her daughter Meiping, a ballet dancer, who had been born while the Chengs were in Australia. Nien Cheng left China in 1980 and died in Washington aged 97, on 2 November 2009.[10]

As the Giblins developed their own circle of compatible friends, Eilean found the rituals of Canberra entertaining less and less attractive. By 1943 she accepted these invitations only rarely and usually only if the occasion offered more than social interaction. She was happy to go to a dinner arranged by Mrs Tillyard to meet anthropologist Camilla Wedgwood, the principal of Sydney University Women's College. Apart from their mutual interest in the operation of women's colleges they also had in common an interest in the fate of the *Dunera* internees. A Quaker and a pacifist, Camilla Wedgwood had been involved in moves to resettle German refugees in Australia and had joined public protests against the treatment of those on the *Dunera*.

---

[8] MS366/6/2, 13 October 1943.
[9] MS366/6/2, 18 October 1943.
[10] Nien Cheng, *Life and Death in Shanghai*, Grove Press, New York, 1986; *Canberra Times*, 13 November 2009.

Eilean found her 'a breezy cheerful person with an emphatic and downright manner' and invited her to lunch the following day 'to eat bread and cheese with me, outside the back door in the sun'.[11] This was a relatively infrequent interaction, however. Eilean indicates in a diary entry that she was tired of the obligatory afternoon teas that were a conventional way of receiving and returning hospitality among acquaintances. 'Last Thursday,' she wrote, 'Messrs Johnson, Edwards, Frederickson and Miss Mitchell came to tea, but I never seem to get any further with anybody on these occasions, and sometimes I wonder why I do it, that is ask people.'[12]

In August 1943 she recorded the landslide victory of the Curtin Labor Government at the general election with the comment, 'Australia has decided with no uncertain voice that John Curtin is the man to lead the government of the Commonwealth.' She noted the election of the first women to Federal Parliament, a long-awaited moment for feminists. Dame Enid Lyons was elected for the Liberal Party in the House of Representatives and Senator Dorothy Tangney for the ALP in the Senate and for a while, as counting continued of absentee and postal votes from far-flung places in Australia and from the troops overseas, Eilean recorded the possibility that Jessie Street might be elected for the ALP in the Sydney seat of Wentworth. She noted that the advent of women was a problem for a formerly all-male institution. The officials of Parliament were 'scratching their heads over the problem of providing accommodation,' she wrote.[13]

Soon after the election there was another event of note with the arrival of one of the most distinguished wartime visitors to the National Capital, Mrs Eleanor Roosevelt, wife of the President of the United States. Eilean describes the excitement the visit caused in Canberra but also the Giblins' antipathy towards social events and celebrities. She wrote:

> As we approached the Hotel [Canberra], lines of cars edged Commonwealth Avenue, so I turned to the right and crossed to the road on the other side ... People were standing about outside the Hotel, and at the entrance we had to show our card of invitation. Inside we found a queue which we joined, but L. said I cannot stand this, I am off – and he left. The queue moved slowly, and I looked round at the hotel lounge (or hall) which was roped off, and every seat seemed to be taken and was crowded with

---

[11] MS366/6/2, 30 May 1943.
[12] MS366/6/2, 3 August 1943.
[13] MS366/6/2, 1 September 1943.

Figure 9.1   Eleanor Roosevelt with Prime Minister John Curtin, Canberra in 1943.
(Portrait of John Curtin with Eleanor Roosevelt at a State Luncheon, Parliament House, Canberra, September 1943. BibID: 3601808. National Library of Australia.)

> people watching the visitors progress towards the reception. Soon I saw by an open door the tall figure of Mrs Roosevelt wearing her grey Red Cross uniform cap. I shook hands with Mr Johnson, the American Ambassador, then with Mrs R, and got an impression of grey hair and a colourless face and moved on to Mr Curtin who smiled …

She explained her husband's absence to the Prime Minister and to the United States Minister, Nelson Johnson, then moved through the throng of people, drinking a glass of fruit drink and noting a few people before she left. As she drove home along Commonwealth Avenue she saw her husband walking near West Block and stopped to pick him up. The Giblins were home in National Circuit less than half an hour after they had left and Eilean wrote her verdict:

> Really I am getting a bit tired of Mrs Roosevelt; the newspaper correspondents report every detail of her movements, and what she says, to Jim or John, who may be small boys who have pushed

through crowds to ask for autographs. If she had not been the wife of the President nobody outside America would have heard about her. She is, no doubt, able and charming, hardened to crowds and publicity, and so is natural and simple under any circumstances. And this morning I heard that Melbourne's Lord Mayor had said that she, Madame Chiang Kaicheck (I can't spell it) and Queen Elizabeth were the three outstanding women of today which seems to be nonsense, in reference to the last, who is as far as I know a worthy sensible woman, but I have never heard of any outstanding quality about her. No one would have heard of her if she had remained a Bowes Lyons.[14]

It may not be coincidental or an oversight that Eilean Giblin included two references in this one entry to women whose roles in public life depended on the positions their husbands occupied. It was something she had endeavoured to avoid throughout her life in Australia.

Eilean Giblin's diary ended abruptly in October 1943. During that year she had made less frequent entries and there were some long gaps including a period of more than a month between March and April. Her explanation was that there was not much to write about or she was 'too lazy or too tired, or there were too many papers to read, or too many letters to write'.[15] When she came across the diary ten years later she wrote that she had abandoned it as she found it 'a labour'. The Second World War did not finally end until nearly two years after she ceased writing her diary, when Japan surrendered in September 1945. Even the Second Front in Europe with the massive landings at Normandy did not begin until June 1944, more than six months after her diary ended. If she had had the motivation she would have found much to write about. Two factors may have influenced her to abandon her diary. She may have been, as she wrote, 'too tired'. She had already had a number of colds and attacks of influenza, one bout necessitating a hospital stay. In the next few years she had several illnesses and was in hospital several times and it seems likely she was beginning to suffer from the first signs of the debilitating illness that eventually overtook her. The other reason for abandoning her diary may have been that she had heard that the manuscript of the first section of her diary had been rejected by an American publisher.

---

[14] MS366/6/2, 5 September 1943.
[15] MS366/6/2, 26 April 1943.

From the start of her diary in 1940, Eilean Giblin was conscious not only that she had the opportunity to observe and record a nation at war from the nation's capital but she believed others would want to read her diary because of the uniqueness of her record. She had sent the first volume, 'Canberra Calling', in high hopes to Angus & Robertson. Although her instinct was correct in thinking a wartime diary could be worth publishing, it is not surprising that eventually her 1940–41 manuscript was rejected with the well-worn excuse that not enough copies would sell to make publishing pay.[16] Publishing in Australia, always a marginal proposition because of the limited market, had become much more difficult with the wartime shortage of paper. As early as the middle of 1940 Angus & Robertson told a hopeful author that it had 'too little paper to indulge in speculative publishing' and this situation got progressively worse as paper imports ceased and Australian-made paper was in ever growing demand to cope with the huge expansion of government publishing.[17]

Angus & Robertson's reply to Eilean did not arrive until close to the end of March 1942 when Australia was at the height of the greatest crisis the nation had ever faced. The obvious reason for the rejection of the manuscript was that it covered a period when the Second World War was still confined to Europe and the Middle East, before the start of the war in the Pacific with its direct threat to Australia. If published in 1942 it would have been strangely out of date and its tenor would not have suited the times. Wartime propaganda campaigns were at their most strident portraying the enemy as barely human, capable of the most horrendous acts. Hatred of the enemy was actively encouraged. The ABC broadcast a series of 'hate talks' during a propaganda campaign emphasising the cruelty and viciousness of the Japanese,[18] and there was no questioning of the basis for the war. Eilean Giblin was out of step with this view, recording the destructive forces on both sides and agonising over the cost of war not only in the loss of millions of lives and the destruction of cities and industries, ships and planes, but in the deterioration of moral judgment.

There were other problems with her manuscript. She recorded interesting vignettes of life but she did not write with sufficient awareness of the audience she was attempting to reach, often not explaining the significance

---

[16] MS366/6/2, 28 March 1942.

[17] Jacqueline Kent, *A Certain Style: Beatrice Davis a Literary Life*, Viking, Richmond Vic., 2001, pp. 58–9.

[18] Michael McKernan, *All In! Australia During the Second World War*, Thomas Nelson, Melbourne Vic., 1983, p. 141.

of her observations or the people about whom she wrote. The conversations she recorded were often not quite pointed enough and her descriptions were sometimes inverted and awkward. She expressed her instinctive abhorrence of the waste of war in human life and resources strongly and she conveyed the paradoxes of wartime life, juxtaposing the ordinary routines of life with cities bombed, ships blown up and countries falling to invasion. She had difficulty, however, in conveying an overall sense of either war strategies or in interpreting the local political scene, although she made some incisive comments on both. These drawbacks were added to when she followed her husband's advice that names of some well-known people should be indicated only by initials, taking away a sense of reality from some sections.

She seemed to take the rejection by Angus & Robertson in March 1942 in her stride and very soon sent the manuscript to a major American publisher, G.P. Putnam's Sons, based in New York. Although she does not record the result in her diary, it seems likely that she heard of its second rejection sometime in 1943 and this may have left her with little motivation to continue. Discouraged at the rejection she did not send her second diary to any publisher although, with its description of the dramatic period from the Japanese attack on Pearl Harbor to late 1943 when the Allies were recording major successes, it was intrinsically more interesting than the earlier section.

* * *

When the Second World War ended in September 1945, Lyndhurst Giblin's role in government began to wind down. The Commerce Graduates' Association arranged for William Dobell to paint his portrait and the Giblins began planning their return to Hobart. Originally intended to occur in early 1946, their move was delayed for nearly a year as Eilean suffered recurring bouts of ill health. After one attack of influenza she was admitted to hospital no less than three times, the last time for a lengthy stay suffering from 'post-influenza depression'.[19] Later in the year she was in hospital again with 'a vicious cold' and when she came out Yseult Bailey took her to the Baileys' home to recover. Lyndhurst Giblin described his wife's illness as 'mysterious' and 'the doctors unable to help'.[20] Ominously, he described

---

[19] MS366/3, n.d. [?1946], LFG to Edith Hall.
[20] MS366/3, 4 November 1946.

his wife as 'so shaky' that it seemed unwise to face the disruption of moving house. Later, however, she regained her strength and Giblin wrote to his sister, 'unless she has a relapse we shall have broken up the household here and be coming over on 16th [November 1946]'.[21]

Lyndhurst Giblin, by then in his seventies, was also in poor health. He had recurring bronchitis and suffered from 'soft feet', a legacy of the First World War. At the best, he told his sister, his feet were 'poor things to walk on these days' and gardening was his remaining outdoor activity.[22] Nevertheless after a short break in Hobart he was back in Canberra early in 1947 to finalise his wartime work with the Financial and Economic Committee, which was being disbanded. He was farewelled at an all-male party, held in sweltering heat in February, at the home of a colleague. 'Nearly everyone was there with whom I had had much to do from Garran and Mac to the junior people like Whitelaw and Brand,' he wrote to Eilean. 'Everyone was of course very kind and many greetings to you: a round of 6 or 8 "tributes".' The refreshments were 'very suitable' – biscuits, rolls and cheese and a hard to get, nine-gallon keg of beer set up in the middle of the back lawn.[23]

Soon after, he began his last major work, the writing of a history of the development of the Commonwealth Bank as a central bank,[24] which required him to be in Sydney almost continuously to work on Bank records. He was also needed, intermittently, in Melbourne to present statistical evidence on behalf of the Commonwealth to the standard hours inquiry which was heard by the Commonwealth Court of Conciliation and Arbitration at numerous sittings between February and July 1947.[25] The Court's decision resulted in a 40-hour week, to take effect from the beginning of 1948.

Meanwhile in Hobart, Eilean had many challenges dealing with problems that had accumulated in a house in which they had not lived for any considerable time since the late 1920s and a garden that needed re-establishing on poor soil. She also had the problem of setting up her pottery studio in its new location, although this was delayed as her kiln did not arrive at The Side until nearly four months after her departure from Canberra. She

---

[21] MS366/3, 15 November 1946.
[22] MS366/3, 24 February 1944, LFG to Edith Hall.
[23] MS366/1, 14 February 1947.
[24] L.F. Giblin, *The Growth of a Central Bank: The Development of the Commonwealth Bank of Australia 1924–45*, Melbourne University Press, Carlton, Vic., 1951.
[25] Commonwealth Court of Conciliation and Arbitration, 'Judgment – Standard Hours Inquiry, 1947', *Commonwealth Arbitration Reports*, Vol. 59, Part III, July–December 1947, pp. 597–8, 606.

was in hospital twice in Hobart during 1947, the second time for a prolonged stay. The cause of her illness was undiagnosed – her husband referred to her 'mysterious cold'. After she had a 'serious' setback he suggested that she should get in touch with her friend, Dr Marion Wanliss, a physician in Melbourne, whom she had consulted ten years before, even suggesting organising for her to fly across to Tasmania to give an opinion.[26] When Eilean left hospital early in December after a stay of about two months she went to the home of Giblin's nephew, Cyril ('Copper') Giblin and his wife Violet in Sandy Bay, to convalesce, returning to The Side when her husband flew to Tasmania for the Christmas holidays.

* * *

A new horizon opened the following year with the return of international shipping to some normality after the huge disruptions of war and its aftermath. At the first opportunity Eilean Giblin started to plan to visit England. Her pattern of visits had been disrupted by the war and it was not until ten years after her last visit that she was able to travel from Australia again. During the long separation the dynamics of her family had changed. In December 1943 she heard of the death of her mother, inevitably bringing to her mind the length of time since her last visit to Homefield. Then, just as the war in Europe was ending she heard of the sudden death of an older brother, Brigadier Colin Burton CBE DSO, who died aged 61 on 4 May 1945 after a long career in the RASC.[27]

After her mother's death, Homefield became the home of her eldest brother Kenneth Burton who, with his cousin, had inherited the family's tobacco business of Pritchard and Burton. Kenneth and another brother Esmond met her when she arrived in England on the *Stratheden* on 27 March 1948. Her first visit was to her elderly MacRae aunts at Polegate where, influenced by her closest friend, her artist aunt Mary MacRae White, she took up painting again. Although she did not reach professional status as she had in pottery, painting gave her great interest and enjoyment. She did 'some delightful works', Eveline Syme wrote.[28] During the four or five months she was in England she alternated between staying with her aunts at

---

[26] MS366/1, 14 November 1947.
[27] Obituary, London *Times*, 8 May 1945.
[28] Eveline Syme, 30 November 1955.

Polegate and Kenneth at Homefield and she also visited her brother Esmond at Kensington, where he shared an elegant house with architect Christopher Wright, and her youngest brother Clive and his family in Essex. These visits were interspersed with several attacks of illness but, although she had blood tests and cardiograms in London, the nature of her illness remained undiagnosed.

Esmond Burton's reputation as a carver in stone and wood had blossomed during the inter-war years when he received several commissions for ecclesiastical work from major architects. He was responsible for four near life-size figures above the main altar in Wells Cathedral, seven figures in stone embellished in colour for St Mary's, Oxford; and a statue of St Edmund of Canterbury for Salisbury Cathedral. In 1948 he was still completing a major work for Ripon Cathedral in Ancaster stone, consisting of eight large figures representing bishops and patrons and 24 small figures suggesting a heavenly choir. From the end of the Second World War he was increasingly in demand for work on war memorials, including the extension of existing First World War memorials to cover the losses in the recent war, and on the restoration of churches destroyed by enemy action. He was commissioned for additional sculpture for the major Naval Memorial at Portsmouth to commemorate those lost in the Second World War and for a nine-foot-span stone eagle weighing over two tons surmounting the RAF memorial at Brookwood Military Cemetery, the largest Commonwealth war cemetery in the United Kingdom. He executed the Royal monograms for the rebuilt Dutch Church in London, which had been completely destroyed in an air raid, and the tympanum over the central archway of Belfast Cathedral. While Eilean was in England, Esmond took her to see some of his work. A contemporary article describes how much this absorbed him:

> Burton lives for his work and all his hobbies are ancillary to it, the reading of history, the collection of old furniture, the loving examination of any old church house, or cottage in whatever neighbourhood he may find himself, and the discovery of anything from the ghost of an old mass dial on a church porch to a Sheraton tea-caddy in a back-street shop.[29]

During Eilean's visit to England the Giblins' house in Hobart was let for six months and when she returned she was again its sole occupant. Lyndhurst Giblin had spent most of 1947 in Sydney as he began work on his history of

---

[29] Bashford, *Country Life*, 27 January 1950.

the Commonwealth Bank and for the following two years and a considerable part of 1950 he was almost continuously in Sydney with only short breaks in Hobart for the Christmas holidays and other occasional visits. During what was effectively a separation in these years, Eilean and her husband kept in touch by mail usually at least weekly. As with all their correspondence, only her husband's side has been preserved but some aspects of Eilean's life are apparent through comments in his letters.

When Eilean returned to The Side in September 1948, she threw herself into re-establishing her studio pottery but the hard physical work became too difficult for her. In February 1949 her husband wrote from Sydney: 'I have been wondering whether it would be useful to enlist a faithful disciple for pottery – an active girl (or boy) – who would do the hard work under instruction ... you could put the finishing touches.'[30] He noted, however, that her health was better: 'Your letters record increasing activity without bad effects', he wrote. '– walking, night-driving without a collision and so on'.[31]

During 1949 Lyndhurst Giblin became involved in arrangements for a lecture tour of Australia by the eminent philosopher, mathematician and controversial public intellectual Bertrand Russell, whom he had last encountered during the First World War. Giblin's friend, Edward Dyason, then living in England, had persuaded Russell to undertake the tour but, before it began, Dyason died suddenly on 3 October 1949 on board the *Queen Mary*, after leading the Australian delegation to the British Commonwealth Relations Conference in Ontario. Giblin continued with the arrangements for the tour in collaboration with the Australian Institute of International Affairs and the Dyason Trust.[32] His letters to Eilean indicate that this involved considerable stress.[33]

Russell's tour of Australia, which began in Sydney on 23 June 1950 and ended with a farewell broadcast on 26 August, was a tremendous success. There was great popular demand for seats at his lectures, with overflow crowds listening to relayed broadcasts and huge press coverage of his speeches, broadcasts and interviews. He gave two major lectures in Sydney and Melbourne and one each in Brisbane, Canberra, Adelaide and Perth. Strangely, in view of Giblin's strong links with Tasmania, Hobart was the

---

[30] MS366/1, 10 February 1949.
[31] MS366/1, 13 May 1949.
[32] NLA MS1648, F.S. Keighley, 'Left-wing Liberal: Bertrand Russell in Australia, 1950', ANU thesis, November 1973.
[33] MS366/2, 21, 25 January 1950.

only capital city excluded from the tour. Despite complaints, Giblin stuck to his decision to leave Tasmania out because it did not have an active Institute of International Affairs.[34] If Eilean heard any of Bertrand Russell's lectures, it would have been one in Melbourne, which she visited occasionally.

The public persona of the man who toured Australia in 1950 at the age of 78 was very different from the pacifist Bertram Russell whom Giblin had known during the First World War, when Russell was imprisoned for his anti-war activities. In 1950 Russell was awarded the Nobel Prize for Literature and the previous year he had given the prestigious Reith lectures for the BBC and been awarded the high British honour of the Order of Merit. Although arrangements for Russell's tour began while the Chifley Labor Government was still in power, by the time he came to Australia the Menzies Liberal/Country Party Coalition had won government at the Federal election held in December 1949 and Australia was at the beginning of a long conservative era that was to last for more than two decades. Nevertheless even conservative opinion makers welcomed Russell's lectures as a contribution to public discussion on the gravity of the problems facing the world.[35] The previous month the Korean War, sometimes then regarded as a prelude to a third world war, had begun. According to a chronicler of his Australian visit, Russell was an amiable visitor who liked meeting people who engaged him intellectually.[36] Giblin told Eilean that Russell's Sydney lecture on population as an obstacle to world government was 'very well done & pleased people generally'.[37]

At the same time as he was overseeing Russell's visit, Lyndhurst Giblin began revising his central bank history, following comments from readers of his manuscript and in order to comply with instructions from the publisher, Melbourne University Press. 'All well with MUP', he told Eilean, 'but they want certain things done with the text – spellings, capitals & printing details, which will take longer than I reckoned on. ... It seems you can't leave things to the modern printer in the old way.'[38] His monumental work apparently nearly over, he left Sydney and was back in Hobart by mid-February 1950, bringing Eilean a copy of a newly released Pelican book, *Pottery and ceramics:*

---

[34] MS1648, Keighley.
[35] Melbourne *Argus*, 27 July 1950.
[36] Alan Wood, *Bertrand Russell: The Passionate Skeptic*, George Allen & Unwin, London, 1957, pp. 211–12.
[37] MS366/2, 25 June 1950.
[38] MS366/2, 21 January 1950.

From common brick to fine china, by Ernst Rosenthal, which he described as 'not artistic but technical'.[39] He soon found, however, that he had to return to Sydney for further checking in the Commonwealth Bank records.[40] Apart from Bank comments he had to take into account views ranging from those of Raymond Kershaw, the Australian-born aide to the Bank of England's Sir Otto Neimeyer, who had forced deflationary measures on Australia during the Great Depression, to those of the recently defeated Labor Prime Minister Ben Chifley. By early July 1950 he had sorted out most of the difficulties with 'the Bank people' but while he was consolidating all the corrections onto the final proof, he became ill. During the years in Sydney he had suffered several periods of severe ill health including being hospitalised for a suspected heart attack. After the latest episode of illness he told Eilean he was able to sit up and sip brandy and after two days of dry toast and brandy was able to finish the proofs. With the task completed he left Sydney late in July 1950 to return to Hobart.

As the book progressed through the stages of publication during the remainder of 1950, he made occasional visits to Melbourne but the trips were draining. In October when he was in Melbourne to tackle a large pile of papers from Roland Wilson to clear up some 'doubtful' dates in the history, he found the tram journey to and from the university 'exhausting'. 'I never loathed a big city so much as I did yesterday,' he wrote, '... I'm so slow in getting about & getting things done.'[41] In what appears to be his final trip to Melbourne in December 1950 he complained prophetically that his dental plate was continuing to disintegrate, although 'not fatally so far', and his watch had stopped 'dead' the day after he arrived. Much reduced in energy, he attended a Dyason Trust meeting in the city but was unable to undertake any other activity that day. 'I have stuck to works of necessity so far,' he told Eilean, 'but I hope to drop in to *Shoe-Shine* [an Italian realist film] some time before I go.'[42]

Despite his deteriorating health, Lyndhurst Giblin, during his visits to Melbourne, made several strenuous trips to Eltham, then a semi-rural suburb on the outskirts of the city, to see a young boy who had become his protégée, the Australian child film star, Nicky Yardley, who had appeared in some famous Australian films including *Bush Christmas*. His long-standing

---

[39] MS366/2, 12 February 1950.
[40] MS366/2, 20 June 1950.
[41] MS366/2, 25 October 1950.
[42] MS366/2, Kew, Monday [December 1950].

Figure 9.2 Lyndhurst Giblin at Betty Roland's Eltham home in December 1950 with (from left) Gilda Baracchi (Betty Roland's daughter), Nicky Yardley and Gavin Bowie. (Reproduced from *The Eye of the Beholder* by Betty Roland, Hale & Iremonger, Sydney, 1984, courtesy Gilda Baracchi.)

interest in the development of boys, together with his love of the theatre, combined to underwrite his interest in Yardley. Giblin had been a leading advocate for the establishment of a National Theatre, an idea that was supported by John Curtin when he was Prime Minister but which fell out of favour after his death. He had been enchanted when he saw Yardley playing Tyl Tyl in Sydney in Maurice Maeterlinck's *The Blue Bird*, the story of a magical quest for the fabulous Blue Bird of Happiness. After the death of his father, Edgar Yardley, and the departure of his mother for England, Nicky was cared for in Eltham by Betty Roland, a founder of Melbourne's left-wing New Theatre and the former de facto wife of the wealthy Marxist intellectual Guido Baracchi. When Roland's income became precarious Giblin paid the fees for Nicky to board at Ivanhoe Grammar School, a few suburbs distant from Roland's house. He described Roland to Eilean as 'obviously sensible & competent & a good sort'.[43] Roland wrote of Giblin;

---

[43] MS366/2, 20 June 1950.

'I was helped by a remarkable old man, Professor Giblin, who, having no children of his own, got great pleasure out of helping other people's children.'[44] Giblin provided for the ongoing expenses of Nicky Yardley's education in his will.

An earlier protégée, Tony Melville, remarked on this affinity between Lyndhurst Giblin's interest in the arts and in boys. 'It was always an experience to go to the theatre with Giblin,' he wrote. 'One might almost say, in fact, that his love of the Arts and his interest in children went together. For it was the education of the young that interested him, the slow process by which appreciation of the arts is formed in the mind of a child.'[45] At the time he wrote this appreciation for Douglas Copland's commemorative volume, A.E. (Tony) Melville was a teacher at Haileybury College, Hartfordshire, England, and from 1969 to 1987 he was Headmaster at The Perse School, Cambridge. Giblin had taken an interest in him since his schooldays at Geelong Grammar and later at Cambridge and corresponded with him from the late 1930s, his letters to him always closing with 'Love Giblin'.[46]

Lyndhurst Giblin's interest in the education and development of boys is well-documented. In Melbourne he was a friend of James Darling, Headmaster of Geelong Grammar, and a supporter of his education reforms. He visited the school frequently and interstate boarders often stayed at his South Yarra home on their way to and from school. He took boys to plays and concerts, particularly those he considered had musical or cultural interests. A son of one of the Giblins' friends remembers as a young boy meeting Giblin in the city and being taken to Wirth's circus in Melbourne. In Canberra he was a friend of the Reverend W.J. Edwards, Headmaster of Canberra Grammar, and he arranged for boys to help with gardening and odd jobs and he took them camping. The only time Eilean mentions this in her diary, she wrote, 'L. went off this morning by producer gas car to Coppins Crossing, on the Molonglo, to camp for the night, with Hugo and (at the last minute) Warwick. I refused to go – for one night it did not seem worthwhile, and my bed is more comfortable'.[47]

---

[44] Betty Roland, *The Eye of the Beholder*, Hale & Iremonger, Sydney, 1984, p. 274.
[45] A.E. Melville, 'Giblin and the Arts', in Copland, *Giblin The Scholar and the Man*, pp. 68, 69.
[46] NLA MS6225 Papers A.E. Melville, Box 4.
[47] MS366/6/2, 28 March 1942. Many people attached gas producers to their cars to supplement the small wartime ration of petrol.

Soon after his last visit to Melbourne and with his Commonwealth Bank history in the final stages, Giblin's health deteriorated rapidly. A friend, James Bartley, wrote: 'With the task completed, but with the book not yet in print, it seemed that his strength quickly ebbed away.'[48] He was diagnosed with bowel cancer and when it spread to his liver his death became inevitable. He spent the last months of his life at The Side, the house Eilean and he had built a quarter of a century before, only being moved to hospital a few days before his death. His last letter was to Roland Wilson, who wrote of him:

> He made a unique mark in government, in economics, in central banking, in statistics and in war. But above all, from his vast knowledge and experience was distilled a wisdom which was put without stint at the disposal of those who knew and loved him. I am proud to have been one of them.[49]

Lyndhurst Giblin was 78 when he died in Hobart on 1 March 1951. He was universally praised for his clear thinking and intellectual honesty and described as 'a natural leader of men', 'a superb teacher', 'a fabulous old man' who had 'almost single handedly founded an Australian political economy'.[50] His 'reach and grasp of mind' would have made him 'distinguished in any generation', but he 'never lost the common touch, his sense of fellowship and his zest for experience', his friend J.M. Garland wrote. In character he described him as having a 'habit of reticence' and being 'on guard against self-revelation'.[51] Keith Archer, Commonwealth Statistician from 1962 to 1970, whom Giblin had recruited as a teenage clerk in Tasmania, described him as 'one of the most remarkable men of the century'. He told an oral history interviewer 'he was a big man in every way, he was big physically and he was big in his outlook, he was a tremendous judge of a man'.[52] When Paul Hasluck wrote his volumes for the official history on the political and social aspects of the Second World War he described Giblin running the influential Financial and Economic Committee during the Second World War from a small room 'at the sunny corner of the top floor of West Block,

---

[48] T.J. Bartley, 'Giblin and the Commonwealth Bank' in Copland, *Giblin The Scholar and the Man*, p. 63.

[49] Wilson, *Search*, 7/7, p. 315.

[50] William Coleman, 'Lyndhurst Falkiner Giblin', *The Companion to Tasmanian History*, ed. Alison Alexander, 2007.

[51] J.M. Garland, 'Giblin and John Smith' in Copland, *Giblin The Scholar and the Man*, p. 222.

[52] NLA Oral Transcript 121/38, Keith Archer interviewed by Mel Pratt, 1971.

Canberra', as he 'crouched over a pipe among a litter of papers'. He credited Giblin's wisdom and experience, his human qualities and his professional standing with making the Committee 'not only a cell of economic thought but a place where many departmental and inter-departmental tangles were unwound by honest and straightforward common sense'.[53]

Amid the profusion of tributes to her husband, Eilean faced the fact that his death left her alone in Hobart and inevitably led her to question her future.

---

[53] Paul Hasluck, *The Government and the People*, Vol. I, 1939–1941, Australia in the War of 1939–1945 Series Four Civil, Australian War Memorial, Canberra, 1952, p. 452.

Chapter 10

'My roots are in England'

Australia, England 1951–1955

After her husband's death Eilean Giblin set about collecting letters from people with whom he had corresponded, depositing these in the National Library of Australia and encouraging others to deposit their letters. Douglas Copland also sought letters and published some of those Lyndhurst Giblin had written to his sister, Edith Hall, in the tribute he edited, *Giblin: The Scholar and the Man*.[1] The book consisted of three sections: a series of biographical essays by people who had known him from his days as a student at Cambridge, in the Yukon, at the First World War, as Ritchie Professor of Economics, on the Grants Commission, at the Commonwealth Bank and in the arts; selected writings of Giblin and evaluations of his contribution to economic policy by academics and economists.

Apart from collecting letters, there is no record of Eilean Giblin's reaction to her husband's death. On the surface their marriage appeared a companionable union between two compatible people with a similar outlook on world events who kept themselves well informed on liberal and socialist opinions and ideas. They had common interests ranging from walking and gardening to reading and music. Eilean's diaries confirm the surface impression of a compatible marriage between two people who shared many attitudes and values but who maintained separate interests and lived intertwined but largely separate lives. In their latter years in Canberra an observer noted that Eilean was not usually present at the gatherings Lyndhurst Giblin held at their home. At these exclusively male gatherings, guests listened to music played on the Giblins' EMG gramophone with its

---

[1] Douglas Copland, ed., *Giblin The Scholar and The Man: Papers in Memory of Lyndhurst Falkiner Giblin*, Cheshire, Melbourne, 1960.

huge horn, held earnest discussions, drank port and coffee and ate Giblin's specialty, a very heavy fruitcake which he baked himself.²

When Eilean moved from Canberra to Hobart at the end of 1946 and her husband lived for some years almost entirely in Sydney, their lives were effectively separated. On the surface this appeared to be from necessity. Giblin needed to be in Sydney and Eilean, by then aged over 60, is unlikely to have wanted to add another Australian city to those to which she had already adapted. It could also have been a continuation of the separation that had become apparent even when they occupied the same house in Canberra. In keeping with the enigmatic nature of their marriage, however, surface indications may not be correct.

During the years of separation they maintained an exchange of letters, at least weekly, often more frequently. Only Giblin's letters have been preserved but from this one-sided view it appears that the correspondence, while never emotionally intimate, nevertheless portrayed entwined lives in which they reported in detail on their health, their social activities, their acquaintances and their work. In the style he had adopted since his first letters during the First World War they contained no salutation and no ending apart from his initials. Unlike his letters to Tony Melville they did not end with 'Love'. To one observer the Giblins were 'a fine couple with a narcissistic devotion to each other',³ while to another they appeared to live separate lives.

Late in 1951, Eilean visited England and was away for about a year. After she returned to Australia she helped Sidney Crawford, a South Australian businessman and philanthropist, and chair of the South Australian Harbors Board, who intended writing about Lyndhurst Giblin, to access letters and other material. Crawford had been a friend of Giblin's since they first met at the Brisbane ANZAAS Conference in 1930 when Crawford gave a paper on running his motor trade business to an audience of economists. As Brigden, Copland and Giblin sat listening, he described how business was actually transacted, contrasting this with the logical way academic economists assumed would be the case. Giblin was so taken by Crawford's talk he sat 'convulsed' with 'the tears rolling down his face' and Crawford's close friendship with him remained 'uninterrupted till the end'.⁴

---

2   Peter Bailey, 18 June 2007.
3   Australian diplomat, James Cumes, quoted in Coleman, Cornish and Hagger's *Giblin's Platoon*, p. 19.
4   Sidney Crawford, 'Giblin and profit sharing', in Copland, *Giblin the Scholar and the Man*, p. 197.

The correspondence between Eilean and Sidney Crawford reveals the tension, even resentment, that Edith Hall, who regarded herself as the custodian of her brother's memory, felt towards her sister-in-law. When Sidney Crawford proposed visiting Hobart in 1953, Edith wrote to him, 'By all means go to Eilean first but on no account ask her to be present when we meet. Tactful, thoughtful & considerate – no further. I don't know how much she knows or cares but all the information I can give you is distinctly pre-Eilean.'[5] Eilean tactfully told Sidney Crawford not to tell Edith that she had read the letters that he had lent her after having them typed. 'I think it would be wise not to mention to her that I have them. That depends on what sort of mood she may be in when I next meet her,' she wrote.[6]

In a letter to Sidney Crawford, Eilean Giblin disclosed that she found little to keep her in Australia and would leave for England towards the end of the year. 'It is very difficult to know what to do with ties at either end of the world,' she wrote. 'But my roots are in England & I have no strong ties here now. I am attached to L's neices [sic] and nephews[7] – but they are of another generation & must lead their own lives. They are I can say attached to me.' In the same letter she revealed that she was being treated for high blood pressure which, she believed, accounted for her constant giddiness for which she took tablets prescribed by her Hobart doctor but which only made her feel 'dazed'.[8] By this time, it appears that Parkinson's disease may have been well established but had not yet been diagnosed. Before she left for England she burned the accumulated papers of a lifetime in a bonfire in the backyard including, it may be assumed, her unpublished manuscripts. If her husband had kept the letters she wrote to him, as she had kept his, she burned those as well. Either scenario – her husband not keeping her letters or, alternatively, Eilean's burning of her own letters – indicates the pervasive hierarchy that dictated that men's records were worth keeping but those of women were not.

In February 1954 when Eilean arrived in England her brother Kenneth, who met her at Tilbury, found her very 'dicky'. She 'had a job to walk

---

[5] MS366/5/342, Edith Hall, Littlegrange, Hobart, to Mr Crawford, n.d.
[6] MS366/5/278, The Side, Lynton Avenue, EG to Sidney Crawford, 5 April 1953.
[7] The children of Lyndhurst's brother, Alan, nieces Elaine (Ross), Deidre (Mackinnon) and Audrey (Salter) and nephews, Desmond and Cyril ('Copper') Giblin.
[8] MS366/5/278, 5 April 1953.

down the gangway', he wrote.⁹ Eilean went to live with her elderly aunts, Elizabeth MacRae and Mary MacRae White, at their home, Grey Cottage, Milton Street, near Polegate on the Sussex Downs. 'They are dears & I am much attached to them,' she wrote to her husband's nephew, 'Copper' Giblin, in Hobart.¹⁰ But she was always glad to get away when the routine of life in the MacRae household became more than ordinarily monotonous, or her aunts more testy as they became increasingly deaf, or the house more chilly than ever. Her brother Kenneth often drove down to collect her for a break at Homefield. She visited her niece Sheila Burton in London and drove to churches and cathedrals with her brother Esmond to see his sculptures. She was a guest at the wedding of her brother Clive's daughter, Gillian Burton, when she married Christopher Pole-Carew in April 1954, an occasion for meeting relatives she had not seen for many years. After the wedding she decided to change the English part of her will. She had intended to divide the £300 a year she had been left by her father between her three nieces, Sheila Burton and Nancy Gough, daughters of her brother Colin, and Gillian, daughter of her brother Clive but, after realising how successful Clive was on his citrus farm in South Africa, she decided it would be ridiculous to leave a small sum to Gillian and instead would divide the sum between the other two nieces.¹¹

In England, Eilean was without a car for the first time for many years. From the time when she was among the first women in Hobart to drive regularly, she had never been without a car. Just before the Second World War she changed to a new Morris, the car she drove to Canberra and took adventurously on interstate trips and shipped to Tasmania when possible for Christmas holidays. While in Canberra she drove it on many trips into the country in search of clay before severe petrol rationing made car travel an infrequent luxury. In England she longed to be able to take her aunts for drives but her nerve failed her and she felt 'incompetent', although she missed the independence of a car. When she needed to see a specialist she had to order a hire car.¹² When Kenneth offered to come and drive her to Homefield and back to Sussex she was grateful but distressed that she was considered 'rather a helpless old woman', not able to look after herself.¹³

---

9   Kenneth Burton to Mr and Mrs Desmond Giblin, n.d. [1955], copy with author.
10 EG to 'Copper' Giblin, 7 April 1954, copy with author.
11 EG to 'Copper', 7 April 1954.
12 EG to 'Copper', 14 September 1954.
13 EG to 'Copper', 25 September 1954.

Figure 10.1 Eilean Giblin beside her car, c.1950
(Courtesy Elaine Ross)

From the time Eilean Giblin arrived back in England early in 1954 it became increasingly clear that she would never return to Tasmania. She arrived at this decision gradually and relayed it in a series of letters to 'Copper' Giblin. She gave the cottage at Seven Mile Beach to 'Copper' Giblin and decided to sell off the remaining blocks of land, some of which went to the Giblin family where they formed a buffer around the cottage. She was grateful when 'Copper' told her she could stay at Cobblers End if she wanted to return to Tasmania, but, she wrote, 'I cannot plan far ahead & one drifts as one gets older.'[14] The big decision remained the Giblins' house in Hobart, The Side. Giving it up would be the final break with Australia. Eventually after 'thinking a lot' about her future, Eilean decided to sell the house and contents after the latest tenants left. 'I feel more & more that I am not fit enough to undertake the journey to Tasmania & to settle down alone in the Side,' she wrote.[15] 'I do not see that I can settle there alone – so it had better be sold.' The decision to sell was a bitter one. 'I hate getting rid of it,' she wrote, 'after all we built it in 1925, but did not live in it much until

---

[14] EG to 'Copper', 4 November 1954.
[15] EG to 'Copper', 25 September 1954.

recent years'.¹⁶ When it was sold she wrote, 'I can't realise at times that the little house is no longer mine. We were attached to it.'¹⁷

When Eilean visited a doctor in Eastbourne in February 1955 he told her she had Parkinson's disease. By then writing was becoming difficult and she was unable to 'concentrate on anything'. The doctor explained that the disease was causing her shaky hands and feet and the slowness in her movements.¹⁸ After her death the doctor told her brother Kenneth Burton that the disease had been developing for years and he had suspected she had Parkinson's disease at the time she saw him on her visit to England in 1951.

As Eilean's condition deteriorated it became impossible for her aged aunts (then 88 and 81) to look after her and her brother arranged for her to go to a nursing home at Surbiton, near Kingston-on-Thames. Although she improved mentally and physically and put on weight after becoming extremely thin, she died on 4 October 1955, aged 71, after suffering a stroke from which she did not regain consciousness.

Kenneth described his sister's death as 'a happy release'. Just days before she died her youngest brother, Clive, who was visiting from South Africa, took her for a long drive through parts of the Surrey countryside she had not seen since the First World War forty years before.

Although she left no instructions, the Burton family believed she would have wanted to be cremated. They thought it a great compliment that one of Lyndhurst Giblin's fellow officers from the First AIF, Colonel William C. Ruddock, who was visiting England, represented the Tasmanian 40th Battalion at her cremation at Woking Crematorium.¹⁹

The only public tribute to Eilean Giblin appears to be Eveline Syme's short obituary published in the *University Gazette* in Melbourne in which she acknowledged her work in leading the committee and later the Council of University Women's College :

> During her six years of office she was instrumental in the raising of funds to build the first wing, in its planning, building, and furnishing, and its establishment during the first three years of its existence. Her wisdom, tact and the signal service which she

---

¹⁶ EG to 'Copper', 28 October 1954.
¹⁷ EG to 'Copper', 29 December 1954.
¹⁸ EG to 'Copper', 6 February [1955].
¹⁹ Kenneth Burton to Mr and Mrs Desmond Giblin.

rendered are gratefully remembered by all who worked with her on the first Council of University Women's College.[20]

The obituary was based on Syme's address to the first meeting of the Council after Eilean's death. Her 'Tribute to Mrs L.F. Giblin' was published in the minutes. On a motion of the President, Mrs D. Leggatt, the Council agreed a copy would be placed on the College Notice Board in the following term 'to acquaint students with Mrs Giblin's invaluable work for their college'.[21]

* * *

'We cannot reduce any woman's life to a single story,' the distinguished American librarian Sarah Pritchard said in summing up a conference on 'Revealing Women's Life Stories' at Smith College, the renowned American liberal arts college for women. '[T]he lives and histories of women are central to understanding our individual and collective histories and cultures'.[22]

Women's lives in the earlier part of the twentieth century, in the era between the first wave of suffrage successes and the transformative influences of the second wave of feminism in the second half of the twentieth century, were not a simple story. Many women, despite having similar aspirations to those of a later era, were bound by the assumptions that marriage brought in its train. Although independent in outlook and often with great organising ability, they were also tied to their presumed role as homemakers.

For Eilean Giblin this meant uprooting herself from one country to another, then from one city to another, in each case starting again in finding a role that enabled her to pursue her feminist vision. She lived on the edge of achievement, her work for equal citizenship buried in old records, honoured only in a very reserved way for her work in founding University Women's College and largely unacknowledged during her lifetime as a potter.

Although her life was unique, it was also typical of that of many talented and activist women between the wars. Emancipated to the extent that they had the right to vote and to be elected to parliament, very occasionally considered for public appointments, they were still largely tied by the ethos of the era to

---

[20] *University Gazette*, February/March 1956, p. 10.
[21] Eveline Syme, 'Tribute', UC Archives, 30 November 1955.
[22] Sarah Pritchard, 'Closing Remarks', in *Revealing Women's Life Stories: Papers from the 50th Anniversary Celebration of the Sophia Smith Collection*, Smith College, Northampton, Massachusetts, September 1992, pp. 77–78.

domestic arrangements that limited their consistent involvement in feminist causes and certainly circumscribed their potential employment.

A few achieved fame, some were honoured, but most like Eilean Giblin worked with little recognition for small, incremental but essential feminist advances.

Bibliography

Manuscripts
Burton, Clive Mence, 'Burton family history', [1978] typescript, copy with author.
Burton, Kenneth, letter to Mr and Mrs Desmond Giblin, copy with author.
Burton, Peter, letters Eilean Burton to parents, copies with author.
Gibbney, H.J., Papers, National Library of Australia (NLA) MS3131.
Giblin, Eilean, Diaries, NLA MS366/6/1-2.
Giblin, Eilean, Letters to 'Copper' Giblin, copies with author.
Giblin, L.F., Papers NLA MS366/1-7.
Ingamells Collection, Flinders University Library.
Keighley, F.S., 'Left-wing Liberal: Bertrand Russell in Australia, 1950', ANU thesis, November 1973. NLA MS1648.
Melville, A.E., Papers NLA MS6225.
National Archives of Australia (NAA) World War I records; Migration records.
Rapke, Julia, 'Papers on various Australian women', NLA MS842.
Rischbieth, Bessie, Papers, NLA MS2004.
Royal Melbourne Institute of Technology University (RMIT) Archives.
Rudduck, Loma, Papers NLA MS907.
University College, University of Melbourne, Archives.

Books
Akinson, Diane, *The Suffragettes in Pictures*, Museum of London, Stroud, Glos., 1996.
Alexander, Alison, ed., *The Companion to Tasmanian History*, Centre for Tasmanian Historical Studies, University of Tasmania, Hobart Tas., 2005.
Allen, Alexandra, *Travelling Ladies*, Jupiter, London, 1980.
Australian Dictionary of Biography, Melbourne University Press, Carlton, Vic. [various dates].
Australian Federation of Women's Societies, The Federation, Perth, [1924].
Beauman, Katherine Bentley, *Women and the Settlement Movement*, Radcliffe Press, London, 1996.
Bennett, Daphne, *Emily Davies and the Liberation of Women, 1830–1921*, Andre Deutsch, London, 1990.
Birkett, Dea, *Off the Beaten Track: Three Generations of Women Travelers*, Hardie Grant Books, South Yarra, Vic., 2004.
Blakeskey, Rosalind P., *The Arts and Crafts Movement*, Phaidon Press, London, 2006.
Boulton, James ed., *The Letters of D.H. Lawrence, Vol. I, 1901–1913*, Cambridge University Press, Cambridge, 1979.
Bowerman, Elsie, *Stands There a School: Memories of Dame Frances Dove DBE*, Wycombe Abbey School, High Wycombe, Bucks [1996].
British Commonwealth League, *Women and Oversea Settlement and Some Problems of Government*, Report of the Conference, London, 1926.
Brown, Nicholas, *Richard Downing: Economics, Advocacy and Social Reform in Australia*, Melbourne University Press, Carlton Vic., 2001.

Butler, Roger, *Woodcuts and Linocuts of the 1920s and 1930s*, National Library of Australia, Canberra, ACT, 1981.
Caine, Barbara, *Australian Feminism: A Companion*, Oxford University Press, Melbourne, 1998.
Caine, Barbara, *English Feminism 1780–1980*, Oxford University Press, Oxford, 1997.
Campbell, Margaret ed., *University Women's College: A Record of Events – The First Year*, University College Association, Parkville Vic., 1988.
Cheng, Nien, *Life and Death in Shanghai*, Grove Press, New York, 1986.
Clarke, Patricia, *Tasma: The Life of Jessie Couvreur*, Allen & Unwin, North Sydney, 1994.
Cochrane, Grace, *The Crafts Movement in Australia: A History*, NSW University Press, Kensington NSW, 1992.
Coleman, William, Cornish, Selwyn, Hagger, Alf, *Giblin's Platoon: The Trials and Triumphs of the Economist in Australian Public Life*, ANU E Press, Canberra ACT, 2006.
Coltheart, Lenore, ed., *Jessie Street: A Revised Autobiography*, Federation Press, Annandale NSW, 2004.
Copland, Douglas, ed., *Giblin, The Scholar and the Man: Papers in Memory of Lyndhurst Falkiner Giblin*, Cheshire, Melbourne, 1960.
Cornish, Selwyn, *Sir Roland Wilson: A Biographical Essay*, ANU, Canberra, 2002.
Davis, Richard, *Open to Talent: The Centenary History of the University of Tasmania, 1890–1990*, University of Tasmania, Hobart, 1990.
Deutsch, Regine, *International Woman Suffrage Alliance: Its History from 1904 to 1929*, Alliance Board, London, 1929.
Deutsher, Chris, and Butler, Roger, *A Survey of Australian Relief Prints 1900–1950*, Deutsher Galleries, Armadale, Vic., 1978.
Dow, Hume, ed., *Memories of Melbourne University: Undergraduate Life in the Years since 1917*, Hutchinson, Richmond Vic., 1983.
Eldershaw, M. Barnard, *Plaque with Laurel*, George G. Harrap & Co., London, 1937.
Flint, Lorna, *Wycombe Abbey School 1896–1986: A Partial History*, Wycombe Abbey School, 1989.
Garnett, David, *The Familiar Faces*, Chatto & Windus, London, 1962.
Garnett, David, *The Flowers of the Forest*, Chatto & Windus, London, 1955.
Garnett, David, *The Golden Echo*, Chatto & Windus, London, 1953.
Garnett, Richard, *Constance Garnett: A Heroic Life*, Sinclair-Stevenson, London, 1991.
Gibbney, Jim, *Canberra 1913–1953*, AGPS, Canberra ACT, 1988.
Giblin, L.A., *Tracing my Giblin Ancestors*, Lagpress, Sandy Bay, Tas., 1982.
Giblin, L.F., *The Growth of a Central Bank: The Development of the Commonwealth Bank of Australia 1924–45*, Melbourne University Press, Carlton Vic., 1951.
Giblin, L.F., *The Problem of Maintaining Full Employment*, No. 5 in *Realities of Reconstruction*, Melbourne University Press in association with Oxford University Press, Melbourne, 1943.
Gillman, Mark A., *Envy as a Retarding Force in Science*, Avebury, Aldershot, Hants, 1996.
Green, Frank C., *Servant of the House*, Heinemann, Melbourne, 1969.
Green, Frank C., *The Tasmanian Club 1861–1961*, Tasmanian Club, Hobart Tas., 1961.
Green, Frank C., *The Fortieth: A Record of the 40th Battalion AIF*, 40th Battalion Association, Hobart Tas., 1922.
Harrison, Brian, *Prudent Revolutionaries: Portraits of British Feminists between the Wars*, Clarendon Press, Oxford, 1987.

Hasluck, Paul, *Diplomatic Witness: Australian Foreign Affairs 1941–1947*, Melbourne University Press, Carlton, Vic., 1980.
Hasluck, Paul, *The Government and the People 1939–1941: Australia in the War of 1939–1945*, Vol. 1, Australian War Memorial, Canberra ACT, 1951.
Havighurst, Alfred F., *Radical Journalist: H.W. Massingham 1860–1924*, Cambridge University Press, London, 1974.
Heath, E.M., *Thirty Paintings, with a Foreword by Edward Garnett*, Jonathon Cape, London, 1935.
Heaton, Herbert, *Economic History of Europe*, Harper & Bros, London, 1936.
Holden, Colin, *The Outsider: A Portrait of Ursula Hoff*, Australian Scholarly Publishing, North Melbourne, 2009.
Hood, Kenneth, *The Arts in Australia: Pottery*, Longmans, Melbourne, 1961.
Hyams, Edward, *The New Statesman: The History of the First Forty Years 1913–1963*, Longmans, London, 1963.
Isaacs, Victor, *How We Got the News: Newspaper Distribution in Australia and New Zealand*, Australian Newspaper History Group, Brisbane, 2008.
Jefferies, Richard, *Bevis*, intro. Herbert Strang, Oxford University Press, London, 1939.
Jefferson, George, *Edward Garnett: A Life in Literature*, Jonathon Cape, London, 1982.
Jerome, Jerome K., *Three Men in a Boat (To Say Nothing of the Dog)*, J.W. Arrowsmith, Bristol, 1889.
Kennedy, Thomas C., *The Hound of Conscience: A History of the No Conscription Fellowship 1914–1919*, University of Arkansas Press, Fayetville, 1981.
Kent, Jacqueline, *A Certain Style: Beatrice Davis a Literary Life*, Viking, Richmond Vic., 2001.
Koestler, Arthur, *The Case of the Midwife Toad*, Hutchinson, London, 1971.
Lake, Marilyn, *Getting Equal: The History of Australian Feminism*, Allen & Unwin, St Leonards NSW, 1999.
Lake, Marilyn, *A Divided Society: Tasmania during World War I*, Melbourne University Press, Carlton Vic., 1975.
Leach, Bernard, *A Potter's Book*, Faber, London, 1948 (first published 1940).
Lothian, E. I. and Syme, Eveline, *University Women's College, University of Melbourne: A Brief History*, The College, Parkville Vic., 1954.
McArthur, Milford, *Prominent Tasmanians*, G. J. Boyle, Hobart, 1924.
MacKenzie, Norman and Jean, *The First Fabians*, Weidenfeld and Nicholson, London, 1917.
McKernan, Michael, *All In! Australia during the Second World War*, Thomas Nelson, Melbourne, 1983.
McMullin, Ross, *The Light on the Hill: The Australian Labor Party 1891–1991*, Oxford University Press, South Melbourne, 1991.
McNeill, Barry and Woolley, Leigh, *Architecture from the Edge*, Montpelier Press, North Hobart Tas., 2002.
Melbourne Technical College, *Art Prospectus*, 1939, 1940.
Merrylees, Caroline, comp., *Haywire: The War-time Camps at Hay*, Hay Historical Society, Hay NSW, 2006.
Palmer, Sheridan, *Centre of the Periphery: Three European Art Historians in Melbourne*, Australian Scholarly Publishing, North Melbourne, 2008.
Pearl, Cyril, *The Dunera Scandal: Deported by Mistake*, Angus & Robertson, Sydney, 1983.
Penton, Brian, *Advance Australia – Where?*, Cassell and Co., London, 1943.

Queensland Parks and Wildlife Service, *Moorrinya National Park Management Plan*, Queensland Department of Environment, Brisbane, 1998.
Phillips, Ray (Mrs M.M. Phillips), *The White Feather*, Melville & Mullen, Melbourne, 1917.
Poynter, John and Rasmussen, Carolyn, *A Place Apart. The University of Melbourne: Decades of Challenge*, Melbourne University Press, Carlton Vic., 1996.
Public Hospital Hobart, *Annual Report*, 1924–25; 1925–26.
Pugh's Queensland Almanac, 1904.
Raeburn, Antonia, *The Militant Suffragettes*, Michael Joseph, London 1973.
Revealing women's life stories. Papers of the 50th anniversary celebration of Sophia Smith Collection, Smith College, Northampton, Mass, September 1992.
Rischbieth, Bessie, *March of Australian Women: A Record of Fifty Years' Struggle for Equal Citizenship*, Paterson, Brokensha, Perth WA, 1964.
Robson, Lloyd, *A Short History of Tasmania*, updated by Michael Roe, Oxford University Press, Melbourne, 1985.
Roland, Betty, *The Eye of the Beholder*, Hale & Iremonger, Sydney, 1984.
Royal Commission on Child Endowment or Family Allowances, *Minutes of Evidence*, Government Printer, Canberra, 1928–29.
Royal Commission on Child Endowment or Family Allowances, *Report of the Royal Commission on Child Endowment*, Government Printer, Canberra, 1929.
Selleck, R.J.W., *The Shop: The University of Melbourne 1850–1939*, Melbourne University Press, Carlton Vic., 2003.
[Shaw, Flora], *Letters from Queensland*, Macmillan, London, 1893.
Shone, Richard, *Bloomsbury Portraits: Vanessa Bell, Duncan Grant and their Circle*, Phaidon Press, London, 1976.
Spalding, Frances, *Duncan Grant*, Chatto & Windus, London, 1997.
Stephens, Jennifer, *The Peckham Settlement 1896–2000*, Stephens Press, Bickton, Hants, 2002.
Stephenson, Freda, *Capital Women: A History of the National Council of Women 1939–1979, NCW (ACT)*, National Council of Women, Canberra, 1982.
Strahan, Lachlan, *Australia's China: Changing Perceptions from the 1930s to the 1990s*, Cambridge University Press, Cambridge, 1996.
Torrens Creek State School Centenary 1891–1991, Torrens Creek State School, Torrens Creek Qld, 1991.
United Kingdom, Board of Education, *Report of First Inspection of Wycombe Abbey School, High Wycombe, Buckinghamshire, 3–5 June 1908*.
University Women's College, *First Annual Report*, 1937; Annual Reports 1939–57.
Victoria Government Gazette, 1936.
Walch's Tasmanian Almanac, 1925.
Ward-Jackson, Philip, *Public Sculpture of the City of London*, Liverpool University Press, Liverpool, 2003.
Wetherell, David and Carr-Gregg, C., *Camilla*, New South Wales University Press, Kensington, NSW, 1990.
Wood, Alan, *Bertrand Russell: The Passionate Skeptic*, George Allen & Unwin, London, 1957.
Woolf, Virginia, *A Room of One's Own*, Penguin, Camberwell Vic., 2009.
Woollocott, Angela, *On Her Their Lives Depend: Munitions Workers in the Great War*, University of California Press, Berkeley, 1994.
Wren, Denise K. and Wren, Rosemary D., *Pottery Making: Making Pots and Building and Firing Small Kilns*, Pitman, London, 1952.

Articles

Anderson, Jaynie, 'Obituary – Ursula Hoff (1909–2005)', *Symposium*, No. 30, July 2005.
Bartley, T.J., 'Giblin and the Commonwealth Bank' in Copland, Douglas, ed., *Giblin, The Scholar and the Man: Papers in Memory of Lyndhurst Falkiner Giblin*, Cheshire, Melbourne, 1960.
Bashford, Sir Henry, 'The Sculpture of Esmond Burton', *Country Life*, 27 January 1950.
Camsell, Charles, 'Giblin in North British Columbia 1898–99', in Copland, Douglas, ed., *Giblin, The Scholar and the Man: Papers in Memory of Lyndhurst Falkiner Giblin*, Cheshire, Melbourne, 1960.
Clarke, Patricia, 'Canberra in the 1930s: A fictional look at the National Capital', *Canberra Historical Journal*, May 2012, pp. 15–22.
Clarke, Patricia, 'Colonial connections with the *London Times*: Flora Shaw', *Canberra Historical Journal*, September 2004, pp. 22–27.
Clarke, Patricia, 'The Queensland Shearers' Strikes in Rosa Praed's Fiction', *Queensland Review*, May 2002.
Clarke, Patricia, 'Tillyard, Pattie (1880–1971)', *Australian Dictionary of Biography*, Vol. 12, MUP, 1990.
Coleman, William, 'Lyndhurst Falkiner Giblin', *The Companion to Tasmanian History*, ed. Alison Alexander, University of Tasmania, 2007.
Crawford, Sidney, 'Giblin and Profit Sharing', in Copland, Douglas, ed., *Giblin, The Scholar and the Man: Papers in Memory of Lyndhurst Falkiner Giblin*, Cheshire, Melbourne, 1960.
Dever, Maryanne, 'The Case for Flora Eldershaw', *Hecate*, Vol. XV, No. 2, 1989, p. 40.
Dollery, E.M., 'Giblin, William Robert (1840–1887)', *Australian Dictionary of Biography*, Vol. 4, Melbourne University Press, Carlton Vic., 1972.
Dove, Frances, 'The Modern Girl: How Far are We Fitting Her for Her Varied Duties in Life?' Paper read to The Association of Head Mistresses, June 1907, *Wycombe Abbey Gazette*, Vol. III, No. 9, November 1907.
Dyason, Anne, 'It Might Happen to Anyone', *Austral-Asiatic Bulletin*, June–July 1941.
Dyason, Anne, 'The Private Persistence of Man', *Austral-Asiatic Bulletin*, April–May 1941; August–September 1941.
Dyason, Anne, 'Wanted – A Minister', *Austral-Asiatic Bulletin*, June–July 1941.
Forster, Ian, 'From the Archives: The Letters of Edna Walling', *Frappe Fort*, February 2010.
Garland, J.M., 'Giblin and John Smith' in Copland, Douglas, ed., *Giblin, The Scholar and the Man: Papers in Memory of Lyndhurst Falkiner Giblin*, Cheshire, Melbourne, 1960.
Giblin, E.M., 'Tasmania: News of the Women's Movement', *International Woman Suffrage News*, July 1923.
Giblin, L.F., 'John Maynard Keynes', *Economic Record*, Vol. XXII, June 1946.
Giblin, L. F., 'Port Davey in Wartime' in Copland, Douglas, ed., *Giblin, The Scholar and the Man: Papers in Memory of Lyndhurst Falkiner Giblin*, Cheshire, Melbourne, 1960.
Giblin, L.F., 'Reconstruction in Australia', *Agenda*, 1943.
Giblin, L.F., 'Reconstruction in Australia: A Pisagh View', *Australian Quarterly*, September 1943.
Green, F.C., 'Giblin in Politics and War', in Copland, Douglas, ed., *Giblin, The Scholar and the Man: Papers in Memory of Lyndhurst Falkiner Giblin*, Cheshire, Melbourne, 1960.
Green, F.C., 'Lyndhurst Falkiner Giblin', *Stand-to*, August–September 1952.

Gregory, Alan, 'Getting the College on the Ground: Background to the Establishment of a Non-denominational Residential College for Women', in *University Women's College: A Record of Events – The First Year*, ed. Margaret Campbell, University College Association, Parkville, Vic., 1988, pp. 4–13.
Hoff, Ursula, 'Hort, Greta (1905–1967)', *Australian Dictionary of Biography*, Vol. 14, Melbourne University Press, Carlton Vic., 1996.
Marshall, Gerard, 'Obituary, Eric Stadlen', *Independent*, 23 January 1995.
Martin, John Stanley, 'Greta Hort: Scholar and Educationist', *Nordic News*, Centre for Scandiavian Studies, Vol. 8, 2004.
Melville, A E., 'Giblin and the Arts', in Copland, Douglas, ed., *Giblin, The Scholar and the Man: Papers in Memory of Lyndhurst Falkiner Giblin*, Cheshire, Melbourne, 1960.
Moore, Alison, 'Feetham, John Oliver (1873–1947)', *Australian Dictionary of Biography*, Vol. 8, Melbourne University Press, Carlton Vic., 1981.
Northcott, Bayan, 'Obituary – Peter Stadler', *Independent*, 23 January 1996.
Parsons, Jonathan, 'Aboriginal Motifs in Design: Frances Derham and the Arts and Crafts Society of Victoria', *La Trobe Library Journal*, Vol. 11, No. 43, Autumn 1989.
Petrow, Stefan, 'Boiling over: Edith Waterworth and Criminal Law Reform in Tasmania 1912–1925', *Tasmanian Historical Studies*, 4.2, 1994.
Public Hospital Hobart Annual Report, 1924–1929.
Reynolds, John, 'L.F. Giblin: A Plea for an Adequate Biography', Ingamells Collection, Flinders University Library.
Rudduck, Loma, 'A Short Story About a Long Time Ago 1943–1988,' *Canberra Historical Journal*, March 1989, pp. 8–15.
Smart, 'James, Elizabeth Britomarte (1867–1943)', *Australian Dictionary of Biography*, Supplementary Volume, Melbourne University Press, Carlton Vic., 2005.
Stadlen, Peter, 'Obituary, Dr R. Vaughan Williams', London *Times*, 5 September 1958.
Stent, Roland, 'Obituary – Peter Stadlen', *Independent*, 27 January 1996.
Syme, Eveline, 'Women and Art', *Centenary Gift Book*, eds Frances Fraser and Nettie Palmer, Women's Centenary Council/Robertson & Mullens, Melbourne Vic., 1934.
White, Kate, 'Bessie Rischbieth: The Feminist', in *Westralian Portraits*, ed. Lyall Hunt, UWA Press, Nedlands WA, 1979.
Wilson, Sir Roland, 'L.F. Giblin: A Man for all Seasons', Giblin Memorial Lecture, 47th ANZAAS Congress, 12 May 1976, Hobart, Tasmania, pp. 1–39; also *Search*, Vol.7 No.7, pp. 307–315.
'Victorian Government's New Tourist Bureau: Distinctive Australian Motifs the Keynote of the Architectural Treatment', *Decoration and Glass*, February 1940.
Wyllie, Freeman, 'The Community Spirit – Social Service Idealism in Canberra 1925–1929', *Canberra Historical Journal*, September 1997, pp. 7–17.

Internet sources

Betty Churcher, *Hidden treasures*, 'Linocuts of Black, Syme & Spowers', video clip, 2008.
John Stanley Martin, 'Greta Hort: Scholar and educationalist', *Nordic Notes*, Vol. 8, 2004, http:diemperdidi.info.nordicnotes.
Queensland Parks and Wildlife Service, *Moorinya National Park*, Department of Environment, Brisbane, 1998, http://www.qld.gov.au/parks_and_forests/find_a_park_or_forest/moorinya.
Queensland Racing, Oakley Amateur Picnic Race Club, http://www.queensland.com.au/raceclubs/show.asp?id+52792.

Journals and newspapers
Advertiser, Adelaide
Age, Melbourne
Agenda
Argus, Melbourne
Austral-Asiatic Bulletin
Australian Quarterly
Canberra Times
Daily News, Perth
Daily Telegraph, Sydney
Dawn, Perth
Decoration and Glass
Frappe Fort
Independent, London
International Woman Suffrage News
Jargon
Katoomba News (shipboard)
La Trobe Library Journal
London Gazette
Mercury, Hobart
Nation
Overseas: The Monthly Journal of the Overseas Club and Patriotic League.
Queensland Review
Recorder
Search
Sunday Times, Perth
Symposium
Times, London
Tribunal
University Gazette, Melbourne
Victoria Government Gazette
Votes for Women

Index

Page numbers in bold indicate illustrations.

Aberfoyle, 30, 33
Aboriginal motifs, 100, 133, 198
Absent Without Leave (AWL), ix, 52
Acton, ACT, 129, 130, 139
aeroplane crash (1940), 104
Agar, Professor Wilfred, 161, 163
air raid trenches, 151, 166
air raids
    Australia, 145–6, 149, 166
    England, 2, 34, 107, 108, 115, 141
Air Raids Precautions (ARP), ix, 150, 151
Albury, NSW, 124, 143, 146, 157
Alexander, Joe, 76, 110
Alfriston, 49, 69
    see also Polegate
All Quiet on the Western Front, 72
Allen, Dr Eleanor, 59
Allen, Mary Cecil, 86
Angell, Dr Herbert, 134–5, 137, 140
Angell, Kate, 134, 137, 140, 150
Angus & Robertson, 143, 144, 173, 174
Anschluss, 115
ANZAAS, ix
    1930 Conference, 186
    47th Congress, xviii, 52, 55, 198
Anzac Day, 141
Apostles, 39
Archer, Keith, 183
Argus, Melbourne, 86, 87, 88, 90, 91, 115, 179, 198
Argyle, Sir Stanley, 80, 83
Armentières, 36, 41
Arnold, Dr Thomas, 5
Art Workers' Guild, 11–12
arts and crafts movement, xxi, 11–12, 20, 67, 99, 193
Arts and Crafts Society, 86, 100, 136, 139, 198
Arts and Crafts Society Gallery, 86, 136
Ashmolean Museum, 159
Asquith, Herbert, 14
Atlee, Clement, 9
Austral-Asiatic Bulletin, 112, 197, 198

Australian Army
    see Australian Imperial Force (AIF)
Australian Federation of Women's Societies for Equal Citizenship, 58, 61, 193
    First Triennial Conference (1924), 61
    Second Triennial Conference (1927), 63–4
Australian Federation of Women Voters, 58, 63, 74, 76, 81, 105
    see also Australian Federation of Women's Societies for Equal Citizenship
Australian Imperial Force (AIF), ix, 28, 53, 104, 190
    40th Battalion (1st AIF), xv, 28, 36, 38, 44, 45, **46**, 47–9, 50, 51, 52, 73, 190, 194
    2/30th Battalion (2nd AIF), 150
    8th Division (2nd AIF), 140, 149, 150
Australian Institute of International Affairs, 112, 178, 179
Australian Intelligence Corps, 28
Australian Jewish Welfare Society, 119
Australian Labor Party, ix, xiii, 25, 53, 65, 73, 74, 76, 77, 104, 110, 113, 195
    Federal conference (1912), 25
    Federal conference (1919), 53
    Federal Labor governments, 143, 170, 179, 180
    Non-Communist, 113
    Tasmania, 24, 25, 26, 34, 52, 62, 63
    Women's Organising Committee, 83
Australian National University, ix, 140, 152, 161
Australian Parliament, 64, 103, 104, 107, 110, 143, 170, 171, 179, 180, 191
    House of Representatives, xx, 65, 73, 142, 170
    Senate, xx, 170
    see also Provisional Parliament House
Australian Pre-School Association, 139–40
Australian Society of Psychology and Philosophy, 162

The Australian Tariff: An Economic Enquiry, 73
Australian War Memorial, 46, 131, 184, 195
   architecture, 104, 109
   Hall of Memory, 127
   purpose, 109
Australian Women's National League, 83

Bage, Freda, 88
Bailey, Sir Kenneth, 88, 111, 137, 138
Bailey, Peter, viii, 139, 186
Bailey, Yseult (Lady), 137, **138**–40, 174
Balfour, Arthur, 40
Baracchi, Gilda, **181**
Baracchi, Guido, 181
Barcaldine, Qld, 33
Barcoo, Qld, 30
Barnard, Marjorie, 93, 104, 148
Barnett, Canon Samuel, 9
Barrett, Sir James, 90, 95
Barry, William P. (Bill), 82, 83, 87
Bartley, T. J. (James), 183, 197
Barton, ACT, 76, 148
Bateson, William, 160
Bean, Charles, 50
Beasley, John Albert (Jack), 113
Beddington Lane, 3
de Beer, Dora, 99
Belfast Cathedral, 177
Bell, Angelica, 22, 98
Bell, Gertrude, 20
Bell, Vanessa, xxi, 12, 22, 42, 43, 48, 98, 196
Bennett, Mrs Emily, 59
Bennett, General Gordon, 150
Benghazi, 142
Berrima, HMAT, 36
Beveridge, Sir William, 9, 168
Bevis, 26, 195
Birmingham, UK, 46
Bishop, Isabella Bird, 20
Bismarck Sea, Battle of, 166
Black, Clementine, 13
Black, Constance
   see Garnett, Constance,
Black, Dorrit, 99, 198
'Black Friday', UK, xii, 14, 16
blackout, 150
   see also brownout
Blitz, England, 107, 141
Bloomsbury, London, 12,
Bloomsbury Group, xiii, xxi, 12–13, 20, 22, 26, 38, 42, 43, 48, 91, 98, 196
Boar's Head Shag, 2
boating, 1, 3–4, 7
Boer War, 11, 12
Borneo, 146
Botanic Gardens, Melbourne, 71, 72
Bourke, Pte John Thomas (Jack), 44

Bowden, Phillip and Margot, 159
Bowie, Gavin, **181**
Boyd, Biddy Compton, vii
Boyd, Merric, 126–7
Brailsford, H. N., 39
Bray-sur-Somme, 49, 51
Brest, 149
Brigden, James B., 56, 73, 100, 102, 186
Brighton, Tas., 124, 165
Britannia, 11
British Broadcasting Corporation (BBC), ix, 123,179
British Commonwealth League, 59, 64, 193
British Labour Party, 20
British Medical Association, 63
British Museum, 13, 22
Broodseinde Ridge, 44
Brookwood Military Cemetery, 177
Broome, WA, 145
Brown, Nicholas, xvi, 193
Browne, J.T., 102
brownout, 166
Bruce, S. M., 73
Bruce-Page Government, 64, 73
Buna, 158
Bungendore, NSW, 128, 129, 136
Burma, 111, 147, 153
Burnell, Eliza, 63
Burton, Ada Maude, xii, 1, 3–4, 5, 17–18, **20**, 29, 31, 34, 48, 68, 69, 176
Burton, Alfred, 1–3
Burton, Alfreda Mary, 66
Burton, Clive Mence, 4, 12–13, **20**, 66, 69, 177, 188, 190
   as family historian, vii, 1, 12–13, 17, 18, 19, 190
Burton, Brigadier Colin CBE, DSO, vii, 4, 5, 11, **20**, 66, 176, 188
Burton, Edward Pritchard, xi, 1, 3–11, 17, 18, 19, **20**, 31, 32, 48, 52, 66, 111, 188
Burton, Eilean Mary
   see Giblin, Eilean Mary
Burton, Esmond, 4, 5, 11–12, **20**, 48, 52, 66, 176, 177, 188, 197
Burton, Frank, 3, 11, 66
Burton, Geoffrey Edward, 4, 11, **20**, 66
Burton, Gillian
   see Pole-Carew, Gillian
Burton, Gladys Astley, **20**, 66
Burton, Guy, 11
Burton, Kenneth, 4, 5, 11, 19, **20**, 27, 45, 48, 66, 69, 176, 187, 188, 190, 193
Burton, Lovick, 66
Burton, Nancy,
   see Gough, Nancy
Burton, Peter, vii, 29, 69, 101, 193
Burton, Phyllis, 69

Burton, Sheila, 66, 188
Bush Christmas, 180

Cairns, Qld, 29, 30
Calvert, Frances Elizabeth (Betty), 150
Calvert, Dr Joseph (Pat), 150
Camberwell, London, 9,
Cambridge Magazine, 38
Cambridge University, 7, 22, 23, 24, 26, 27, 38–9, 40, 43, 72, 86, 98, 182, 185
    see also Girton College; King's College; Newnham College
Camden, London, 11, 42
Canada, 21, 24, 26, 45, 51, 94
    see also Royal Commission on Dominion/Provincial Relations
Canberra
    accommodation, xiv, xviii, 101–2, 103, 131
    buildings, 103–4, 128,133–4
    as capital, xiv, xvi, 73, 103, 104, 105–6, 106–7, 108, **110**, 148, 168, 170, 173, 196, 197
    culture, 105, 126, 130, 134, 135, 178
    diplomatic presence, 168–9
    gender divide, xiv, 113
    government services, 103, 107, 126, 127, 128
    history, xv, xvi, xxi, 76–7, 106, 134, 148, 194, 196, 198
    public servants, 128, 131, 142, 148, 149, 157
    isolation, 73, 101, 104, 108, 125, 128
    natural environment, xviii, 73, 101, 104, 107–8, 109
    in Second World War, xv, 100, 105, 106, 129, 136, 146–7, 149–51, 153, 154, 166, 168, 170–1, 175, 184–5
    silence, 108, 125
    society, xv–xvi, 76–7, 105–6, 112–13, 115, 116, 157–8, 168, 169, 185–6
    women, xiv, 105–6, 112, 113, 116–17, 118, 127, 135, 139–40, 148, 152, 196, 198
Canberra Brickworks, 134
'Canberra Calling', 143–4, 173
Canberra Community Hospital, 101, 106, 129, 140
Canberra Girls' Grammar School, 113, 152, 168
Canberra Grammar School, 118, 150, 182
Canberra Mothercraft Society, 105, 106
Canberra Nursery Kindergarten Society, 139
    see also Australian Pre-School Association
Canberra Times, xiv, 111, 112, 119, 169
Canberra University College, 105
Capital Hill, ACT, 73, 109, 131
Captain's Flat, NSW, 128, 129, 130
Carlton, Vic., 81, 82, 83, 163, 164

Carlton Cricket Club, 80, 83, 87
Carlton Land Bill, 83
Carnegie Institute, 85
Carrodus, J. A., 132
The Case of the Midwife Toad, 160, 161, 163–4, 195
Castieau, Mrs, 151
Catalysts, 160
Catherine Helen Spence scholarship, 59
'Cearne', 22–3, 35, 41, 42, 45, 50–1
censorship
    see wartime censorship
Centaur, 166
Chamberlain, Neville, 99
Chaplin, Charlie, 2
Charleston, East Sussex, 42, 43, 48, 98
Chekhov, Anton, 22
Chiang Kai-shek, General, 112
Chiang Kai-shek, Madame, 172
Chifley, J.B. (Ben), 157, 180
Chifley Labor Government, 179, 180
child endowment, xx, 57, 64–6, 196
    see also Royal Commission on Child Endowment
Child Welfare Association, Tas., 56
Children's care committee, 10, 11
Children's Court magistrates, Tas., 58
China, 196
    Communist, 169
    Nationalist, 112, 169
Chinese Cultural Revolution, 169
The Choice Before Us, 38,
Chungking, 112
Churchill, Winston, xii, 14, 16, 164
Clapham, Elizabeth, Cr, 59
Clapham, Sir John, 43
clay
    see pottery
Clemens, Lady, 113, 150
Clemens, Lt P. C., 150
Clemens, Sir William, 113
Clermont, Qld, 33
Cloister House, 7
'Cobblers End', 27, 36, 38, 124, 145, 164, 189
    see also Seven Mile Beach
Coles, Arthur, 143
collegiate life, 82, 91
    see also University Women's College
Cologne, 155
Comforts Cottage, 41
Commerce Graduates' Association, 174
Commission of Inquiry (Darwin), 146
Commonwealth Bank, xix, 100, 101, 113, 133
    Central bank history, 175, 177–8, 180, 183, 194
Commonwealth Bank Board, 100, 101, 113, 132–3, 185, 197

Commonwealth Bureau of Census and
    Statistics, 54
Commonwealth Court of Conciliation and
    Arbitration, 175
Commonwealth Film Unit, 122
Commonwealth Franchise Act, 57
Commonwealth Grants Commission, 100,
    185
Commonwealth Literary Fund, 149, 169
Conrad, Joseph, 22
conscientious objectors, 28, 42–3, 98
conscription, 38, 39, 42–3, 55
    Australia, 39, 55
    Britain, 38
    see also No Conscription Fellowship
Copenhagen, 161
Coombs, Dr H.C. (Nugget), 100, 105, 150
Coombs, Mary Alice, 105, 128, 135
Copland, Douglas B., 22, 26, 28, 41, 54, 56,
    73
Coral Sea, Battle of, 153, 156
cosmetics, xviii, 154, 155
Cotter River, ACT, 128
Country Women's Association, 83
Cowling, Mrs Muriel, 85, 87
Crane, Stephen, 22
Crawford, Professor R. M. (Max), 95, **96**
Crawford, Sidney, 186–7, 197
Crete, 141
Crockham Hill, 23
Croydon, Surrey, 3, 30
Cunningham, Una, 135
Curtin, John, 65, 168, 170, **171**, 181
Curtin Labor governments, 113, 143, 170
Cusacks' store, 150

Daily Telegraph, London, 45,123
Dalton, Sir Llewellyn, 117
Darling, James, 182
Darmstadt Summer School, 123
Darwin, NT, 145, 146, 149, 150, 166
Davey, Constance, 59
Davies, Emily, 91, 193
Dawn, The, 58, 60, 62, 63, 64, 74, 76, 77, 199
Defence, Department of, 103, 148
Defence of the Realm Act (DORA), ix, 40,
    45–6
Denison electorate, Tas., 24, 58
Dennis, Mary, 2
Derby, WA, 145
Derham, Enid, 95
Derham, Frances, 100, 198
Derham, Rosemary, 94
Derwent River, Hobart, 124
desert uplands, Qld, 30, 32
deserted wives, 62, 64, 65
Dickinson, G. Lowes, 26, 38–9, 43

Disarmament Conference, 1932, 77
Dobell, William, xvii, 174
Dostoevsky, Fyodor, 22
'Dostoevsky Corner', 23
double moral standard
    between sexes, 57
    in war, xxi, 166
Dove, Dame Frances, 5–7, 9–10, 193, 197
Downing, Richard, xvi, 129, 136, 157, 193
drought, 31, 32, 34
Dunbabin, Professor R.L., 56
Duncan, Constance, 118
Dunera, HMT, xvii, 103, 114–24, 161,
    169–70, 195
    see also enemy aliens
Dunkirk, 107, 141
Duntroon, ACT, 108
Dutch Church, London, 177
Dutch East Indies, 145, 147, 149
Dyason, Anne, 111–12, 197
Dyason, Diana, 94, 162
Dyason, Edward C., 73, 112, 178
Dyason Trust, 178, 180

Eagle House Boys' School, 3
East Clandon Church, 12
East Molesey, 1, 3–4, 20, 37, 48
    see also 'Homefield'
Eastern Front, 146
Edenbridge, Kent, 13, 22, 41, 45
Edinburgh School of Art, 6
Edwards, Frances, 58, 63
Edwards, Mrs, 118, 150, 170
Edwards, Canon W. J., 118, 182
Eilean Donan, 3
Eldershaw, Flora, 93, 104, 148–9, 194, 197
Eldershaw, M. Barnard, 93, 104, 148, 194
Eliot, T. S., 43
Elliott, Alice Gordon, 63
Ellis, Dr Constance, 83, 95
Eltham, Vic., 180, 181
Empire Circuit, Canberra, 77, 102, 103, 112,
    126, 130, 131
enemy aliens, 115–17, 119, 161
    see also Dunera
England, xv, xxi, 22, 23, 27, 59, 98, 176–7,
    185, 187–90
    female suffrage, xiii, 21, 60
    in First World War, 2, 36–7, 39, 45–6,
        47, 52, 53
    in Second World War, 114, 115–16, 119
Epstein, Jacob, 134
equal citizenship, xi, xix-x, 57, 58, 61, 63, 68,
    106, 191, 196
equal educational opportunities, 106
equal moral standard, 57
equal pay, 57, 61–2

eugenics, 64–5
Evans, Ivor, 65
evolution, 153, 160
    see also Kammerer, Paul; Lamarkian theory
External Affairs, Department of, 105, 113, 152

Fabian Society, xxi, 12, 13, 20, 22, 26
Fadden, Arthur, 142, 143
Fairbairn, James, 104
Fairbairn aerodrome, ACT, 153
Falk, Rabbi L.A., 119
family allowances
    see child endowment
Federal Capital Commission, 105–6
Federal elections, 109, 179
Feetham, Bishop John Oliver, 29
Fellowship of Australian Writers, 148–9
female suffrage
    see woman suffrage
feminism, xxi, 57, 58, 91, 191, 194, 195
feminist goals, xv, xix, xx, xxi, 56, 68, 70
fifth column, 114–15, 119
Financial and Economic Committee, 100, 148, 175, 183–4
Finton, Maria Lacerta, 159, 160, 161, 163–4
Finton, Paul Jacques, 161
first wave feminism, xv, xxi, 191
First World War, xv, xxi, 2, 11, 25, 28, 33–4, 36, 38, 66, 103, 104, 144, 175, 177, 190
    see also Australian Imperial Force, 40th Battalion; Western Front
Fison, Miss, 14–16
flax industry, 135
Flight, Claude, 99
For Valour medal, 14, 16
force feeding, 13, **15**, 17, 21, 60
    see also hunger strikers
Ford, Ford Madox, 22
Forrest, ACT, 73, 77, 78, 101, 103, 126, 129, 131
Forster, E.M., 26, 43
Foulis, Jane, 6
Frankl, Erich, 122
Frederickson, Mrs, 170
Froghole, 23, 35
Frohlich, Ernst, 120
Fry, Roger, 43

Gallipoli, 141
Galsworthy, John, 22
Garden City ideas, 67
Garland, J.M., 183, 197
Garnett, Arthur, 22, 23, 27, 36, 38
Garnett, Constance, 13, 22–3, 41, 42, 50–1, 98, 194

Garnett, David (Bunny), 22, 23, 26, 42–3, 48–9. 98, 99, 114, 194
Garnett, Edward, 13, 22–3, 35, 41–2, 43, 51, 98, 114, 195
Garnett, Ray, 98
Garnett, Dr Richard, 22
Gauss, Clarence E., 113, 146
Geelong Grammar School, 182
Gemas, 150
George, Stella, 59
Gibbney H.J. (Jim), xvi, 34, 107, 131, 193, 194
Giblin: The Scholar and the Man, 25, 28, 41, 182, 183, 185, 186, 194, 197, 198
Giblin, Alan, 187
Giblin, Cyril ('Copper'), vii, 67, 176, 187, 188, 189, 190, 193
Giblin, Desmond, 27, 187, 188, 190, 193
Giblin, Edith
    see Hall, Edith
Giblin, Eileen Mary
    and arts and crafts movement, xxi, 12, 20, 67–8, 72, 86, 99, 100, 136, 139
    attitude to war, xiv, xv, xvi, xxi, 38–9, 47–8, 108, 116, 124, 126, 140, 142, 147, 149–50, 151, 153–4, 155–6, 158, 164–5, 166–7, 173, 174
    birth, 1, 4
    and Bloomsbury Group, xxi, 20, 91
    and British Commonwealth League, 64
    and Burton family, xii–xiii, 1–2, 19, **20**, 66–7, 68, 101, 176–7, 187–8, 190–1
    and Canberra society, xiv, xxi, 76–7, 78, 102, 103–5, 106–13, 131–2, 142–3, 157,168–72
    car driver, xiii, xix, 73, 103, 119, 124, 128–9, 131, 139, 158, 188, **189**
    and carpentry, 7, **10**, 130, 133
    character, xiii-iv, xvii, xviii, 11, 19, 27, 56, 72, 81, 91, 151, 154, 169–70, 171–2
    and Constance Garnett, 13, 50–1
    cook, xviii, 33, 34
    death, 190, 191
    derivation of name, 3
    diarist, vii, xv-xviii, xx, xxi, 34, 66, 106, 107–13, 118, 121, 123, 126, 141–2, 143–4, 145–6, 149, 155, 172–4, 185, 193
    dress, 27, 60, 94
    and *Dunera,* xvi-xvii, xix-xx, 114–24
    education, 5–8, **9, 10**
    and equal citizenship, xix-x, 57–9, 62–3, 68, 106, 191
    feminist, xv, xx, xix, xxi, 56–7, 59, 64, 68–9, 70, 74, 75, 78, 80, 81–2, 91, 172, 191
    and Hobart society, xiii, xix, 53, 55–7, 63

hospital board member, xx, 63, 68–9
illness, 50, 68, 69–70, 73, 78, 139, 172, 174–5, 175–6, 178,187–8, 190
and International Woman Suffrage Alliance, ii, 55, 58, **59**, 60–1, **62**, 63, 144, 168
and League of Nations, 64, 70, 77, 118
letter-writer, vii, xiii, xvii, 29, 30, 31–4, 36, 37, 47, 70, 75–6, 82, 84, 87–8, 90, 97, 172, 178, 186, 187, 189
marriage, xiii, xv, xvi, xvii, xviii, xix, xxi, 13, 26–7, 36–8, 45, 48, 49, 53, 70, 185–6, 191
and nationality of married women, xx, 61–2, 64
and natural environment, xvi, 108–9, 132, 168
painter, 8–9, 100, 176
potter, xiv, xvi, 99–100, 101, 106, 126–31, 132–40, 147, 149, 167, 175, 178, 179–80, 191
in Queensland, 22, 29–34
and Second World War, 103–4, 106, 107–12, 113, 140–4, 145–57, 158, 159, 161, 166–8
social worker, 9–11, 19–20
traveller, xiii, xix, 20–2, 26–8, 29–35
and University Women's College, xiii-xiv, xvii, xx, 79, 80–5, 87–94, 94–5, **96**, 97, 101, 105, 118, 148, 152, 156, 158–62, 164, 190–1
and Victorian Women's Citizens Movement, 74–6, 77, 80, 105
visits to England, 59, 60, 68, 76, 85, 176–7, 189–90
war bride, xiii, xv, 52, 53
war work, 45, 46–7
and woman suffrage, xv, xxi, 12, 18, 21, 55, 58, 59, 61–3, 144, 191
and Women's Non-Party Political League, 57–8,60–2, 63–4, 81, 105
and women's rights, xi, xiii, xiv, xix, xxi, 18, 57, 91, 106, 191
writer, xiii, 20–1, 34, 35, 38, 43, 97–8, 99, 172–4, 187
Giblin, Ella, 27, 36–7
Giblin, Lyndhurst Falkiner
attitude to war, 28, 38–40, 44, 45–6, 47–8, 49–50, 98
and Bloomsbury Group, xxi, 26, 38, 42, 43, 48, 98
in British Columbia, 22, 23, 24, 185
at Cambridge 22, 23, 24, 26, 27, 43, 72, 92, 98, 182, 185
career, 53–4, 68, 71, 73, 74, 76, 78, 80, 100, 131, 185
and Central Bank history, 175, 177–8,
179, 180, 183
character, xiii, xviii-xix, 22, 23, 25, 26, 27, 37, 38, 40, 43, 55–6, 113, 183–4
and Cobblers End, 27, 36–7, 38, 52, 54, 124, 164
Commonwealth Bank Director, xix, 100, 101, 113, 132–3, 185
death, 183
dress, 27, 43
early life, 22, 23, 24–5, 48
and Financial and Economic Committee, 100, 148, 175, 183–4
at First World War, xiii, xv, 28, 36–8, 40–1, 44–5, **46**–7, 49–50, 51–2
decorated, 37, 41, 44–5, 47, 48, 51–2
wounded, 40–1, 42–3, 49–50
and Garnetts, 13, 22, 23, 26, 36, 38, 41, 42–3, 48–9, 50–1, 98–9
illness, 69, 77, 101, 180, 183
and Labor Party, 25–6, 52, 53
letters, xvii, 36–40, 45, 46, 48, 49, 50, 52, 68, 69, 82, 101, 178, 182, 185, 186
marriage, xii, xv, 48–9, 51, 53
and Nicky Yardley, 180, **181**, 182
orchardist, 23, 25, 52, 54
parliamentarian, 23–4, 25–6, 28, 34, 52, 53
and post-war reconstruction, 148, 168
relationship with wife, xiii, xxi, 13, 23–4, 26–8, 35, 36–8, 43–4, 45–6, 68–70, 72, 73–4, 82, 93–4, 98–9, 101–2, 109–10, 113, 128, 129, 131, 139, 142–3, 178
Ritchie Professor of Economics, xvii, 68, 71, 74, 86, 100, 105, 112
sexuality, 26, 185–6
statistician, 53–4, 76, 78
and University of Tasmania, 26, 54, 56
and wrestling, 23, 24–5
Giblin, Violet, vii, 176
Giblin, Lt Colonel Wilfred Wanostrocht, 56
Giblin, William R., 24, 197
Giblin pots, 139
see also pottery
Gibson, Professor Boyce, 162
Gilmore, Mary, 35
Girton College, Cambridge, 7, 80, 91, 92, 93, 94, 159
Goffe, Dr E.G.L. (Leopold), 48
Goldstein, Vida, 61
The Golden Echo, 23, 42, 114, 194
Gollancz, 99
Gona, 158
Goring, Dr Charles, 43
Gorman House, ACT, 153
Gough, Nancy, **20**, 66, 188
Gowrie, Lady, xx, 90, 91
Grainger, Martin, 24–5, 26

gramophone, ix, xix, 73, 102, 150, 185
Grant, Duncan, 22, 42, 48, 98, 196
Great Depression, xxi, 70–1, 73, 74, 76, 85, 92, 103, 180
Greater Asia Co-prosperity Scheme, 140
Greece, 34, 97, 141, 147
Green, Florence, 135
Green, Frank, 25, 27, 41, 44, 51, 56, 73, 135, 194, 197
Greenwich Settlement House, 10
Grey, Sir Edward, 14–6
Griffin, Murray, 127
Grosvenor School of Modern Art, 99
Guam, 140
Gullett, Sir Henry, 104

Haig, Sir Douglas, 47
Hain, Mrs Gladys, 83
Hall, ACT, 134
Hall, Edith, 27–8, 36, 74, 139, 174, 175, 185, 187
Hall, Pte John (Dick), 44
Hall, Radclyffe, 72
Hall, Robert, 27–8
Hammersley, Mrs, 112
Hampton Court station, 3, 19
Harris, Sir Arthur, 155
Harry, Elsie, 153
Hasluck, Sir Paul, 183, 184, 195
Hay, NSW, viii, 116, 119
  Internment Camp, 118, 120–3, 195
Heath, Ellen Maurice (Nellie), 42, 114, 195
Heath, Richard, 42
Heaton, Herbert, 26, 195
Henderson, A. and K., 84
Henderson, Kingsley A., 88, 95
Heucke, Albert, 4
Heucke, Amy, 4
Herbst, Peter, 161
hitch-hikers, 124
Hobart, xiii, xvii, xix, xx, 25, 26, 27, 53, 62–4, 66–8, 74, 102, 175–6, 183, 186, 188, 189–90, 196
  society, 53, 55–7, 71
  in wartime 124–5, 164–5
Hobart Public Hospitals Board, xx, 63, 68–9, 196
Hoff, Dr Ursula, 94, 159–60, 161, 162–3, 195, 197
Hoffman Brick, Tile and Pottery Company, 126–7
Holloway Gaol, 15, 17, 18
Holloway Medal, 14
'Homefield', 4, 18, **20**, 37, 48, 50, 51, 66, 69, 98, 176, 177, 188
Hong Kong, 146
Hood, John D.L., 105, 113

Hood, Mrs, 105, 113
Hort, Dr Greta, 92–4, **96**, 101, 159–60, 161–2, **163**, 164, 197, 198
  appointment, 92–3, 162
  opinions of, 93–4, 162
Hotel Canberra, 73, 77, 102, 110, 111, 170
Housewives' Association, 83
Hughenden, Qld, 29, 32, 33
Humphreys, Travers, 16
hunger strikers, xii, 13, 14, 17, 60
  see also force feeding
Huntingfield, Lady [Eleanor], 84, 85, 86, 88
Hurst, Lucie Evelyn, 63
Hutchins School, 24

Iceland, 24, 86
India, 45, 153
influenza pandemic, 50, 53
Institute of Anatomy, Canberra, 133–4
Interior, Department of, 107, 126, 131, 132, 152
International Council of Women, 61
International Council on Monuments and Sites, ix, xvi
International Labour Office, 70
International Woman Suffrage Alliance, ix, 58, 61, 144, 194
  Berlin conference (1904), 61
  Rome (Ninth) Congress (1923), **ii**, 55, 58, 59, 60–2
  Washington (inaugural) conference (1902), 60–1
International Woman Suffrage News, 55, 63, 197
internment camps
  see Hay, NSW; Tatura, Vic.
invasion threat
  to Australia, xvi, 126, 129, 145, 146–7, 150, 152, 153, 154, 155, 158, 164, 168
  to Britain, 107, 109, 115, 116, 154
Ivanhoe Grammar School, 181

James, Elizabeth Britomarte, 74–5
Jamieson-Williams, Mrs, 59, 77
Janet Clark Hall, 80
Japan
  advance through Asia, xvi, 126, 140, 143, 145–7, 149–54, 156, 158, 164
  submarine attacks, 145, 155, 166
  surrender, 172
  threat to Australia, xvi, 147, 154, 158, 168, 173
Japanese wrestling, 23, 25
Jardine, Lizzie, 33
Java, 145, 149, 151
Jenkins, Herbert, 35
Jerome, Jerome K., 4

Jervis Bay, HMS, 141
Jewish refugees, xvii, 94, 115, 116, 122, 159–60, 164
Johnson, Mrs, 146, 170
Johnson, Nelson T., 146, 168, 171
Jones, Kathleen Gilman, 75, 77
Joyner, Mrs A.E., 59
Junee, NSW, 119, 122, 124
justices of the peace, ix, xix, 57, 58, 63, 75

Kammerer, Dr Paul, 160–1, 163–4
Kang-chi Cheng, 169
Katherine, NT, 145
Katoomba, HMAT, xv, 52, 53
Katoomba News, 53
Kershaw, Raymond, 180
Keynes, Maynard, xvii, 43, 48, 197
Kindergarten Society
   see Canberra Nursery Kindergarten Society
King George V, 51–2
   statue, 128
King's College, Cambridge, 22, 24, 39, 43, 92, 98
Kingston-on-Thames, 4, 17, 48, 190
Klondike, 23, 24, 26
Knight, John Arthur Barnard (Jack), 100, 126–7
Knowles, Sir George, 113
Knowles, Lady, 113, 150
Knowles, Ft Lt Lindsay, 150
Koestler, Arthur, 161, 163–4, 195
Kokoda, 145, 158, 166
Korean War, 179
Kuttabul HMAS, 155

Labour and National Service, Department of, 78, 128
   Division of Industrial Welfare, 149
   Division of Reconstruction, 148
Laby, Professor Thomas H., 120
Lady Gowrie Services Club, Canberra, 113
lady travellers, 20–1
Lake, Marilyn, 25, 55, 58, 68, 195
Lamarkian theory, 160, 161
Lammermoor, 30
Lansdowne, Lord, 45–6
Launceston, Tas., 63, 124, 164
Lawrence, D.H., 22, 42, 193
Lawrence, T.E., 98
Lawson, Henry, 43–4
Layton, Major Julius, 122
Leach, Bernard, 128, 195
League of Nations, 61, 70
League of Nations Union, 64, 118
Legacy, 114–15
Leitch, Sir Walter, 85

Lethaby, William, 11
Letters from Queensland, 21
Life and Death in Shanghai, 169, 174
Lillingston, Jessie
   see Street, Jessie
Limpsfield, 23
Lindsay, Daryl, 160
linocuts, 99, 194, 198
Lloyd George Government, 39, 40
London, xi, xix, 1–3, 9, 10–11, 12–13, 14, 17, 17, 19, 34, 52, 196
   in Second World War, 107, 108, 109, 112, 123, 177
London, City of, 1–2, 3, 12, 16, 17, 19, 34, 196
London County Council, 10–11, 12
London Gazette, 41, 45, 47
London School of Economics, 10, 169
London *Times*, xiv, 8, 21, 33, 50, 111, 115, 118, 123, 176, 197, 198
Lord Mayor, London, 3
Lothian, Elizabeth, 79, 82, 84, 90, 195
Lowe. Mr Justice, 146
Lucas, Edward Verrell, 35, 43
Ludbrook, Nelly, 134–5, 152
Lyceum Club, Melbourne, 83, 85, 160
Lyndhurst, Lord, 23
Lynton Avenue, Hobart
   see 'The Side'
Lyons, Dame Enid, xx, 63, 86, 170
Lyons, Joseph A., 25–6, 62, 76, 77, 104
Lyons Government, 149

Macartney, Mervyn, 11
MacArthur, General Douglas, 153, 167
McArthur, Norma, 152, 157
McCarthy, Desmond, 43
McCredie, Nell, 134
MacFarland, Sir John, 79, 83
McFarlane, Mary, 134
McInnes, W.B., 95
Mackinnon, Deidre, 171, 187
McMullin, Ross, 25–6, 195
MacRae, Ada
   see Burton, Ada
MacRae, Elizabeth (Betty), 12, 49, 69, 176, 188
MacRae, Georgiana
   see Roberts, Georgiana
MacRae, Georgina, xii, 5, 7, 12–18, 41, 60
MacRae, Helen, xii, 5, 7, 12–18, 21, 41, 60
MacRae, James, 3
MacRae, Mary (Molly)
   see White, Mary (Molly) MacRae
Maeterlinck, Maurice, 181
Malaya, 140, 145, 147, 150
Manchester, 45, 46
Manchester Guardian, xiv, 111

Mann, Thomas, 116
Manuka, ACT, 77, 102, 103, 109, 118, 151
Marlborough College, 4–5
married women (war), 152
Massingham, H. W., 18, 27, 38, 42, 195
Master Carvers' Association, 12
maternal mortality, 64
Mehaffey, Mrs Alma, 128
Meiping Cheng, 169
Melbourne, xx, 21, 24, 70, 71–2, 74, 75, 80, 84, 85, 91, 99–100, 113, 143
   in wartime, 107, 125, 149, 152–3, 156–7, 158–62
Melbourne Centenary (1934), 81, 84
Melbourne Contemporary Artists, 99–100
Melbourne General Hospital, 79–80
Melbourne Grammar School, 71
Melbourne *Herald*, 72–3, 76, 111
Melbourne Technical College, x, 100, 126, 127, 135, 195
Melbourne University Press, 168, 179
Melville, A.E. (Tony), 182, 186, 193, 198
Melville, Leslie, 100
Menuhin, Yehudi, 116
Menzies, Robert G., 101, 104, 109, 110, 142, 143
Menzies Government, 104, 110, 142, 179
Mercury, Hobart, 56, 61–2, 71, 164
Messines, Battle of, 37, 41, 43, 44, 46
Methuen, 35
Meyer, Hans, 120
midget submarine attack, 145, 155
Midway, Battle of, 156
Migration and Government Conference, 64
militant suffragettes, xii, xix, 5,13–15, 16, 17, 18, 57, 60, 193, 196
Mills, Stephen, 65
Milne Bay, 145, 156, 166
Ministry of Labour (Britain), 45, 46–7
Mitchell, Una, 113
modernism, art, 99–100
Molesey Lock, 4
Mollison, Edith, (nee MacRae), 69
Molonglo River, ACT, 103, 109, 182
Monash, Sir John, 44
Moore, Sir Harrison, 79
Moorrinya National Park, 30, 196
Morlancourt, 47–8
Morris, Dr Ethel Renfry, 59
Morris car, xiii, xiv, xix, 73, 119, 124, 139, 188, **189**
Moscheles, Dr Julie, 159, 161, 162
motherhood endowment
   see child endowment; Royal Commission on Child Endowment
Mt Ainslie, ACT, 131
Mt Anne, Tas., 71

Mt Stromlo Observatory, ACT, 120, 152
Mugga Way, ACT, 102, 108
Mulberry Cottage, 71–2, 73
Mulligan's Flat, ACT, 128
Munich, 98
munitions, 108, 135, 147, 149, 152, 164, 196
   manufacture, 46–7
   optical, 120
   workers, 46–7
Murdoch, Mrs Lesley, 58, 64
Murphy, Mrs Beatrice, 113, 136
Murphy, James F., 113
Muscio, Mrs Mildred, 65
Museum of London, vii, 13, 14, 15, 193
Mussolini, Benito, 61

Naas, ACT, 128
Narrandera, NSW, viii, 119
Nation (to 1931), 18, 27. 33, 38, 39, 42, 47
   see also New Statesman and Nation (from 1931)
National Council of Clothes Styling, 155
National Council of Women, x, 65, 83, 106
   in ACT, 106, 148, 196
National Gallery, London, 123
National Gallery of Australia, viii, x, xvi, 137, 140
National Gallery of Victoria, 94, 160, 162
National Library of Australia, ii, vii, viii, x, xv, xvii, 49, 59, 60, 110, 130, 131, 138, 171, 185, 193
national theatre, 181
Nationalist/Country Party Government, 64
nationality of married women, xx, 57, 61–3, 64
Nationality of Married Women Committee, xx, 61
Naval Memorial, Portsmouth, 177
Neimeyer, Sir Otto, 180
'New Australia' settlement, 34–5
New Republic, 38
New South Wales, 59, 68, 116, 128
   female suffrage, 21
New Statesman (to 1931), 38
New Statesman and Nation (from 1931), xiv, xvi, 111, 116, 158, 195
New Theatre, 181
New Zealand, 7, 21, 35, 141, 169
Newcomb, Harriet, 59
Newman College, 80
Newnham College, Cambridge, 22, 79, 80, 86, 89, 91, 92, 112
newspaper delivery, 111, 195
newsprint rationing, 164
Nien Cheng, 169, 194
Nimmo, Jim, 136
No Conscription Fellowship, 38, 40, 195
   see also Tribunal

Noble, Dr G.K., 160
Northcliffe, Lord, 39

O'Grady, Sir James, 71
O'Halloran, T.S., 65
Old Parliament House, Canberra
  see Provisional Parliament House
Ormond College, 80
Optical Munitions Panel, 120
  see also Mt Stromlo Observatory
Overseas Club, Melbourne, 21

Pacific war, 140, 141, 143, 145, 156, 164, 173
  see also invasion threat
pacifists, 38, 39, 43, 98, 144, 164, 169, 179
Palmer, Nettie, 86, 169, 198
Pankhurst, Christabel, 13
Pankhurst, Emmeline, 13, 16, 60
Pankhurst, Sylvia, 13
Papua New Guinea, 145, 147, 150, 158, 165, 166
Paraguay, 34
Paris, 7, 8, 9, 12, 42, 107
Parkville, Vic., 80
Passchendaele, 43, 44, 45
Patriotic League of Britons Overseas, 21
Pearl Harbour, 143, 145, 146, 167, 174
Peckham Settlement, 9–11, 12, 19, 196
  Apprenticeship committee, 10
  Children's care committee, 10
People's Palace of Delights for Eastenders, 13
Perham Downs, 43
Petherick Room, viii
Petoe, Stefan, 115, 119, 122, 123
Petrococino, Phyllis
  see Burton, Phyllis
petrol rationing, 119, 129, 135, 154, 188
Philip Morris Inc., 2
Philipp, Franz, 161
Phillips, Mrs M.M. (Ray), 85, 196
Piesse, Mrs Amelia, 63
Pilcher, Bishop Charles Venn, 118
Pipe Clay Lagoon, Tas., 135
Plaque with Laurel, 104, 148, 194
Pole-Carew, Christopher, 188
Pole-Carew, Gillian, vii, 20, 69, 101, 188
Polegate, 67, 69, 176–7, 188
Polglaze, Jean, 148
political prisoners, 13, 17, 40
police
  Britain, xii, 14, 16
  Queensland, 33
  Russia, 42
policewomen, 57, 68
Port Davey, Tas., 28, 197
Port Hedland, W.A., 145
Port Moresby, 145, 153

post-war reconstruction, 148, 168, 194, 197
Post War Reconstruction, Department of, 148, 168
Potter Museum, xvii
A Potter's Book, 128, 195
Pottery and Ceramics, 179
pottery, viii, xiv, xvi, 99–100, 105, 106, 126–40, 147, 153, 176, 178, 195, 196
  arts and crafts influence, 100
  Canberra studio, 106, 126, 134
  clay, xiv, 127, 128–30, 133, 134, 135–6, 139, 140, 156, 158, 188
  designs, 100, 133–4, 139
  glaze, 132, 136
  kiln, xiv, 127, 130, 131, 132, 135, 136, 140, 175
  market, 136, 139–40
  training, 100, 126–7, 135
  wheel, 126, 127, 128, 130, 132, 133, 134, 136–7, 139, 140, 142
  women potters, 127, 128, 134, 135, 137–40
potting, solace of, 126, 140, 149, 167
Praed, Rosa, 33
Prairie, Qld, 29, 30
Presbyterian Church, Forrest, 129, 135, 136
Presbyterian Ladies' College, Burwood, 148
Presbyterian Ladies Guild, 106
Priest House Museum, 17
Priestley, Raymond E., 88
Prime Minister's Lodge, Canberra, 73, 136
Prince of Wales, HMS, 147
prisoners of war, 116, 118, 141, 149
Pritchard, Edward, 1–2
Pritchard, Sarah, 111, 191
Pritchard and Burton, 2–3, 11, 34, 66, 176
Provisional Parliament House, Canberra, 103, 104, 109, **110**, 113, 128
Putnam's G.P. Sons, 174

Quakers, 119, 169
Queanbeyan, NSW, 128, 131
Queen Alexandra's Imperial Military Nursing Service, 12
Queensland, 30, 59, 196
  female suffrage, 21
  North, xiii, 29, 153
  Western, viii, xiii, 22, 29–33, 35, 196, 197, 198
Rabaul, 145, 147
Rapke, Julia, 60, 74, 75, 76, 193
Rankin, Jeannette, 144
rationing, 145, 154, 155
  see also newsprint rationing; petrol rationing
Ratten, Dr Victor,
Recorder, The, 99, 100

Red Cross, 49, 113, 136, 171
Rendel, Lord, 12
Reparation and Debt Conference (1932), 77
Repulse, HMS, 147
Revealing Women's Life Stories, iii, 191, 196
Reynolds, John, 55, 56, 198
Rhodes scholarship, 56, 127
Rich, Ruby, 77
Ripon Cathedral, 177
Rischbieth, Mrs Bessie, ii, 58, **59**, 60, 61, 75–6, 77, 81, 193, 196, 198
Roberts, Alan Griffydd, 31, 32
Roberts, Amy
  see Heucke, Amy
Roberts, Arthur, 30
Roberts, Dr Daniel, 3
Roberts, Dr George, 30
Roberts, Georgiana, 3, 8
Roberts, Grace Adelaide, 29, 30–2
Roberts, Harold Griffydd, 22, 29, 30–3
Roberts, Shirley Desiree, 31, 32
Rockefeller Institute, 85
Rogerson, Joan, 129, 152
Roland, Betty, 181, 182, 196
Rommel, Field Marshal, 147, 158
A Room of One's Own, xx, 81–2, 85, 86–7, 91, 196
Roosevelt, Eleanor, 116, 170, **171**
Ross, Elaine, vii, 67, 187, 189
Royal Air Force, x, 147, 155, 177
Royal Army Service Corps, x, 11, 48, 66
Royal Australian Air Force, x, 124, 146, 151
Royal Commission on Child Endowment or Family Allowances, xx, 57, 64–5, 196
Royal Melbourne Hospital, 161
Royal Melbourne Institute of Technology (RMIT) University
  see Melbourne Technical College
Royal Navy, 25, 66, 111
Royal Society of Tasmania, 71
Royal Warwickshire Regiment, 11
Ruddock, Colonel William C., 190
Rudduck, Loma, 134, 140, 191, 198
Russell, Bertrand, 38, 39–40, 178–9, 193, 196
Russia, 22, 39, 40, 42, 142, 143
Russian Legation, 169
Rutzen, Sir Albert de, 14

St Bartholomew's Church, London, 2
St Christopher's Church (later Cathedral), Manuka, 151
St Edmund of Canterbury Church, 177
St John's Ladies Guild, Canberra, 106
St Mary's Hall, University of Melbourne, 80
St Mary's University Church, Oxford, 177
St Michael's Grammar School, St Kilda, vii, 160, 161, 163

St Paul's Cathedral, London, 11
Salisbury Cathedral, 177
Salter, Audrey, vii, 187
Samoa, 140
Schoenberg, Arnold, 123
  Medal, 123
Scotland, 1, 3, 53, 66, 98
Scott, Lt Colonel W. P., 118
Scullin, James, 73
Scullin Labor Government, 76
sculpture, 11, 12, 138, 177, 196, 197
Second Front, 155, 166, 172
second wave feminism, xv, xxi, 191
Second World War, xiv, xv, xvii, xviii, xx, 34, 78, 95, 107, 135, 142, 149, 172, 173, 174, 177, 183
  Canberra, xv, 100, 103, 105, 106, 128, 129, 136, 146–7, 149–51, 153, 154, 166, 168, 170–1, 175, 184–5
  England, 107, 108, 109, 112, 115, 116, 154
  Europe, 99, 101, 104, 107, 108, 114, 124, 140, 141, 143, 151, 172, 173, 176
  Melbourne, 107, 125, 149, 152–3, 156–7
  Middle East, xvi, 98, 104, 107, 125, 140, 141, 142, 146, 150, 173,
  Tasmania, 124–5, 146–7, 164
  toll of, 141, 150
settlement movement, 9, 10, 19, 29. 193, 196
Seven Mile Beach, Tas., 23, 27, 37, 54, 124, 146
sex education, 61
Shann, Sir Keith (Mick), 157, 158
Shaw, Bernard, 22
Shaw, Flora, 21, 196, 197
shearers' strikes, 33, 197
'Shirley' station, Qld, 22, 30–4
Shoe-Shine, 180
Sickert, Walter, 42
'The Side', Hobart, **67**–8, 175, 176, 178, 183, 187, 189–90
Sietz, John A., 88
Simon, Hedi, 123
Singapore, 145, 147, 149, 150, 164
Sino-Japanese War, 112
Slade School, 138
Smith College, 191, 196
Smith, Mrs Ella Louisa, 63
Solomon Islands, 22, 24
South Africa, vii, 21, 188, 190
South Australia, 59, 65
  female suffrage, 21
South Australian Harbours Board, 186
South Yarra, Vic., xix, 71, 103, 161, 182
  see also Mulberry Cottage
Spain, 69
Spender, Dale, xi–xiv

Spowers, Ethel, 99, 198
Stadlen, Erich, 115, 119, 120, 121, 122, 123, 124, 197
Stadlen, Peter, 115, 116, **117**, 119, 120, 122, 123, 124, 198
Standard Hours Inquiry, 175
Star, Melbourne, 83
Stepniak, Sergei, 42
Sternberg, Kurt, 122
Stewart, Sir Frederick, 113
Strachey, Lytton, 43
Strauss, Johann, 123
Street, Brigadier G.A., 104
Street, Jessie, 6, 7, 170, 197
strikes
    wartime, 142, 152
    see also hunger strikers; shearers' strikes
Stubbington House School, 11
submarine attacks, 145, 155, 166
suffrage movement, xv, xxi, 12, 13, 16–18, 21, 59, 60, 61, 144, 191
    see also International Woman Suffrage Alliance; militant suffragettes; woman suffrage
Suffragette, The, 60
Sumatra, 146, 149
Sussex Downs, 43, 69, 188
Sweet, Dr Georgina, 79, 80, 81, 84, 86, 88, 89, 90, 95, 156, 160
Sydney, HMAS, 143
Sydney Morning Herald, xiv, 111
Syme, Eveline, 80, 84, 85, 86, 88, 90, 99, 156, 160, 164, 195, 198
    tribute to Eilean Giblin, 33, 81, 91, 94, 95, 176, 191
Synge, J. M., 50

Tagg, Thomas, 4
Tagg Island, 4
Tangney, Senator Dorothy, ix, 170
tariff, 73
Tasmania, vii, xiii, xx, 23–4, 25, 26–7, 36, 38, 59, 63, 81, 105, 176, 178–9, 188–9, 194, 195, 196, 197
    economy, 55–6, 71
    female suffrage, 21, 56, 57
    politics, 23–4, 25, 26, 57, 58, 123–5
    social conditions, xix, 55–6, 62–3, 67–8, 71
Tasmanian Club, 56, 194
Tasmanian Labor Government, 62–3
Tasmanian Women's Non-Party Political League
    see Women's Non-Party Political League
Tatura, Vic.
    Internment Camp, 116, 118, 123, 161
Teece, Rev. Aubrey, 28

Teece, Muriel Kathleen (Cush), 28
telephone communication, 31, 33–4, 84, 133
Thames, River, 1, 3–4, 188
Thane, Lt Col Charles S., 119
Themistocles, 123
Thorpe, Mavis, 134
Tillyard, Pattie, 112, 116–7, 169, 197
tobacco
    manufacture, xviii, 1–3, 19, 176
    proposed rationing, 155
    smoking, xviii, 2, 43, 49, 56, 121, 184
Tobruk, 142, 146
Tolstoy, Leo, 22
Torrens Creek, Qld, 29, 30, 33, 196
total war, 119, 142, 145, 148, 152
Tours-en-Vimeu, 50, 52
Townsville, 29, 145
Toynbee Hall, 9
train travel
    to and from Canberra, 90, 100, 101, 124, 134, 136, 141, 143, 146
    in England, 41, 42, 66
    to Hay, viii, 119–20, 124
    in Queensland, 29
travel permits, 156
Treasury, Department of, 78, 103, 128, 134, 136, 157
Tribunal, The, 38, 39–40
    see also No Conscription Fellowship
Trinity College, University of Melbourne, 80
Turner, Lawrence, 11
Tynan, Mrs Ida Mary, 63

United Australian Party/Country Party Government, 76, 77, 104, 143
    see also Menzies Government
United Girls' Schools Settlement, 9–10
    see also Peckham Settlement
United Kingdom Parliament, 8, 13, 64, 191
United States of America, 30, 61, 73, 86, 116
    diplomatic representation, 108, 113, 146, 168, 169, 171
    Second World War, 129, 140–1, 144, 146, 147, 165, 170–1
    see also MacArthur, General Douglas
Universities Bureau of the British Empire, 92
University Association, Canberra, 111
University College, London, 12, 22, 23, 24, 35, 43, 48
University College, Melbourne (from 1975), viii, x
    Archives, 82, 89, 92, 163
    coat of arms, 2
    see also University Women's College
University College School, London, 23
University of London, 13, 59, 138
    see also Slade School

University of Melbourne, viii, xvii, xx, 68, 71, 79, 80, 83, 85, 92, 100, 105, 106, 148, 161, 196
University of Queensland, 80, 88
University of Sydney, 80, 89, 169
University of Tasmania, 56, 67, 194
  Commemoration Day ceremony, 56
  Council, 26, 54, 56, 58
University of Vienna, 164
University Women's College, Melbourne
  appeal, 85–7, 88, 90, 92
  building, 84, 86, 88, 89, 90, 95, 97
  Constance Ellis Wing, 95
  design, 84, 86
  Council, xx, 81, 88, 89, 90, 91, 93, 95, 97, 99, 105, 143, 156, 160, 162, 164, 190–1
  Executive committee, 84, 85
  foundation stone, 88
  garden, 90
  Georgina Sweet Wing, 79–80, **89**, 90, 95
  management committee, 88, 89
  opening, xx, 90–1, **92**
  principals
    Greta Hort, 92–4, **96**, 101, 159–60, 161–2, **163**, 164
    Susie Williams, 89–90, **92**, 94–5, **96**
  provisional committee, 79–80, 80–1, 82, 84, 85, 89
  purpose, 87–8, 91
  and *A Room of One's Own*, xx, 86–7, 91
  scholarship fund, 90
  site, 79–80, 82–84, 88
  and University of Melbourne, 80, 84, 85

Victoria, 59, 58, 126, 135, 143, 161
  female suffrage, 21
Victorian era, xxi, 1, 2, 4
Victorian Government Tourist Bureau, 123, 198
Victorian International Refugee Emergency Committee, x, 118
Victorian Parliament, 79, 80, 82, 83, 88
Victorian Women's Citizenship Movement, x, 74–6, 80, 81, 105
Vintners' Company, 3, 52
Votes for Women, 14, 16–17, 60
Votes for Women campaign, xii, 13, 14–18

Walker, Bernard, 67–8
Wallace, Robert, 16
Waller, Napier, 127
Walling, Edna, 90, 197
Wandsworth Army Hospital, 41, 50
Wanliss, Dr Marion, 153, 176
Wanostrocht, Felix, 23
war brides, xiii, xv, 51, 52, 53
War Cabinet, 148
The War of Steel and Gold, 39

The War of the Worlds, 155–6
wartime censorship, 45–6, 47–8, 145
wartime regulations, xvi, 150
Waterworth, Edith, 57, 58, 64, 198
Wau, 166
Webb, Jessie, 79, 81, 88, 95
Webern, Anton, 115
Wedd, Nathaniel, 43
Wedgwood, Camilla, 169, 196
Weisz, Dr Edward, 122
The Well of Loneliness, 72
Wells, H. G., 13, 155
Wells Cathedral, 177
Wells Station, ACT, 134
West Block, Canberra, 104, 171, 183
West Hoathly Museum, 17
Western Australia, 58, 59, 60, 143
  female suffrage, 21
Western Front, xv, 28, 35, 36, 40, 44, 45, 46, 72, 97
Westralian Worker, 65
Whiskard, Sir Geoffrey, 111, 118
White, Sir Brudenall, 104
White, James Martin, 8
White, Joan, 8
White, Mary (Molly) MacRae, 8, 10, 49, 69, 176, 188
White, Oliver, 8
Whitelaw, Anne W., 7
Wickens, C.H., 73, 76
widows, 64, 65
von Wiederspenger, Baroness Felicitas, 160
Wigmore Hall, London, 115
Williams, Sir Ralph Vaughan, 116, 123, 157, 198
Williams, Susannah Jane (Susie)
  death, 156
  and University Women's College, Melbourne, 88, 89–90, **92**, 93, 94–5, **96**, 156
  and Women's College, Sydney, 89
Wilson, Alex, 143
Wilson, Sir Roland, xviii, 52, 55, 56, 77–8, 100, 122, 127–8, 135, 180, 183, 194, 198
Wilson, Valeska, 77, 135
Wiltshire, 52
wireless, 109
Wodehouse, Dr Helen, 93, 159
woman suffrage, 12–18, 21, 56, 57, 60–1
  see also International Woman Suffrage Alliance
Women and Overseas Settlement Conference, 64, 193
women parliamentary candidates, xv, xx, 21, 57, 58, 61, 170, 191
Women's Association for the Reform of the Criminal Law, Tasmania, 56–7, 58

women's education, xiii, 72
    see also equal education
Women's Health Association, Tas., 56
women's liberation, xix, 91, 193
Women's Non-Party Political League, Tas., x, 57, 58, 60, 62–5, 81, 105
Women's Service Guilds of Western Australia, 58
Women's Social and Political Union (WSPU), x, xii, 13–15, 16, 17, 18
Woolley, Dr Richard, 120, 157
Woolf, Leonard, 12, 43
Woolf, Virginia, xx, xxi, 12, 18, 22, 43, 81, 85, 86, 91, 196
Woolnough, Dr Walter, 128
Workers' Educational Association, 26
world wars
    see First World War; Second World War
Wright, Christopher, 177
Wycombe Abbey, vii, xi, 5–8, **9**, **10**, 27, 138, 193, 194, 196, 197
    see also Dove, Dame Frances

Wycombe Abbey Gazette, 5, 7, 197
Wyndham, W.A., 145

Yardley, Edgar, 181
Yardley, Nicky, 180, **181**, 182
Young Women's Christian Association (YWCA), x, 106, 134, 136
Ypres, Third Battle of, 37, 41, 43, 44, 45
Yukon River, 22, 24, 185

Zealandia, HMAT, 124
Zeppelin air raids, 2, 34

2/30th Battalion
    see Australian Imperial Force (AIF), 2/30th Battalion
40th Battalion
    see Australian Imperial Force, 40th Battalion
8th Division
    see Australian Imperial Force, 8th Division

About the author

Dr Patricia Clarke OAM is a writer, historian, editor and former journalist who has written extensively on women in Australian history. Several of her books are biographies of women writers, and others explore the role of letters and diaries in the lives of women. She edited poet Judith Wright's autobiography and is joint editor of two books of Judith Wright's letters. She has also written widely on media history.

She is an Honorary Fellow of the Australian Academy of Humanities and a Fellow of the Federation of Australian Historical Societies. A former President and Councillor of the Canberra & District Historical Society, she edited the Society's *Canberra Historical Journal* for fourteen years. She was Founding Honorary Secretary of the Independent Scholars Association of Australia and was elected a Life Member.

Patricia Clarke has been a member of the Commonwealth Working Party for the *Australian Dictionary of Biography* since 1987, a member of the National Library of Australia's Fellowship Advisory Committee since 1996 and in 2010 was appointed to the ACT Historic Houses Advisory Committee.

Patricia Clarke
Courtesy National Library of Australia, Bib ID 6192468.
Photographer Craig Mackenzie.
© 2012 National Library of Australia

Books by Patricia Clarke

The Governesses: Letters from the Colonies 1862–1882, Hutchinson, Melbourne, 1985; paperback edition, Allen & Unwin, North Sydney, 1989; print on demand, 2012.

A Colonial Woman: The Life and Times of Mary Braidwood Mowle 1827–1857, Allen & Unwin, North Sydney, 1986; paperback edition, 1991; Eden Killer Whale Museum and Historical Society, Eden, NSW, 2001; ebook, 2013.

Pen Portraits: Women Writers and Journalists in Nineteenth Century Australia, Allen & Unwin, North Sydney, 1988; Pandora, London, 1988; print on demand, 2012.

Pioneer Writer: The Life of Louisa Atkinson, Novelist, Journalist, Naturalist, Allen & Unwin, North Sydney, 1990.

Life Lines: Australian Women's Letters and Diaries 1788–1840 (with Dale Spender), Allen & Unwin, St Leonards, NSW, 1992; new edition, 1996.

Tasma: The Life of Jessie Couvreur, Allen & Unwin, St Leonards, NSW, 1994.

Tasma's Diaries, Mulini Press, Canberra, 1995.

Rosa! Rosa! A Life of Rosa Praed, Novelist and Spiritualist, Melbourne University Press, Carlton, Vic., 1999.

Steps to Federation: Lectures Marking the Centenary of Federation, ed., Australian Scholarly Publishing, Melbourne, 2001.

The Equal Heart and Mind: Letters between Judith Wright and Jack McKinney, ed. with Meredith McKinney, University of Queensland Press, St Lucia, Qld, 2004.

With Love and Fury: Selected Letters of Judith Wright, ed. with Meredith McKinney, National Library of Australia, Canberra, 2007.

Eilean Giblin: A Feminist between the Wars, Monash University Publishing, Clayton, Vic., 2013.